Reproduction & Responsibility

REPRODUCTION
AND
RESPONSIBILITY

The Regulation of New Biotechnologies

A Report of
The President's Council on Bioethics

Washington, D.C.
March 2004

www.bioethics.gov

CONTENTS

PART II

LETTER OF TRANSMITTAL TO THE PRESIDENT OF THE UNITED STATES

The President's Council on Bioethics
1801 Pennsylvania Avenue, N.W., Suite 700
Washington, D.C. 20006
March 31, 2004

The President
The White House
Washington, D.C.

Dear Mr. President:

I am pleased to present to you *Reproduction and Responsibility: The Regulation of New Biotechnologies,* the latest report of the President's Council on Bioethics, and one that contains a set of unanimous policy recommendations. The product of two years of research, reflection, and deliberation, we hope that it will prove a worthy contribution to understanding and addressing important ethical and social issues arising at the intersection of assisted reproduction and genetic knowledge.

This report differs from, yet complements, the Council's work in its previous publications. In *Human Cloning and Human Dignity*, we addressed the limited topic of human cloning—what to think and what to do about it—and offered specific legislative recommendations. In *Monitoring Stem Cell Research*, we answered your request for an update on developments concerning human stem cell research, both in basic and clinical research and in the ethical and policy debates, as these have emerged under the current federal policy. In *Beyond Therapy: Biotechnology and the Pursuit of Happiness*, we surveyed growing capacities that biotechnologies are providing to serve non-medical goals—such as the desires for "better children," "superior performance," "ageless bodies," and "happy souls"—and sought to raise public awareness of the challenges such pursuits might pose to the meaning of our humanity. And in *Being Human*, we offered a rich anthology of readings to help the nation better appreciate and promote those aspects of our humanity affected by the coming age of biotechnology. Only in this report do we address the large social and political question: how can we monitor, oversee, and regulate these burgeoning new technologies, so as to reap their benefits while avoiding their harms, both overt and subtle? How can we exercise responsible control over where biotechnology may be taking us, in order to both serve and preserve our humanity?

In investigating the general subject of the regulation of biotechnology, we have taken as our specific focus the intersection of the technologies of assisted reproduction, human genomic knowledge and technique, and human embryo research. Advances in biotechnology are providing new capacities for altering and influencing the beginnings of human life, especially life initiated outside the body, in the clinic, or in the laboratory. The well-established procedures of in vitro fertilization are being rapidly augmented by abilities to test the genetic make-up of embryos, to screen them for genetic diseases, to select them for their sex or (in the future) for some other desired traits, and to alter them in many other ways. These new capacities increase the variety and complexity of the options facing infertile couples and others seeking assisted reproduction, and they raise the prospect of changes in human reproduction that may have great significance not only for the parents and children involved, but also for society as a whole.

The Council has sought to understand the public policy implications of these developments in human reproduction and, in particular, the ways in which the technologies in question are currently monitored and regulated. Surveying this domain in our report on human cloning, we noted that

> we lack comprehensive knowledge about what is being done, with what success, at what risk, under what ethical guidelines, respecting which moral boundaries, subject to what oversight and regulation, and with what sanctions for misconduct or abuse. If we are to have wise public policy regarding these scientifically and medically promising but morally challenging activities, we need careful study and sustained public moral discourse on this general subject, and not only on specific narrowly defined pieces of the field.

Since the release of that report, the Council has conducted a comprehensive inquiry into the current regulation of those biotechnologies that touch on human reproduction. This report is the fruit of that inquiry.

The Council finds that our regulatory institutions have not kept pace with our rapid technological advance. Indeed, there is today no public authority responsible for monitoring or overseeing how these technologies make their way from the experimental to the clinical stage, from novel approach to widespread practice. There is no authority, public or private, that monitors how or to what extent these new technologies are being or will be used, or that is responsible for attending to the ways they affect the health and well-being of the participants or the character of human reproduction more generally. Our existing regulatory institutions, such as the Food and Drug Administration or local institutional review boards, do not at the present time oversee this area, and the welcome ethical standards promulgated by the professional societies are somewhat limited in scope and not binding on individual member practitioners.

Yet the Council has refrained, at least for the time being, from proposing major new regulatory institutions. Gaps in our current information make doing so premature, and our deep differences over the moral status of human embryos make it problematic. Before either policymakers or the public can address the need for institutional change, we first need much more additional information. What are the true health effects of assisted reproductive technologies on children, mothers, and egg-donors? Are assisted-reproduction patients able to make fully informed choices in the current environment? Could federal intervention be rendered unnecessary by better professional self-regulation? What would be the benefits and the costs of each of the various alternatives either for expanding the responsibilities of our current regulatory institutions or for designing new ones, so as to provide oversight and guidance for responsible practices in reproductive medicine and research? The Council presents a series of recommendations—addressed both to government and to the relevant scientific and medical practitioners—for data gathering, reporting, and professional self-scrutiny. These recommendations are designed to help us get answers to those and other such questions.

But even as we seek answers to these questions and ponder the need for institutional reforms, we do think that the nation would benefit from a series of targeted interim legislative measures that would safeguard certain important ethical boundaries. Accordingly, we propose a series of modest yet precise legislative proposals targeting certain unethical or disquieting practices in human reproduction—for example, attempts to conceive children other than by the union of egg and sperm, to produce a hybrid animal-human embryo, to initiate a human pregnancy for any purpose other than to produce a live-born child, or to try to grow human embryos in the bodies of animals. (The full list of the targeted legislative measures—and of all the other recommendations—is provided in the Executive Summary.) Based on our deliberations to date, we believe these targeted measures will find support on all sides—pro-choice as well as pro-life, secular as well as religious, scientist as well as humanist, left as well as right. Like the nation at large, our members hold differing views about certain foundational questions, especially the moral standing of human embryos. Yet despite our great differences, we all support these proposals and urge their swift adoption.

The issues surrounding the beginnings of human life are notoriously controversial in our country, as they are on the Council. By design, this Council consists of Members with strongly held yet divergent views on these subjects. Yet precisely because of these differences, we have sought in this report—and especially in its recommendations—to find a common ground in certain aims and formulations that all sides could accept, without anyone having to compromise on a matter of principle or having to repudiate what they have said in previous reports. Rather than allow continuing disagreements to blind us to possible significant points of agreement, we have sought precisely to find those goods we all hold dear and to highlight them for the country, so that some progress might be made where it is possible, while public debate and attempts at persuasion continue on the issues that still divide us.

The Council stands behind these recommendations unanimously, even though different members come to them from different premises and with different aims and hopes—as they articulate in their personal statements in the appendix to this document. This discernment of practical common ground in the midst of meaningful disagreement and debate is an accomplishment of which the Council is very proud. We hope it might point the way for others to seek and find the responsible way forward in this vexing arena of public policy.

As with our past reports, so in this one we have sought to be—and we hope you will find us—fair in our approach, precise in our language, accurate in our presentation, and thoughtful in our recommendations.

And as always, Mr. President, I send you this report with the good wishes of my Council colleagues and our fine staff. Once again, we thank you for the opportunity to serve.

Sincerely,

Leon R. Kass

Leon R. Kass, M.D.
Chairman

MEMBERS OF THE PRESIDENT'S COUNCIL ON BIOETHICS

LEON R. KASS, M.D., PH.D., Chairman.
Addie Clark Harding Professor, The College and the Committee on Social Thought, University of Chicago. Hertog Fellow, American Enterprise Institute.

*BENJAMIN S. CARSON, SR., M.D.**
Professor and Director of Pediatric Neurosurgery, Johns Hopkins Medical Institutions.

REBECCA S. DRESSER, J.D., M.S.
Daniel Noyes Kirby Professor of Law and Professor of Ethics in Medicine, Washington University, St. Louis.

DANIEL W. FOSTER, M.D.
Professor of Internal Medicine, John Denis McGarry, Ph.D. Distinguished Chair in Diabetes and Metabolic Research, University of Texas Southwestern Medical School.

FRANCIS FUKUYAMA, PH.D.
Dean of the Faculty, Bernard L. Schwartz Professor of International Political Economy, Paul H. Nitze School of Advanced International Studies, Johns Hopkins University.

MICHAEL S. GAZZANIGA, PH.D.
Dean of the Faculty, David T. McLaughlin Distinguished Professor, Professor of Psychological and Brain Sciences, Dartmouth College.

ROBERT P. GEORGE, J.D., D.PHIL.
McCormick Professor of Jurisprudence, Director of the James Madison Program in American Ideals and Institutions, Princeton University.

MARY ANN GLENDON, J.D., M. COMP. L.
Learned Hand Professor of Law, Harvard University.

ALFONSO GÓMEZ-LOBO, DR. PHIL.
Ryan Family Professor of Metaphysics and Moral Philosophy, Georgetown University.

WILLIAM B. HURLBUT, M.D.
Consulting Professor in Human Biology, Stanford University.

CHARLES KRAUTHAMMER, M.D.
Syndicated Columnist.

*PETER A. LAWLER, PH.D.**
Chairman of the Department of Government and International Studies, Dana Professor of Government, Berry College.

PAUL MCHUGH, M.D.
University Distinguished Service Professor of Psychiatry, Johns Hopkins School of Medicine. Professor, Department of Mental Health, Bloomberg School of Public Health, Johns Hopkins University.

GILBERT C. MEILAENDER, PH.D.
Phyllis & Richard Duesenberg Professor of Christian Ethics, Valparaiso University.

JANET D. ROWLEY, M.D.
Blum-Riese Distinguished Service Professor of Medicine, Molecular Genetics and Cell Biology, and Human Genetics, Pritzker School of Medicine, University of Chicago.

MICHAEL J. SANDEL, D.PHIL.
Anne T. and Robert M. Bass Professor of Government, Harvard University.

*Diana J. Schaub, Ph.D.**
Chairman of the Department of Political Science, Loyola College, Maryland.

JAMES Q. WILSON, PH.D.
James A. Collins Professor of Management and Public Policy Emeritus, University of California, Los Angeles. Reagan Professor of Public Policy, Pepperdine University.

* This Council Member did not participate in the report.

Council Staff and Consultants

Dean Clancy
Executive Director

Yuval Levin
Deputy Executive Director

Eric Cohen
Senior Research Consultant

Judith E. Crawford
Administrative Director

Diane M. Gianelli
Director of Communications

Laura Harmon, Esq.
Senior Aide to the Chairman

Emily Jones
Executive Administrator

Michelle Powers
Law Clerk

Richard Roblin, Ph.D.
Scientific Director

Adam Schulman
Research Consultant

O. Carter Snead, Esq.
General Counsel

Catherine Thorp
Receptionist/Staff Assistant

Audrea R. Vann
Information Technology Specialist

Rachel Flick Wildavsky
Director, Education Project

Lee L. Zwanziger, Ph.D.
Senior Research Analyst

PREFACE

Reproduction and Responsibility: The Regulation of New Biotechnologies is a report of the President's Council on Bioethics, which was created by President George W. Bush on November 28, 2001, by means of Executive Order 13237.

The Council's purpose is to advise the President on bioethical issues related to advances in biomedical science and technology. In connection with its advisory role, the mission of the Council includes the following functions:

- To undertake fundamental inquiry into the human and moral significance of developments in biomedical and behavioral science and technology.

- To explore specific ethical and policy questions related to these developments.

- To provide a forum for a national discussion of bioethical issues.

- To facilitate a greater understanding of bioethical issues.

In his executive order, the President specified several areas for possible attention by the Council, including "embryo and stem cell research, assisted reproduction, cloning, uses of knowledge and techniques derived from human genetics or the neurosciences, and end of life issues," and added that the Council may "study broader ethical and social issues not tied to a specific technology, such as questions regarding the protection of human subjects in research, the appropriate uses of biomedical technologies, the moral implications of biomedical technologies, and the consequences of limiting scientific research." The President left the Council free to establish its own priorities among the many issues encompassed within its charter, and to determine its own modes of proceeding.

The inquiry that led to the present report began at the first Council meeting in January of 2002, when, in his maiden comments to the Council, Professor Francis Fukuyama proposed that the group pursue a study of how new biotechnologies are currently regulated, in hopes of advising the President on new regulatory institutions and principles that might outlive the Council.

In a memo to the Council dated April 10, 2002, Professor Fukuyama argued that

> broad legislative bans will not be an appropriate approach for dealing with a number of foreseeable future technologies. For this, a regulatory model (that is, where Congress delegates authority to a regulatory body under broad guidelines) will be necessary. But the current regulatory system in the United States for human biotechnology is inadequate to make some of the decisions that will have to be made.*

Detailing what he regarded as the gaps in the U.S. regulatory system, Fukuyama suggested that new institutions are necessary, but added that "a great deal may be achievable through self-regulation," citing as an example the Recombinant DNA Advisory Committee (RAC), created as a tool for self-policing by scientists after the Asilomar Conference of 1975. And he named five specific areas for possible regulation: preimplantation genetic diagnosis (PGD); germ-line engineering; the creation of human-animal hybrids and chimeras; novel research techniques (as, for example, research cloning or creating female embryos in order to harvest eggs from their ovaries); and security against bioterrorism.

The Council's interest in the general topic of the regulation of biotechnology soon became focused on the area of human reproduction, and in particular, on the intersection of assisted

---

* Fukuyama, F., "An Overview of Biotech Regulation," Memo to the Members of the President's Council on Bioethics, discussed at session 6 of the Council's meeting on April 26, 2002. For more on this theme, see his book *Our Posthuman Future: Consequences of the Biotechnology Revolution*, New York: Farrar, Strauss and Giroux, 2002.

reproduction, genetic testing and selection, and embryo research. In its July 2002 report on human cloning, in addition to recommending a permanent nationwide ban on cloning-to-produce-children and a four-year moratorium on cloning-for-biomedical-research, a majority of the Council called for "a federal review of current and projected practices of human embryo research, preimplantation genetic diagnosis, genetic modification of human embryos and gametes, and related matters, with a view to recommending and shaping ethically sound policies for the entire field." And it offered itself to "undertake the preliminary steps of such a process and to provide advice on further steps."*

In October 2002, staff produced a memo that set forth some tentative findings to date:

1. The need for some system of regulation has been widely felt around the world.

2. Most countries focus their debate and regulation on questions of assisted reproduction and genetics.

3. The experience of other countries shows that diverse approaches are possible, each in line with the character and history of the particular society.

4. Designing and establishing systems of regulation takes a great deal of time and effort.

5. In the United States, existing institutions appear to be insufficient to handle the questions raised by the new biotechnologies.†

After discussing the memo, the Council charged staff with the task of coming back in six months with a thorough description

* The President's Council on Bioethics, *Human Cloning and Human Dignity: An Ethical Inquiry,* Washington, D.C.: Government Printing Office, 2002, p. 205 (also pp. x and xxxvi).

† The President's Council on Bioethics, "Regulating the New Biotechnologies: Observations and Procedural Options for the Council," Staff Working Paper discussed at session 7 of the Council's meeting on October 18, 2002 (available at www.bioethics.gov).

of the entire range of regulatory institutions and activities—governmental and professional—that monitor, oversee, and regulate the uses of biotechnologies touching the beginnings of human life, and perhaps also with some policy options for consideration. In addition, the Council continued to hear invited presentations on various aspects of the subject, including, among others, the activities of the Food and Drug Administration and institutional review boards (IRBs); the patenting of living organisms; professional self-regulation; the concerns of patients with infertility or with children suffering genetic diseases; and the regulatory activities of other countries, with special presentations regarding institutional arrangements in Canada, Germany, and Great Britain. And the Council also received and considered voluminous written submissions in response to its call for public comment, posted in the *Federal Register*.*

At the June 2003 meeting, staff presented the requested diagnostic overview of all current oversight and regulatory activities, in the form of a 132-page discussion document. Further discussion documents were subsequently produced: a summary of the diagnostic findings and an overview of some possible policy options (July); draft recommendations covering data collection, monitoring, oversight, professional self-regulation, and targeted legislative measures (September); revised recommendations for the targeted legislative measures (October); and all recommendations, revised once more (January 2004). All told, twenty-six sessions, of ninety minutes each, were devoted to this topic at public meetings. Transcripts are available at www.bioethics.gov. The present report draws directly upon those transcripts, as well as on writings of Council members, staff, and invited consultants; comments by interested members of the public and outside experts†; and the written submissions responding to the Council's call for public comment.

As noted in Chapter 1, this report does not go so far as Professor Fukuyama had originally recommended. It does not ad-

---

* The President's Council on Bioethics, "Call for submissions," *Federal Register* 68, no. 56 (March 24, 2003): 14239.

† See the Acknowledgments for a list of individuals and organizations that aided the Council in preparing the report.

vocate new regulatory structures or institutions; neither does it recommend any major changes or increased responsibility for existing regulatory institutions. It does, however, set forth detailed findings about the regulatory status quo. It lays out possible policy options for future examination and study. And it makes interim recommendations, to be followed as the investigation seeking improved regulatory institutions and activities proceeds. We view this report as a first step in a continuing national conversation.

We hope this document, with its detailed diagnostic survey of the regulatory status quo, will serve as a source of clear, intelligible, and useful information for both policymakers and the general public. We also hope that policymakers will take action soon to implement the interim recommendations, set forth in Chapter 10, even as that conversation continues.

In creating this Council, President Bush expressed his desire to see us

> consider all of the medical and ethical ramifications of biomedical innovation. . . . This council will keep us apprised of new developments and give our nation a forum to continue to discuss and evaluate these important issues. As we go forward, I hope we will always be guided by both intellect and heart, by both our capabilities and our conscience.

It has been our goal in the present report, as in all of our work, to live up to these high hopes and noble aspirations.

LEON R. KASS, M.D.
Chairman

ACKNOWLEDGMENTS

The Council would like to extend special thanks to two former Council Members, Elizabeth H. Blackburn, Ph.D., and William F. May, Ph.D., who participated in some of the discussions leading to this report and offered very helpful comments during its drafting.

Special recognition is also due the following outside experts who provided helpful comment on certain portions of the report in draft form. (They do not bear any responsibility for the final report nor do they necessarily endorse its contents.):

Sandra Carson, M.D.
President (2003), American Society for Reproductive Medicine (ASRM)

Lee Rubin Collins, J.D.
National Board of Directors, RESOLVE: The National Infertility Association

Marian D. Damewood, M.D.
President (2004), ASRM

Theodore Friedmann, M.D.
Professor, Center for Molecular Genetics, University of California, San Diego; former Chair, National Institutes of Health (NIH) Recombinant DNA Advisory Committee

Erin Kramer
Director of Government Affairs, RESOLVE: The National Infertility Association

Pamela L. Madsen
Executive Director, The American Infertility Association

Richard A. Merrill, L.L.B, J.D., M.A.
Professor of Law, University of Virginia

Phillip D. Noguchi, M.D.
Director, Division of Cellular and Gene Therapies, Center for Biologics Evaluation and Research, Food and Drug Administration (FDA)

Sean Tipton
Director of Public Affairs, ASRM

Daniel E. Troy, J.D.
Chief Counsel, FDA

The Honorable Ron Wyden
United States Senator, Oregon
Judith A. Yost
Director, Division of Laboratories, Centers for Medicare and Medicaid Services

The Council would also like to extend its gratitude to the following individuals who provided valuable testimony used in the production of this report:

George J. Annas, J.D., M.P.H.
Chairman, Department of Health Law, Bioethics and Human Rights, Boston University
Patricia A. Baird, OC., OBC., FRSC., M.D., C.M., FRCPC., FCCMG,
University Distinguished Professor, Department of Medical Genetics, University of British Columbia, Canada
James S. Benson
Former Acting Commissioner, Food and Drug Administration
Robert Bryzski, M.D., Ph.D.
President (2003), Society for Assisted Reproductive Technology (SART)
Francis S. Collins, M.D., Ph.D.
Director, National Human Genome Research Institute (NHGRI), NIH
Richard M. Doerflinger, Ph.D.
Deputy Director, Secretariat for Pro-Life Activities, U. S. Conference of Catholic Bishops
Ezekiel J. Emanuel, M.D., Ph.D.
Chief, Center for Clinical Bioethics, NIH
Karen Hauda, J.D.
Office of Legislative and International Affairs, U. S. Patent and Trademark Office
Steve H. Holtzman
President, Infinity Pharmaceuticals, Inc., Cambridge, Massachusetts
Kathy Hudson, Ph.D.
Director, Genetics and Public Policy Center, Johns Hopkins University
Baroness Helena Kennedy QC
Chair, U. K. Human Genetics Commission
Daniel J. Kevles, Ph.D.
Department of History, Yale University

Andrew Kimbrell, J.D.
President, International Center for Technology Assessment (ICTA)
Lori Knowles, L.L.B., B.C.L., L.L.M.
Former Associate for Law and Policy, Director, Education and Outreach, The Hastings Center
William Kristol
Chairman, The Bioethics Project
Suzi Leather
Chair, U.K. Human Fertilisation and Embryology Authority
Pamela L. Madsen
Executive Director, The American Infertility Association
Mary Briody Mahowald, Ph.D.
Professor Emerita, Department of Obstetrics and Gynecology, MacLean Center for Clinical Medical Ethics, Committee on Genetics, and The College, University of Chicago
Michael Manganiello
President (2003), Coalition for the Advancement of Medical Research; Senior Vice President, Christopher Reeve Paralysis Foundation
Arti Rai, J.D.
Assistant Professor (2002), University of Pennsylvania Law School
Gerald P. Schatten, Ph.D.
Vice-Chair, Obstetrics-Gynecology & Reproductive Sciences and Cell Biology-Physiology, University of Pittsburgh School of Medicine; Director, Pittsburgh Development Center; Deputy Director, Magee-Women's Research Institute
Spiros Simitis, Prof. Dr. Drs. h.c.
Chairman, German National Ethics Council
Maxine F. Singer, Ph.D.
Chair, Committee on Science, Engineering, and Public Policy, National Academy of Sciences
David H. Smith, Ph.D.
Director (2003), The Poynter Center for the Study of Ethics and American Institutions, Indiana University
Michael J. Werner, J.D.
Vice President, Biotechnology Industry Organization

Finally, the Council would like to thank those that answered its call for public comment on the issues touched on in this report:

American Association for the Advancement of Science
American Association of Bioanalysts

American Bar Association
American Board of Bioanalysis
American College of Obstetricians and Gynecologists
American Infertility Association
American Life League
American Medical Association
American Society for Reproductive Medicine
American Society of Human Genetics
Assemblies of God U.S.A.
Biotechnology Industry Organization
Center for Applied Reproductive Science
Center for Bioethics and Human Dignity
William P. Cheshire, Jr., M.D.
Christian Legal Society
Christian Medical and Dental Associations
Church of Jesus Christ of Latter-day Saints
Coalition for the Advancement of Medical Research
College of Reproductive Biology
Concerned Clergy for Choice
Concerned Women for America
Council for Responsible Genetics
Evangelical Lutheran Church of America
Family Planning Advocates of New York State
Family Research Council
Federation of American Societies for Experimental Biology
Focus on the Family
Genetics and Public Policy Center
Greek Orthodox Church of America
Ronald M. Green, Ph.D., Institute for the Study of Applied and Professional Ethics, Dartmouth College
The Hastings Center
Institute for Women's Policy Research
International Center for Technology Assessment
Journal of Assisted Reproduction and Genetics
Lutheran Church - Missouri Synod
Lynne Millican, R.N., B.S.N.
Medical and Health Research Association of New York City, Inc.
Michael J. Fox Foundation for Parkinson's Research
The National Academies
National Catholic Bioethics Center
National Science Foundation
National Women's Law Center
Northwest Women's Law Center

Planned Parenthood
Reproductive Health Technologies Project
RESOLVE: The National Infertility Association
Society for Assisted Reproductive Technology
Society for Reproductive Endocrinology and Infertility
Craig H. Syrop, M.D.
Union of Orthodox Jewish Congregations of America
Yates Family Planning Services

EXECUTIVE SUMMARY

Advances in biotechnology in recent decades have made available an increasing capacity to intervene in the beginnings of human life, especially life initiated outside the body, whether in the clinic or in the laboratory. This capacity emerges from a confluence of work in reproductive biology, developmental biology, and human genetics, and raises ethical issues involving a number of important human goods. There is little question that the way these new technologies are used could have far-reaching consequences, not only for the individuals involved but also for society as a whole.

Yet it is not clear just how the interests of those individuals and of the public at large can best be served as these new technologies are developed and applied. What challenges and public policy concerns arise together with the use of new technologies affecting human reproduction? Whose responsibility is it to monitor, review, and offer guidance where guidance is needed, in order to safeguard the diverse human goods at stake? Should there be more or less oversight and regulation? Should there be any? Just how much is there now? Only partial answers are available to these questions, and much basic data remain to be gathered before they could be answered.

Since its very first meeting, in January of 2002, the President's Council on Bioethics has taken an interest in these subjects, and the Council has sought a way to advance public understanding of the challenges that confront us in this arena—beginning with the most basic information regarding what is being done and with what results. In the Council's report, *Human Cloning and Human Dignity* (2002), members observed that, with regard to assisted reproduction, genetic testing, and human embryo research,

> we lack comprehensive knowledge about what is being done, with what success, at what risk, under what ethical guidelines, respecting which moral

> boundaries, subject to what oversight and regulation, and with what sanctions for misconduct or abuse. If we are to have wise public policy regarding these scientifically and medically promising but morally challenging activities, we need careful study and sustained public moral discourse on this general subject, and not only on specific narrowly defined pieces of the field.

Following the release of that report, the Council decided to undertake a thoroughgoing inquiry into the current regulation of those biotechnologies that touch on human reproduction. This report is the fruit of that inquiry. Its principal aim is to describe and critically assess the various oversight and regulatory measures that now govern the biotechnologies and practices at the intersection of assisted reproduction, human genetics, and human embryo research.

I. WHAT IS AT STAKE?

The Council saw a number of powerful reasons for taking up this subject. It involves some of the key concerns of bioethics and is likely to be an area of increasing importance, one in which both public understanding and public policy lag well behind the rapid advance of technological developments. Among the goods and ideals that are at stake, and that led the Council to point the public's attention toward this subject, are the following:

- The health and well-being of the human subjects directly affected by these technologies, not only the individuals or couples seeking their use, but also and especially the children who may be born with their aid.

- Relief of the suffering and sorrow of those afflicted with infertility.

- Compassion for children with serious genetic diseases, and relief of the sorrows and burdens that they and those who love and care for them must bear.

- The intrinsic value of new knowledge of human development and genetic function in addition to the inestimable practical value of new treatments for diseases and disabilities.

- Privacy of genetic information and reproductive practice.

- The foundational value of human life and the respect owed to it in its various stages.

- Several expressions and avenues of human freedom, including the freedom of parents to make their own reproductive decisions or to use or refuse genetic screening, and the freedom of scientists to conduct research. As important, as well, is the necessity to protect the freedom of children from improper attempts to manipulate their lives through control of their genetic make-up or from unreasonable expectations that could accompany such manipulations.

- The promotion of justice and equality, including equitable access to the use and benefits of new technologies, equal respect and opportunity in a world that places great emphasis on genetic distinctions, and the prevention of discrimination against or contempt for genetic "defectiveness" or "inferiority."

- The protection of human dignity, including the dignity of the human body and its parts, the dignity of important human relationships (parent and child, one generation and the next), and the humanity of human procreation.

The Council's review of the field has been guided and motivated by these concerns.

II. A DIAGNOSTIC OVERVIEW

This report is fundamentally a diagnostic document, and even most of the recommendations with which it concludes aim largely at improving the nation's capacity for future diagnosis of the state of this field. The diagnosis begins by examining policies and practices related to assisted reproduction. This is our starting point because assisted reproduction is, in practice, the necessary gateway to all the newer technologies—present and projected—that affect human reproduction. Preimplantation genetic diagnosis (including sex selection), germ-line genetic modification, human embryo research, and similar techniques all presuppose in vitro fertilization and the existence of developing human life in vitro. As a consequence, any oversight or regulation of the use of genetic technologies in human reproduction will necessarily depend on the systems that oversee and regulate assisted reproduction itself. Also, the addition of genetic technologies to existing techniques of assisted reproduction has made it clear—if it had not been clear before—that we are dealing here with a most unusual branch of medicine. In no other area of medicine does the treatment of an ailment—in this case, infertility—call for the creation of another human being. Our deep concern for the safety and well-being of children suggests to us the need for special attention to the uses and outcomes of these new biotechnologies.

The report then proceeds to review the regulatory policies and practices involved in screening and selecting for genetic conditions and traits; modification of traits and characteristics; research involving in vitro human embryos; and commercial and financial interests in this arena.

In discussing each area we review the relevant techniques and practices, the principal ethical issues, and (especially) the existing regulatory activities. This extended diagnostic discussion explores in detail precisely who currently provides oversight and guidance in each area, pursuant to what authority, according to what principles and values, and with what ultimate practical effect.

III. THE COUNCIL'S FINDINGS

The Council's diagnostic review of these areas has led us to several general conclusions:

- The fields of assisted reproduction, human genetics, and embryo research are increasingly converging with one another.

- There is no uniform, comprehensive, and enforceable system of data collection, monitoring, or oversight for the biotechnologies affecting human reproduction.

- There is minimal direct governmental regulation of the practice of assisted reproduction.

- There is extensive professional self-regulation of the practice of assisted reproduction, but compliance with the standards invoked is purely voluntary.

- There is no comprehensive, uniform, and enforceable mechanism for data collection, monitoring, or oversight of how the new reproductive biotechnologies affect the well-being of the children conceived with their aid, the egg donors, or the gestational mothers.

- There are no nationally uniform laws or policies relating to access to assisted reproduction.

- Given the present framework of regulation, novel technologies and practices that are successful move from the experimental context to clinical practice with relatively little oversight or deliberation. Once in practice, these techniques are used at clinicians' discretion, with little or no external oversight. Use of effective technologies becomes widespread rapidly.

- As in other areas of medicine, there is no uniform system for public review and deliberation regarding the larger human or social significance of new reproductive biotechnologies.

- Preimplantation genetic diagnosis is an unregulated practice.

- Gene transfer research, by contrast, is regulated robustly.

- There is no comprehensive, uniform, and enforceable mechanism for data collection, monitoring, or oversight regarding the use and disposition of in vitro human embryos in the context of clinical practice or research.

- There is no comprehensive mechanism for regulation of commerce in gametes, embryos, and assisted reproductive technology services.

- Patenting of embryonic or fetal human organisms is prohibited for the fiscal year 2004.

The Council does not take these findings in and of themselves to mean that any public policy response is called for, but any consideration of potential public policies in this area must take these basic facts into account.

IV. POLICY OPTIONS AND RECOMMENDATIONS

The Council's findings, combined with the concerns that animate our interest in this area, point toward a fairly wide array of possible regulatory approaches. In this report, the Council considers these options in some detail, laying out a range of potential institutional options—from doing nothing to developing entirely new regulatory institutions—and offering a number of possible aims and principles that might guide future regulators.

However, given the preliminary character of this report, and the fact that our review of the field has turned up a number of areas where crucial data are simply lacking, the Council was not prepared to recommend any sweeping institutional reform or innovation. Rather, members agreed upon a series of modest measures to alleviate some clear and significant present problems, including especially the lack of information on certain key practices and their consequences.

The report concludes, therefore, with a set of recommendations that the Council agrees should be adopted immediately. These recommendations are not for structural or institutional changes; we do not propose the wholesale creation of new regulatory institutions or even the reform of existing ones. Rather, we offer these recommendations as interim measures with two goals in mind: first, to strengthen existing legislation and regulatory mechanisms in order to gather more complete and useful information; and, second, to erect certain legislative safeguards against a small number of boundary-crossing practices, at least until there can be further deliberation and debate about both the human goods at stake and the best way to protect them.

The recommendations fall into three general categories: studies and data collection, oversight and self-regulation by professional societies, and targeted legislative measures. In each case, the Council has detailed its precise recommendations in the report and has offered extensive supporting arguments and reasons. The recommendations are as follows.

A. Federal Studies, Data Collection, Reporting, and Monitoring Regarding the Uses and Effects of These Technologies

As the Council's findings demonstrate, the incompleteness of basic information on the uses and impact of new reproductive technologies makes any conclusive policy judgments very difficult to formulate. The Council therefore recommends that the federal government take a number of specific steps to improve our knowledge and understanding:

- Undertake a federally funded longitudinal study of the impact of assisted reproductive technologies on the health and development of children born with their aid.

- Undertake federally funded studies on the impact of assisted reproductive technologies on the health and well-being of women.

- Undertake federally funded comprehensive studies on the uses of reproductive genetic technologies, and on their effects on children born with their aid.

- Strengthen and augment the Fertility Clinic Success Rate and Certification Act to better protect consumers and patients:

    - Provide more user-friendly reporting of data.
    - Require the publication of all reported adverse health effects.
    - Require the reporting of the average prices of the procedures and the average cost (to patients) of a successful assisted pregnancy.
    - Include information on novel and experimental procedures.
    - Require more specific reporting and publication of the frequency of, and reasons for, uses of specialized techniques such as ICSI, preimplantation genetic diagnosis, and sperm sorting for sex-selection.
    - Provide model forms for decision-making.
    - Provide stronger penalties to enhance compliance with the Act's reporting requirements.
    - Increase funding for implementation of the Act.

B. Increased Oversight by Professional Societies and Practitioners

Most oversight in this area currently takes the form of self-regulation by professional societies, and as far as the Council can determine the vast majority of practitioners abide by these guidelines and standards and are dedicated to the welfare of their patients. Yet the Council has identified a few ways in which self-regulation could be meaningfully improved:

- Strengthen informed patient decision-making.
- Treat the child born with the aid of assisted reproductive procedures as a patient.
- Improve enforcement of existing guidelines.
- Improve procedures for movement of experimental procedures into clinical practice.
- Create and enforce minimum uniform standards for the protection of human subjects affected by assisted reproduction.
- Develop additional self-imposed ethical boundaries.

C. Targeted Legislative Measures

In the course of its review, discussion, and findings, the Council encountered and highlighted several particular practices and techniques (some already in use, others likely to be tried in the foreseeable future) touching human reproduction that raise new and distinctive challenges. Given the importance of the matter, we believe these require special attention, and we therefore recommend that Congress should consider some limited targeted measures that might institute a moratorium on certain particularly questionable practices. The report includes an extensive discussion of the reasons for these recommendations as well as the aims we hope they might serve. The Council recommends that the Congress should, at least for a limited time:

- Prohibit the transfer, for any purpose, of any human embryo into the body of any member of a non-human species.

- Prohibit the production of a hybrid human-animal embryo by fertilization of human egg by animal sperm or of animal egg by human sperm.*

- Prohibit the transfer of a human embryo (produced ex vivo) to a woman's uterus for any purpose other than to attempt to produce a live-born child.

- Prohibit attempts to conceive a child by any means other than the union of egg and sperm.†

- Prohibit attempts to conceive a child by using gametes obtained from a human fetus or derived from human embryonic stem cells.†

- Prohibit attempts to conceive a child by fusing blastomeres from two or more embryos.†

- Prohibit the use of human embryos in research beyond a designated stage in their development (between 10 and 14 days after fertilization).‡

---

* It bears noting that, in testing for male-factor infertility, practitioners of assisted reproduction now use hamster eggs to test the capacity of human sperm to penetrate an egg; yet there is no intent to produce a human-animal hybrid embryo, and there is negligible likelihood that one might be formed, given the wide genetic gap between the species. Thus, we do not believe that such procedures run afoul of the letter or spirit of the above recommendations.

† Operationally, in each of the three cases listed, the prohibited act comprises the creation ex vivo of any such human embryo *with the intent* to transfer it to a woman's body to initiate a pregnancy.

‡ Some members of the Council are opposed to any experimentation that harms or destroys human embryos, but, recognizing that it is legal and active, they see the value in limiting the practice. Other members of the Council favor allowing such experimentation during the early stages of embryonic development, but nonetheless recognize the need to establish an upper age limit beyond which such research should not proceed. Some Council members believe that this upper limit should be 14 days after the first cell division; others favor 10 (or less).

- Prohibit the buying and selling of human embryos.*

- Prohibit the issuing of patents on claims directed to or encompassing human embryos or fetuses at any stage of development; and amend Title 35, United States Code, section 271(g) (which extends patent protections to products resulting from a patented process) to exclude these items from patentability.†

---

* This provision is not intended to preclude patients who receive donated embryos from reimbursing donors for reasonable expenses, storage costs, and the like. Also, because the compensated giving of sperm is a long-established practice, and because payment to egg donors is now also fairly common, efforts to ban payment to gamete providers would likely prove controversial and untenable for purposes of actual legislation. Thus, we decline to recommend such a ban here. That is not to say, however, that the Council approves of the buying and selling of gametes. Indeed, many Council members have raised serious concerns regarding this species of commercialization in the domain of human reproduction.

† The language of any such statute would in our view need to take some care not to exclude from patentability the processes that result in these items, but only the products themselves. Similar language has been included in a component of the federal budget for fiscal year 2004 (the Consolidated Appropriations Act of 2004, H.R. 2673, 108th Congress [January 23, 2004], Division B, §634), but we believe this provision should also be made a clear and permanent element of the patent law.

1

Introduction

It is by now a commonplace that advances in biomedical science and technology are raising challenging and profound ethical issues—for individuals and families, for scientists and health care professionals, and for the broader society. Many important human goods are implicated, among them health and the relief of suffering, scientific progress, respect for life and the human person, human freedom, and human dignity. The flourishing field of modern bioethics, not yet forty years old, arose to explore these issues, and various bodies, including local research review boards, academic bioethics institutes, and several national commissions, have been wrestling with them. Yet amid all this activity, it is far from clear whose responsibility it is to monitor, oversee, and offer guidance where guidance is needed, in order to safeguard the diverse and often competing human goods at stake. Which institutions, public or private, are now responsible for which sorts of oversight or regulatory activity, and in the name of what? We can readily name some—the Food and Drug Administration, for example—that are responsible for the efficacy and safety of new drugs or devices. But which permanent bodies, if any, are vested with effective authority to protect some of the other goods we care about? And how well are they doing their job?

I. BACKGROUND

At its very first meeting, the President's Council on Bioethics signaled an interest in exploring how, if at all, the existing regulatory mechanisms in the United States address the various ethical and social issues that arise from advances in biomedical science and technology. Some members of the Council suggested that new regulatory institutions might need to be devised. Others were skeptical, especially before we knew how well the current arrangements worked or which principles should guide any such new institutions. In the Council's report, *Human Cloning and Human Dignity*, published in July 2002, a suggestion emerged to pursue this interest regarding regulation in a specific domain. Members observed that, for the activities at the intersection of assisted reproduction, human genetic testing, and human embryo research,

> we lack comprehensive knowledge about what is being done, with what success, at what risk, under what ethical guidelines, respecting which moral boundaries, subject to what oversight and regulation, and with what sanctions for misconduct or abuse. If we are to have wise public policy regarding these scientifically and medically promising but morally challenging activities, we need careful study and sustained public moral discourse on this general subject, and not only on specific narrowly defined pieces of the field.[1]

Three months following the release of that report, the Council decided to undertake a thoroughgoing inquiry into the current regulation of those biotechnologies that touch human reproduction. This report is the fruit of that inquiry. Its principal aim is to describe and critically assess the various oversight and regulatory measures that now govern the biotechnologies and practices at the intersection of assisted reproduction, human genetics, and human embryo research.

II. THE DOMAIN OF INQUIRY

The reason for and focus of this inquiry is the growing capacity to influence and control the beginnings of human life, especially as exercised ex vivo (outside the body), in the clinic and the laboratory. These capacities emerge from a confluence of work in reproductive biology, developmental biology, and human genetics. The well-established practices of assisted reproduction are today being augmented by techniques of genetic screening and selection of embryos; some day, gametes or embryos may be modifiable by directed genetic manipulation. Our focus here is not assisted reproduction as such, nor is it the fate of human embryos or the evolving understanding of human genetics and the novel capacities for genetic diagnosis and manipulation. Rather, we are concerned with the unique interactions among these elements and the new possibilities these interactions create for controlling and perhaps someday altering the character of human procreation and human life.

Our point of departure will be the practice of assisted reproduction. We are well aware that assisted reproduction is not new—indeed, it has over the past quarter-century become firmly established within the practice of medicine, and it is thus subject to the usual formal and informal mechanisms that regulate medical practice. With great success, assisted reproductive technologies (ART) have enabled over one million otherwise infertile couples and individuals to have biologically related children and to participate in the joys of family life. Our purpose here is not to second-guess how this novel and profoundly important practice grew and came to be regulated in the way it has. Neither are we interested in interfering with that practice. However, three reasons, taken together, recommend assisted reproduction as our point of departure. First, all the other activities of interest—preimplantation genetic diagnosis, sex selection, germ-line genetic modification, human embryo research, and a range of potential new modes of human conception—presuppose the creation and existence of human embryos in vitro. The ability to screen and select genetic traits in vitro depends on the prior ability to initiate and sustain embryonic life in the laboratory. Thus, in vitro fertilization and related techniques are the starting point for all the others, both in practice and, hence, in our inquiry. Second, as a consequence, any oversight or regulation of the use of genetic technologies in the context of human procreation will necessarily depend on the systems that oversee and regulate assisted reproduction itself: what they are and how well they work. Third, the addition of genetic technologies to existing techniques of assisted reproduction has made it clear—if it had not been clear before—that we are dealing here with a most unusual branch of medicine. In no other area of medicine does the treatment of an ailment—in this case, infertility—call for the creation of another human being. Here, the therapeutic intervention, addressing the needs and desires of the procreating adults, aims at and consists in the production of a new human child, who may be at risk of harm from the very procedures used to conceive or produce him. It is our concern for the safety and well-being of children that suggests to us the need for special attention—especially now that genetic screening and selection are being added to the practices of assisted reproduction.

III. THE HUMAN GOODS AT STAKE

All regulatory institutions and practices operate, either explicitly or tacitly, in order to promote or protect one or more important human goods. Identifying those goods and the things that challenge them is indispensable for any analysis and evaluation of how—and how well—regulatory activities are conducted. It is therefore useful, at the start of this document, to identify the major goods, values, and ethical concerns that the Council finds pertinent to the subject area, and hence to our assessment. First among these, as already indicated, is the health and well-being of the human subjects directly affected by the biotechnologies, not only the individuals or couples seeking their use but also and especially the children who may be born with their aid. Concern for the bodily health, safety, and well-being of those children is of prime importance, especially in an age in which more and more features of their genetic make-up could be shaped by technical intervention and deliberate human decision.

Other human goods of crucial relevance to this discussion include:* (1) Relief of the suffering and sorrow of those afflicted with infertility, for whom assisted reproductive technologies are an avenue of hope and possibility and offer the chance to enjoy the blessings of rearing (biologically related) children. (2) Compassion for children with serious genetic diseases, and relief of the sorrows and burdens that they and those who love and care for them must bear. (3) The intrinsic value of new knowledge of human development and genetic function in addition to the inestimable practical value of new treatments for diseases and disabilities—the main goals of some of the associated genetic and reproductive technologies under consideration and of research using embryonic stem cells. (4) Privacy of genetic information and reproductive practice. (5) The foundational value of human life and the respect owed to it in its various stages. (6) Several expressions and avenues of human freedom, including the freedom of parents to make their own reproductive decisions or to use or refuse genetic screening, and the freedom of scientists to conduct research. As important, as well, is the necessity to protect the freedom of children from improper attempts to manipulate their lives through control of their genetic make-up or from unreasonable expectations that could accompany such manipulations. (7) The promotion of justice and equality, including equitable access to the use and benefits of new technologies, equal respect and opportunity in a world that places great emphasis on genetic distinctions, and the prevention of discrimination and contempt for genetic "defectiveness" or "inferiority." (8) The protection of human dignity, including the dignity of the human body and its parts, the dignity of important human relationships (parent and child, one generation and the next), and the humanity of human procreation.

IV. SOME SPECIFIC ISSUES

Some of the aforementioned human goods—for example, relieving the sorrows of the infertile or preventing and treating

* Each item on the list that follows is considered important by most, though not necessarily all, Members of the Council. And, of course, we often differ among ourselves as to which goods, values, and concerns are more important than others.

heritable diseases—are, of course, among the primary goals of the practice of ART or the study of human genetics and development. Although many have reaped the benefits of these technologies, many others who seek these benefits still wait in sadness and hope. Other goods—for example, protecting the freedom and privacy of reproductive choice or preventing genetic discrimination—have been the focus of professional self-regulation and legislative enactments. Nevertheless, other relevant human goods appear not to be receiving comparable attention. And, while ethical issues connected with these various goods are identifiable, there appears to be no existing oversight body or significant regulatory activity directly concerned with those issues. Accordingly, throughout our analysis we shall be especially mindful of how various existing regulatory practices address these ethical issues. Some issues are raised by the practice of ART as such, others by the practices of genetic screening and selection, and still others by potential new techniques of human conception. In addition, there are concerns raised by the commercialization of human reproductive services and the advent of commerce in eggs, sperm, and embryos.

Beyond the obvious and important issues of health and safety, there are a number of broader ethical and social concerns that have been called to our attention—some already here, others perhaps on the way. These concerns include the following: (1) The daunting complexity of options confronting would-be ART patients, and the need for full and candid reporting of the successes and failures of different ART treatments and techniques. (2) The adequacy or inadequacy of procedures for informed decision-making by patients. (3) The potential aggravation of existing social inequalities, should such technologies become available only to the wealthy or the privileged. (4) The possible emergence of new grounds for inequality and discrimination based on genetic characteristics. (5) The prospect of making entrance into human life contingent on passing certain genetic tests. (6) The concern that the state, insurance providers, or others may attempt to impose prenatal or preconception testing on prospective parents. (7) The use, cryopreservation, and destruction of embryonic human life. (8) Questions about the boundary between disease-prevention and so-called "enhancement" uses of these technologies—how to define that boundary and what to do about it. (9) The effects of commercialization of aspects of human procreation (such as the sale or patenting of gametes and embryos). (10) The consequences of moving procreation more and more into the laboratory and possibly turning it in the direction of manufacture. (11) The changing expectations of parents regarding children born using—or *not* using—genetic screening and selection. (12) The concern that children born through certain assisted reproductive technologies (for example, cloning) will be denied a share in our common human heritage (such as a biological connection to two adult parents and two clear lineages). (13) A blurring of the line between the human and the animal in certain laboratory research techniques. (14) The fear that a growing emphasis on genetic determinants of human life will exaggerate the primacy of genetic causation over environment, free will, agency, and choice.

Not all of these ethical issues are equally susceptible to regulatory activity, and few of them are likely to be the subject of anything so far-reaching as restrictive legislation. Not all of these concerns are shared or shared equally by every member of this Council. But most, if not all, of these issues are sufficiently serious as to suggest the desirability of monitoring what is going on, with a view at the very least to informing patients and policymakers how well we are handling any possible untoward consequences.

Also animating the following inquiry are concerns about the chilling effect that overbroad or excessive regulation might have on the development and practice of promising and worthwhile technologies. Just as the absence of fitting and effective regulation is ethically problematic, so too is overly burdensome or unjustifiable regulation of practices that alleviate human suffering and bring great joy. The possible costs and drawbacks of potential regulation must themselves be counted among the concerns that drive our interest in this field. *However, while this report will touch on a wide range of subjects, our main focus is on the well-being of children who might be conceived and born with the aid of new reproductive and genetic technologies, and on the possible implications of these biotechnologies for human reproduction considered more broadly.*

V. THE AMERICAN LEGAL LANDSCAPE

Before moving to the substantive analysis of the present regulatory landscape, it is worth noticing briefly some unique aspects of American law that create the backdrop against which the current regulatory mechanisms exist.

First, because practices touching reproduction and developing human life raise questions related to the central themes of the abortion debate, any efforts at regulation are likely to be fraught with political difficulty. Proposed efforts to regulate or monitor assisted reproduction are viewed by many people through the prism of *Roe v. Wade* and the legal-political context it has created, arousing suspicion and concern among individuals on both sides of the abortion conflict. Defenders of reproductive freedom want no infringement of the right to make personal reproductive decisions, and they fear that the regulation of ART might undermine the right to privacy. Pro-life opponents of embryo destruction fear that the federal regulation of assisted reproduction or embryo research might give tacit or explicit public approval to practices that they find morally objectionable. This situation creates a powerful disincentive for any regulation of the uses of reproductive technologies. More generally, there is deep disagreement in our society about the degree of respect owed to in vitro embryonic human life and the weight that respect should carry in relation to other moral considerations, such as helping infertile couples to have children, helping couples to have healthy children, and advancing biomedical knowledge that could well lead to cures for dread diseases. This disagreement is one of the main reasons for the current relatively laissez-faire approach to regulation. While some observers urge that the standoff over the moral status of embryonic human life should not be permitted to hold up appropriate and useful regulation of ART and related practices, others respond that resolution of this dispute is the *sine qua non* of any responsible approach to regulation.

Second, the practice of medicine (now embracing ART) occupies a special place in the American legislative and legal system. The practice of medicine is principally regulated through state licensure and certification of physicians rather than by reference to specific legislative proscriptions or prescriptions of conduct. Legislatures defer to the profession not only because medicine is highly esteemed, but also because of the special expertise of physicians in their various specialties and the relative lack of medical expertise on the part of legislatures or other governmental authorities. Medicine is a profession where crucial judgments must be made on a case-by-case basis by a practitioner familiar with the details and circumstances involved. The law tends to give physicians ample latitude to make such judgments.

Third, the U. S. Constitution has several distinctive features that bear on the present discussion. The American system of federalism has tended to vest principal authority for safeguarding the health, safety, and general welfare of citizens in their respective states. This broad mandate of the states leads to a lack of uniformity across local jurisdictions, but also permits states to serve as "laboratories" for regulatory experimentation. In addition, the enumeration of federal powers in the Constitution sets limits on what the national government may legislate. Only conduct that meets a specific jurisdictional threshold (for example, activities that involve interstate commerce) is reachable by federal mechanisms of regulation. (The authority of the FDA, for example, a key player in the regulation of human biotechnology, is grounded partly in the constitutional power of the federal government to regulate interstate commerce.) On the other hand, the Constitution recognizes certain individual rights inhering in all citizens (or, depending on the right, in all persons), as well as liberties that may be vindicated against both state and federal governments. The assertion of such rights can be controversial, especially in cases in which the rights in question are not explicitly enumerated in the Constitution itself. One such controversial right is, of course, the right to privacy in intimate matters relating to procreation. The relevance of the right to privacy to the regulation of assisted reproduction is easily recognized, while its likely application in actual cases is difficult to predict.

A fourth principal concept in American law, directly relevant to the present inquiry, is that the public and private realms of conduct are legally and ethically distinct. The reach of law is in many ways driven by this distinction: public action may properly be regulated by the government, especially to protect public health, safety, and welfare, and to vindicate individual rights; by contrast, the realm of private conduct (that is, actions undertaken in private, affecting only the particular individuals involved) is the zone of maximum individual liberty. To be sure, this distinction, while simple in theory, proves complicated in practice. The new biotechnologies and practices treated in this report involve human life in its most intimate and private aspects: procreation, child rearing, human suffering, and individual conscience. In such matters, there is a strong legal and cultural presumption in favor of personal liberty. This presumption is only overcome by an equally compelling governmental and societal interest, typically the protection of life and limb. The tension between these concepts—public and private, liberty and the public good—should be borne in mind when considering these technologies and practices.

A fifth concept, related but different, is the distinction often drawn between publicly funded and privately funded activities. Some activities the law chooses silently to tolerate while withholding its official sanction or endorsement through public support; other activities are actively promoted and funded by the government; and still others are regulated or prohibited entirely. This distinction between prohibition, silence, and active endorsement is especially significant in some arenas touched on in this discussion.*

A sixth crucial principle is the special role of parents in American law. They are considered the principal protectors of the well-being of their children, including their as-yet-unborn children. As such, they are granted wide latitude by the law to

---

* Scientific research involving the destruction of human embryos, for instance, is not legally prohibited at the federal level, though federal government funding of nearly all such activity is prohibited. This distinction has played an important role in the political controversies surrounding embryo research, and it is held by many people on all sides of the question to be of great significance. For example, there are some who argue that the proscription of federal funding for such embryo research deters scientists from undertaking valuable studies of the safety and efficacy of various techniques of assisted reproduction. Moreover, it is argued that this limitation on funding deprives the federal government of a useful opportunity to provide meaningful oversight in this domain. Others, not persuaded by these observations, respond that research involving the destruction of human embryos can proceed in the private sector without any governmental restriction. They argue further that federal funding is not a prerequisite for governmental oversight in this area; indeed, the federal government regulates a number of activities that it does not fund. For a more extensive discussion, see the Council's report, *Monitoring Stem Cell Research*, published in January of 2004, especially Chapter 2, pp. 37-41. See also the commissioned paper by Peter Berkowitz, contained in Appendix F of that report.

make decisions that directly affect their children's well-being, and this is especially true in the context of assisted reproduction. At the same time, however, the law recognizes certain circumstances in which the state may intervene to protect the welfare of children.

A seventh feature of American law relevant to the present inquiry is the presumption in favor of commerce and free enterprise. The values of freedom to contract, to participate in the free market, and to profit from the fruits of one's labors are embodied in the Constitution, statutes, and decisional authorities that constitute U.S. law. Any governmental efforts to regulate biotechnology and related activities would take place against this legal backdrop. Similarly, unlike many other nations, our health care system is not run by the government, and physicians enjoy a large measure of autonomy in their own economic activity. The largely private funding of medical care also places additional obstacles in the way of attempts at government regulation.

An eighth element that informs the present inquiry is the absence of human dignity as an explicit concept in American law. Much of the legal discourse in this country employs operative terms such as liberty, equality, justice, and rights. Unlike some of our European counterparts, "human dignity" is not in our legal lexicon. Thus, legislators and courts lack the language (and therefore the explicit authority) to fashion responses and remedies to conduct solely on the grounds that it threatens the dignity of the human person.

Ninth, it is necessary to bear in mind the range and variety of activities that may be properly deemed "regulation" for purposes of this inquiry. Regulation comes in myriad forms, from various sources, with widely differing results. Regulation can include a variety of mechanisms, ranging from legal prohibition and statutory obligations to mere monitoring and data collection. Methods of enforcement range from criminal prosecution to mere hortatory suggestion. Even information-gathering can serve as a kind of cautionary regulatory function. It signals to practitioners in the field that society is paying attention and has a stake in the underlying activity. In addition, the source of regulation can be governmental (with the coercive power of the state as the principal mechanism for implementation) or nongovernmental (where market forces and peer evaluation are the chief means of implementation).

Finally, another distinctive aspect of regulation in the United States is the nation's deeply ingrained commitment to pluralism. The potential need to regulate assisted reproduction runs up against American individualism and an aversion to "legislating morals." Americans expect their governments to give compelling reasons before restricting individual liberty. Many people also harbor suspicions that governmental regulations and the bureaucracies needed to manage them are harmful, ineffective, and threatening to salutary personal freedoms and economic progress.

All these considerations make thinking about regulating new reproductive biotechnologies extremely complicated, in ways largely peculiar to the United States. Although the Council has heard presentations on regulatory schemes used in other countries, this document does not deal with them. We are eager, first of all, to disclose and assess what is going on in our own country. And, given the noted peculiarities of American law and political culture, there is good reason to doubt whether foreign practices can serve directly as models for what we can and should do here. In any event, there is no consensus among those nations that have chosen to regulate in this domain.*

---

* Approaches vary widely. In the United Kingdom, for example, assisted reproduction and embryo research are regulated through a system of licensure; there are limits on the number of embryos that can be transferred during each cycle, and sex selection for non-medical purposes is forbidden. In Germany, there is an "Embryo Protection Law" that effectively forbids destructive embryo research. In February 2004, the Italian Parliament enacted legislation that prohibits donation of sperm or eggs from third parties, limits in vitro fertilization techniques to cohabiting heterosexual couples, prohibits destructive experimentation on embryos, forbids the creation of more than three embryos at one time, and requires all embryos created to be transferred to the patient's uterus. In March 2004, the Canadian Parliament enacted the "Assisted Human Reproduction Act," a comprehensive piece of legislation that covers the whole field of assisted reproduction. The bill imposes a system of licensure for the creation, alteration, or manipulation of in vitro embryos and provides for the creation of an "Assisted Human Reproduction Agency of Canada" that will administer all the newly enacted regulations. These regulations include, among others, prohibitions of: all human cloning (both to produce children and for biomedical research); sex selection for non-medical purposes; the creation of chimeras (for any reason) and hybrids (for reproductive purposes); the creation of in vitro embryos for any purpose other than reproduction or "improving or providing instruction in assisted reproduction procedures"; the maintenance of an in vitro embryo past 14 days of development; heritable genetic modification; commercial surrogacy contracts; and the buying and selling of gametes. (For further in-

VI. THE CHARACTER AND SIGNIFICANCES OF HUMAN PROCREATION

While following our inquiry into the regulation of new reproductive biotechnologies, it will be important to keep in mind the character and significance of the area of human life we are discussing—namely, human procreation. Thus, before considering the new technologies and how they are regulated, we would do well to reflect (however briefly) on the character of human reproduction itself—especially on the significance of procreation in shaping fundamental human relationships, both familial and social.

Human procreation is an activity of deep biological and anthropological significance. Biologically speaking, as with other animals, human procreation represents life's answer to mortality, perpetuating the human species despite the perishability of every one of its members. In addition, through the genetic recombination produced by the lottery of sexual reproduction, genetic novelty is assured, allowing for the gradual evolutionary emergence of new biological capacities and possibilities. Humanly speaking, because these deep biological facts are lifted up into human self-consciousness, procreation commonly establishes ties of belonging, rooted in begetting, richly significant for parents, children, and the larger society. These last implications deserve further specification.*

---

formation about international models of regulation, see the transcripts of presentations to the Council by Patricia Baird [Canada], Lori Knowles [United Kingdom, Germany, and France], Spiro Simitis [Germany], Suzi Leather [United Kingdom], and Baroness Helena Kennedy [United Kingdom], all available on the Council's website at www.bioethics.gov.)

* The present discussion focuses on the human significance of the *biological* relationship between parents and children, and on the ways in which that relationship takes shape in the context of human procreation. In no way is this meant to suggest that biological ties are the most important (or the only) ties that bind, nor is it meant to devalue the central importance of *child-rearing*, including the bond that exists between parents and children who are not biologically related. Neither does this discussion mean to cast a negative light on the laudable practice of adoption or on those who, for whatever reason, must give up their biological children to be raised by others. The present discussion does suggest, however, that biological ties often do matter, in ways that may significantly affect the subsequent *nurture* of children by their biological parents. It is, indeed, the desire of infertile couples to have "their own (biological) children" that is the major driving force for the use of ART.

Through procreation, each parent (mother and father) acquires a share in a life that transcends his or her own, and thereby also a role in perpetuating the human species. Both parents together wittingly acquire an equal share in their offspring; and, supported by social customs and expectations built on this biological foundation, they also acquire a shared responsibility to nurture, humanize, and civilize the children they generate, by caring for and rearing them well. Each child enters life as a unique, unbidden, and as-yet-mysterious stranger; each child is endowed with both the universal potential for human activity and his or her own unique and unprecedented version of it. The former potential anticipates the common human stage upon which the child now enters; the latter potential foreshadows the individuated, never-before-enacted life that he or she will henceforth live. As the parents' union issues in their child, so the child correlatively stands in immediate and dependent relation to its two progenitors, who are the child's dual and complementary sources. Viewed more broadly and looking *backward*, the child also stands—and can later also understand that he stands—as a singular intersection of long, venerable, and now converging chains of descent; viewed more broadly and looking *forward*, the child stands—and can later also understand that he stands—as a new sprout on the ever-branching and ever-widening family tree—a human-family tree. For any human society, procreation means the renewal of human possibility and the promise of ever-returning youth and freshness. It provides new members who can look upon the community and the world anew, who will be responsible for preserving and transmitting the best of what is past, and who will have the energy and the hope to try to improve upon it for the future.

Human procreation, when viewed most fully, is thus a panorama of wide import and overlapping human meanings. Yet when viewed concretely and on the smallest scale, the immediate focus is on the leading figures: individual parents and their children. At the very center of the picture of human procreation is the newborn child emerging from his or her mother's womb. Even as the child arrives, it is a still-developing new life, derived from the union of "seeds" contributed by the two adults who were and are the child's mother and (biological) father and whose child the newborn baby now becomes. Newly visible to the world after nine months of hidden growth, the child arrives not as "anyone" but as a "someone," with a defined and distinctive (beginning) identity—human, familial, individual, male or female. Part of any child's identity as *this* child lies in its special relationship to two particular human "someones" from whom the child descends. All of the child's being and identity it owes to a continuous developmental process that began with union of egg and sperm and that continued through an unbroken sequence of embryonic and fetal stages enacted within the womb of the mother. Though father and mother are equal contributors of seed, the mother alone brings the child to birth: its developing life absolutely depends on the protection and silent nurturing of her body, its emerging life depends absolutely on her labor.

In this brief synopsis of human procreation, several elements stand out as matters of human worth that are deserving of our respect: the special human attachments that human reproduction both manifests and generates; the special procreative power of women and the special nature of human pregnancy; the singular relationships of parents to child and of child to parents, central to the identity of each; and the (at least) special respect owed to embryonic human life*—and perhaps even some regard for egg and sperm, in view of their standing as the potential seeds of a new child and of a new human generation.

Until the first extra-corporeal fertilization of human egg by human sperm in 1969, the processes of human procreation took place entirely inside a woman's body, not only immune to human intervention but also unobserved by human beholders. Since that time, the beginning of many a human life has been brought outside the body and placed partially in human hands

---

* In using the term "special respect," we do not mean to beg the question, much debated, whether human embryos, from the time of fertilization, are entitled to "full moral status," or whether they are entitled to less than that. (The Council, like the larger American public, is divided on this question.) The term "special respect" is frequently used in these debates by those who deny early human embryos full moral standing, and who hold instead that embryonic human life has some "intermediate worth," between "person" and "thing." Yet whether or not one believes that a human embryo is a person straightaway from fertilization, it is a very special entity precisely because of what it is and where it is directed in its integrated, self-unfolding, and self-directed growth. People of all sorts of opinions about "moral status" see the difference between a growing embryo and any other group of cells multiplying outside of the human body (or in it). It is this agreement that lies behind our formulation here: "(at least) special respect."

and under human control. Undertaken to make procreation possible for infertile couples, in vitro fertilization has been responsible for over a million births worldwide, to the great joy of the parents. Yet by bringing the beginnings of human life outside a woman's body, in vitro fertilization has already had several other consequences, unintended yet foreseeable, and still other possibilities not yet here that are today equally foreseeable. The presence of developing human life in vitro exposed it for the first time to possibilities of manipulation and alteration prior to the initiation of a pregnancy, as well as to utterly novel uses altogether unrelated to procreation—in both cases raising unprecedented and vexing ethical issues.

Among these additional possibilities are the following (those that have already been accomplished or that are today possible are italicized): (1) *The early human embryo can be frozen and stored for later use.* (2) *The early human embryo (at around the eight-cell stage) can be disaggregated into its separate blastomeres (= embryonic cells), which can then be recombined with blastomeres from other human embryos (including those of opposite sex) to produce a hybrid human embryo (of four or more biological parents).* (3) Human blastomeres could potentially be combined with blastomeres from another species (including primates) to produce a cross-species hybrid embryo (an embryonic chimera). (4) *An ex vivo human embryo, altered or not, can be introduced into women other than the donor of the egg.* (5) An ex vivo human embryo could also, in principle, be introduced into the uterus (or other body cavity) of a non-human animal, where it might be grown to later stages for purposes of research or (in due course) for the production of human tissues and organs. (6) *An ex vivo embryo can be grown outside the body for a brief period for purposes of research on early human development or (at the blastocyst stage: five to six days, 100-200 cells) used as a source of embryonic stem cells, themselves usable in research and the pursuit of novel therapies.* (7) *An ex vivo embryo can be genetically screened prior to transfer*, and, in principle, genetically or otherwise *altered by the addition of cytoplasm (ooplasm), genes, or other materials.* (8) Egg and sperm (or their precursors) may be extractable from fetuses or derivable from embryonic stem cells (achieved in mice), making it possible that a child might have a fetus or a five-day old embryo as its biological mother or father. (9) With the aid of synthetic devices (now being pursued) that might serve as an artificial placenta, an embryo could in principle be grown to later stages outside of any living body, for purposes of research or needed tissue or organs. (10) *An ex vivo embryo (and externalized human eggs, as well as sperm) can be treated as an article of commerce.*

These novel technical possibilities, all of them connected with the existence of early human embryos outside the human body, are for many people a source of disquiet. Indeed, whatever one's opinion regarding the propriety or morality of any of these additional uses and practices, one must readily agree that they raise new ethical questions bearing on the character of human reproduction, well beyond anything involved in in vitro fertilization for procreative purposes to help an infertile couple have a child of their own. The ongoing public debate about the ethics of embryonic stem cell research, centering on the morality of destroying embryos to obtain stem cells, concerns only one of the pertinent issues. Other possibilities touch on the respect owed to women and human pregnancy, the respect owed to children born with the aid of assisted reproductive technologies, and the boundary between human and animal life in the context of reproduction.

The enumerated *non*-procreative operations, present and projected, that may be performed on or with ex vivo human embryos not only raise direct ethical questions; they may also have indirect but important implications for our thoughts about and attitudes toward human procreation itself. On the one hand, by gaining new knowledge and understanding of human development through research on human embryos, we can acquire an enhanced appreciation of how nature works in this truly wondrous domain, as well as expanded abilities to help infertile couples to have a child—*and a healthy child*—of their own. On the other hand, and at the same time, should we adopt a merely technical attitude toward the beginnings of human life, we risk a diminution of wonder and awe. The existence of the early embryo in the artificial setting of the laboratory invites an analytic, reductive, and partially disembodied view of the procreative process. It risks isolating and reifying the early stages of human development—"the embryo," "the blastocyst"—thus making it easy to forget their natural place in a continuous, goal-directed, and humanly significant process of human procreation (for example, the natural in vivo link between an early embryo and its mother). And the very fact that the early stages of human life are now partly subject to human manipulation and control invites, at least in some people, a diminished regard for the "naturalness" and awe-inspiring power of the procreative process. Treating as "normal" all the novel things we are learning to do with embryonic human life ex vivo might also desensitize us to still greater departures from the human way of procreating, putting us at risk of weakening, in thought as well as in deed, our regard for the meaning and worth of human procreation. This risk, hard to measure, is not itself subject to any preventive measures. Yet it does provide an additional argument for erecting certain barriers against certain extremely dehumanizing interventions, placing a burden of justification on those who would casually break these barriers in the absence of public debate about the wisdom and propriety of doing so. Erecting such barriers would also require the public to consciously confront the novel possibilities as they occur, rather than complacently acquiescing in the necessity of every fait accompli.*

VII. BRIEF OUTLINE OF THE REPORT

The rest of the report is in two major parts: a diagnostic survey of existing regulatory practices (Chapters 2 through 8) and a discussion of policy options and recommendations (Chapters 9 and 10).

Chapters 2 through 7 explore precisely which institutions currently provide oversight and guidance in this context, pursuant to what authority, according to what principles and values, and with what ultimate practical effect. Those chapters are strictly diagnostic and expository in nature. They seek to describe the current state of affairs, and they are neutral regarding what changes, if any, might be necessary, desirable, or feasible if one should wish to improve upon the present arrangements.

Chapter 8 is a distilled account of the specific findings growing out of the preceding diagnosis.

Chapter 9 is a discussion of the universe of possible public policy options that might be considered in light of the findings and diagnosis.

---

* The Council will offer specific suggestions for regulation regarding such barriers in Chapter 10, Recommendations.

Chapter 10 sets forth a list of recommendations that the Council agrees should be adopted immediately. These recommendations are not for structural or institutional changes; we do not propose the wholesale creation of new regulatory institutions or the reform of existing ones. Rather, these recommendations are offered as *interim* measures with two goals or aims in mind: first, to strengthen existing legislation and existing regulatory mechanisms in order to gather more complete and crucial information, information that patients, policymakers, and the general public do not now have and that is essential to decision-making in the future; and second, to erect certain legislative safeguards against a small number of boundary-crossing practices, at least until there can be further deliberation and debate about both the human goods at stake and the best way to protect them.

ENDNOTE

[1] The President's Council on Bioethics, *Human Cloning and Human Dignity: An Ethical Inquiry*, Washington, D.C.: Government Printing Office, 2002, p. 211.

PART I

2

Assisted Reproduction

In each of the next five chapters—beginning with this one—we will discuss in detail a separate, discrete area of our larger domain of inquiry. Each of these chapters will be structured as follows. First, the chapter will review the relevant techniques and practices; next, it will address the ethical considerations; and finally, it will consider the existing regulatory activities.

For reasons discussed above, we will take the practice of assisted reproduction as our fundamental point of departure. Although readers are no doubt familiar with the main features of assisted reproduction techniques and practices, we will give a detailed account of them in order to clarify which aspects might give rise to a need for monitoring, oversight, or regulation.

I. TECHNIQUES AND PRACTICES

Most methods of assisted reproduction involve five discrete phases: (1) collection and preparation of gametes; (2) fertilization; (3) transfer of an embryo or multiple embryos to a woman's uterus; (4) pregnancy; and (5) delivery and birth. We will discuss each phase separately. Additional issues connected with recruitment, intake, and possible payment of gamete donors will be discussed extensively in Chapter 6 (on commerce).

A. Collection and Preparation of Gametes

The precursors of human life are the gametes: sperm and ova. Parents seeking to conceive through assisted reproduction usually provide their own gametes. In the United States in the year 2001, 75.2 percent of the ART cycles undertaken used never-frozen, nondonor ova or embryos and another 13.7 percent used frozen nondonor ova or embryos. Of the remaining 11.1 percent of cycles using donor embryos, the breakdown is as follows: 3.2 percent of the embryos were previously cryopreserved, and 8 percent were not.[*1]

Sperm are typically acquired directly from the male prospective parent. The minority of men who cannot ejaculate, or who have a blocked reproductive tube, may undergo assisted sperm retrieval (ASR). Alternatively, sperm precursor cells obtained by testicular biopsy may be used for purposes of insemination (though this yields a lower pregnancy rate).

Acquiring ova for use in artificial reproduction is significantly more onerous, painful, and risky than acquiring sperm (though its risks are still low in absolute terms). In the normal course of ovulation, one mature oocyte is produced per menstrual cycle. However in assisted reproduction—to increase the probability of success—many more ova are typically retrieved and fertilized. Thus, the ova source (who is usually also the gestational mother) undergoes a drug-induced process intended to stimulate her ovaries to produce many mature oocytes in a single cycle. This procedure, commonly referred to as "superovulation," requires the daily injection of a synthetic gonadatropin analog, accompanied by frequent monitoring using blood tests and ultrasound examinations. This treatment begins midway through the previous menstrual cycle and continues until just before ova retrieval. The synthetic gonadatropin analogs give the clinician greater control over ovarian stimulation and prevent premature release of the ova.

---

[*] Due to rounding, the total does not equal 100 percent.[1]

A very small percentage of women using assisted reproduction (in 2001, fewer than 1 percent of assisted reproduction patients) opted not to undergo ovarian stimulation prior to ova retrieval.[2] In such "unstimulated" procedures, the clinician monitors the development of an ovarian follicle (via ultrasound) and uses daily blood sampling to predict the moment of ovulation. Only one follicle develops and the timing of maturation and release is not controlled. Because there are fewer embryos for transfer, this process yields a lower success rate than does in vitro fertilization (IVF) following ovarian stimulation.

When blood testing and ultrasound monitoring suggest that the ova are sufficiently mature, the clinician attempts to harvest them. This is typically achieved by ultrasound-guided transvaginal aspiration. In this procedure, a needle guided by ultrasound is inserted through the vaginal wall and into the mature ovarian follicles. An ovum is withdrawn (along with some fluid) from each follicle. This is an outpatient procedure. Risks and complications are low, but may include accidental puncture of nearby organs such as the bowel, ureter, bladder, or blood vessels, as well as the typical risks accompanying outpatient surgery (for example, risks related to administration of anesthesia, infection, etc.).

Once sperm and ova have been collected, they are cultured and treated to maximize the probability of success. Ova are transferred into a culture medium containing the intended mother's blood serum. The seminal fluid is removed from sperm and replaced with an artificial medium. For infertile men, the clinician removes excess material and concentrates the motile sperm.*

B. Fertilization

Once the ova and sperm have been properly prepared, the clinician attempts to induce fertilization—the union of sperm and ovum culminating in the fusion of their separate pronuclei and the initiation of a new, integrated, self-directing organism. It is common practice to attempt to fertilize all available ova.†

---

* There are a number of adjunct screening procedures that may be performed at this stage of assisted reproduction that are discussed extensively in Chapter 3.

† The number of ova collected depends on a number of variables, including

Fertilization can be achieved through a number of means including (1) "classical" IVF, (2) gamete intrafallopian transfer (GIFT)*, (3) intracytoplasmic sperm injection (ICSI), and (4) various other methods of zona pellucida manipulation.†

IVF is the most common method of artificial fertilization. In 2001, it was used by 99 percent of ART patients.[3] As noted previously, both sperm and ovum are cultured to maximize the probability of fertilization. The ova are examined and rated for maturity in an effort to calculate the optimal time for fertilization. They are usually placed in a tissue culture medium and left undisturbed for two to twenty-four hours. The sperm are prepared as described above. Once the gametes are adequately prepared, thousands of tiny droplets of sperm are placed in the culture medium containing a single ovum. After 24 hours, each of the oocytes is examined to determine whether fertilization has occurred.

GIFT was introduced in 1984 as an alternative to standard IVF. Today, attempts at fertilization via GIFT are rare. In 2001, they accounted for less than 1 percent of all attempts at fertilization used by ART patients.[4] As the name suggests, fertilization using GIFT occurs within the woman's body. Ovarian stimulation and retrieval are performed in the same manner as in IVF. In a single procedure, ova are retrieved, combined with the sperm outside the body, and then transferred back into the fallopian tube where it is hoped that fertilization itself will occur. Typically, two or more ova are retrieved and transferred. GIFT requires only one functional fallopian tube to succeed. Because fertilization takes place inside the woman's body, substantially less lab work is required and there is no need for embryo culturing. For the same reason, however, if several ova are transferred, GIFT exposes the patient to a higher-than-normal risk of multiple gestations. Moreover, when GIFT does not succeed practitioners frequently cannot determine why it failed, for example, whether the ovum was not fertilized or the embryo did not implant.

---

the donor's age, health, and other factors. In some cases, ten or more ova are fertilized in a single cycle.

* In GIFT, fertilization occurs in the fallopian tube, beyond the clinician's control.

† ICSI and other forms of zona pellucida manipulation are specialized techniques for inducing fertilization and are adjuncts to conventional IVF.

A new and increasingly popular technique for fertilization is intracytoplasmic sperm injection. As the name implies, with ICSI, ovum-sperm fusion is accomplished not by chance, but by injecting a single sperm directly into an oocyte. The oocyte is treated with an enzyme that removes certain cells that surround it ("nurse cells"). The sperm are placed in a viscous solution that greatly slows their motility. A single sperm is selected and drawn into a thin pipette from which it is injected into the cytoplasm of the ovum cell.

ICSI is indicated in cases of severe male-factor infertility, in which male patients have either malformed sperm or an abnormally low sperm count. ICSI is also ideal for patients whose sperm would not otherwise penetrate the exterior of an oocyte.* ICSI was used in 49.2 percent of all ART cycles in 2001.[5] However, 42.2 percent of those ICSI cycles were undertaken by couples *without* male-factor infertility.[6] The growing popularity of this technique most likely has to do with the wish to increase the control over, and success rates for, fertilization: ICSI, unlike standard IVF, guarantees the entrance of a single sperm directly into a single egg.†

Clinicians can also attempt to induce fertilization artificially through manipulation of the zona pellucida, the thick extracellular covering that surrounds the ovum. To assist the sperm's penetration of the ovum, clinicians perforate the zona pellucida using an acidic solution ("zona drilling") or a needle or pipette ("partial zona dissection"). Alternatively, clinicians inject sperm underneath the zona pellucida, but not directly into the ovum's cytoplasm ("subzonal insemination"). Zona drilling results in few pregnancies and has been linked to inhibition of early embryo growth, perhaps due to the acidic solution entering the ovum itself.[7] Few embryos conceived through

---

* ICSI is also indicated when sperm is acquired through assisted sperm retrieval or in the course of a normal IVF cycle for oocytes that have been mixed with sperm but have not yet fertilized. Some ART clinics require ICSI if patients desire to use preimplantation genetic diagnosis, discussed further in Chapter 3.

† Counterintuitively, the live birth rate for those cycles using ICSI (for patients either with or without male factor infertility) is *lower* than cycles in which such patients used IVF without ICSI. *See* Centers for Disease Control and Prevention (CDC), *2001 Assisted Reproductive Technology Success Rates, National Summary and Fertility Clinic Reports*, Atlanta, GA: Government Printing Office, 2003, pp. 40-41.

partial zona dissection have a normal appearance, but it is not definitively known why this is so or whether the difference is significant in any way to the health of the developing child. Subzonal insemination can be effective in the hands of a skilled practitioner, but frequently results in unfertilized oocytes or fertilization by multiple sperm, rendering the embryo unusable.[8] The safety risks associated with these procedures are discussed below.

A recently developed adjunct to IVF is ooplasm transfer. This procedure has been used for women whose fertilized ova do not develop normally owing to a deficiency in their mitochondria. To remedy this problem at the time of fertilization, the oocyte is injected with donor cytoplasm that contains healthy mitochondria. Because the new cytoplasm contains the donor's mitochondrial DNA, the resulting child will have inherited DNA from three individuals: the father, the mother, and mitochondrial DNA from the ooplasm donor. Moreover, the donor mitochondria could be passed on to future generations through the resulting child. To date, there have been thirty children born worldwide as a result of this procedure.[9] However, for reasons discussed elsewhere in this document, this technique is not currently approved for use in clinical practice in the United States.*

Once fertilization has occurred, the new embryos remain in the culture medium. Nutrients are added to the medium. Some commercially produced preparations exist but, typically, ART clinics make their own on-site. Some clinics co-culture developing embryos: that is, they culture the embryos in a medium containing other cells that enhance the growth of the embryos and remove toxins. Various types of cells have been used for such co-culture, including cells extracted from the uterus or fallopian tubes of patients or donors, rat liver cells, monkey kidney cells, cow uterine cells, and human ovarian cancer cells. The embryos remain in culture and are warmed in an incubator until they are either transferred into the recipient's uterus or cryopreserved.

---

* Research is currently underway on another procedure that would help women with defective ova to conceive. The procedure, called "ovarian nuclear transfer," involves transplantation of the nucleus of a fertilized ovum into an enucleated donor fertilized ovum (including mitochondria).

Because in many cases not all embryos are transferred in each cycle, cryopreservation of embryos has become an integral part of ART.* The American Society for Reproductive Medicine (ASRM) has deemed cryopreservation "essential" to the practice of assisted reproduction and provides extensive guidance to technicians as to the maintenance of cryopreservation facilities. Cryopreservation is a complicated process that requires embryo preparation, sophisticated freezing technology, reliable storage, and meticulous record keeping. To guard against the formation of ice crystals that could destroy the embryo, the clinician introduces a cryoprotectant solution into the early-stage embryo's interior. The prepared embryos are then placed in a straw-like structure that is gradually frozen. Once frozen, these structures are stored in canisters at very low temperature (typically around minus 196 degrees centigrade). Some researchers suggest that it may be possible to cryopreserve embryos safely for fifty years or longer.[10] A recently reported study by the Society for Assisted Reproductive Technology and RAND estimates that 400,000 embryos are in cryostorage in the United States.[11]

Most ART patients do not receive cryopreserved embryos. In 2001, only 14 percent of all ART cycles involved transfer of frozen embryos.[12] The rate of live births for cycles using cryopreserved embryos is significantly lower than it is for never-frozen embryos (23.4 percent versus 33.4 percent).[13] Experts estimate that only 65 percent of frozen embryos survive the thawing process.[14] There are, however, incentives for couples to use cryopreserved embryos; doing so eliminates the cost and effort of further oocyte retrieval. This can decrease the cost of a future cycle by roughly $6,000.[15] Transfer of cryopreserved embryos might be preferable also for recipients who are suffering from ovarian hyperstimulation syndrome (discussed below). Because pregnancy aggravates this disorder, delayed transfer can be helpful, and cryopreservation allows such delay. The additional control over the timing of transfer conferred by cryopreservation is also helpful to women whose uterine lining is not fully prepared to receive an embryo at the time of

* There is not yet a reliable method of freezing unfertilized ova. This is perhaps due to their large size and high water content. Additionally, it seems that freezing an ovum toughens the zona pellucida in a way that can inhibit sperm penetration.

its creation. Cryopreservation also reduces pressure to implant all embryos at once, thus reducing the risk of high-order multiple pregnancies.

C. Transfer

Following the creation of a human embryo by IVF, the next discrete phase in the assisted reproduction process is transfer of the embryo into the uterus of the mother (or gestational carrier*).

Typically, the embryos are transferred on the second or third day after fertilization, at the four- to eight-cell stage. To maximize the probability of implantation, some clinicians cultivate embryos until the blastocyst stage (five days after fertilization) before transferring them to the uterus.[16] Prior to transfer, the clinician evaluates the embryos' shape and appearance. There is believed to be some correlation between the external appearance of an embryo and its likelihood of implantation and successful development, but appearances can also be misleading. Some unhealthy-looking embryos implant and develop into healthy fetuses and children, and some healthy-looking embryos fail to implant or experience developmental problems.[17] Other methods of evaluation include analysis of chemicals produced by the embryos in culture and pre-evaluation of the quality of sperm and ovum.

A more recently developed method of embryo analysis is preimplantation genetic diagnosis. In PGD, one or more cells are extracted from the eight- to sixteen-cell embryo by means of biopsy. The clinician tests the sample cell(s) for chromosomal or genetic characteristics, including the sex of the embryo, with special attention to any genetic disorder for which the relevant mutation has been identified in the parents or an earlier child. (PGD will be discussed further in Chapter 3.)

Prior to transfer, some clinicians attempt to facilitate implantation by means of a process called assisted hatching. Several days after fertilization, an embryo must break out of the zona pellucida so that it can implant into the uterine wall. In some instances, the zona pellucida proves to be too hard to break and implantation fails as a result. To aid in hatching, cli-

---

* In the United States in 2001, gestational carriers were used in 571 ART cycles.

nicians use chemicals, lasers, or mechanical manipulation of the zona pellucida.[18]

Once the embryos have been selected and prepared, they are transferred into the uterus. The total number of embryos transferred per cycle varies, usually according to the age of the recipient. For women under 35, the average number of never-frozen embryos transplanted per transfer procedure was 2.8. For women 35 to 37, 38 to 40, and 41 to 42, the average numbers of never-frozen embryos transplanted per transfer procedure were, respectively, 3.1, 3.4, and 3.7.[19] The Centers for Disease Control (CDC) report notes that in 32 percent of ART cycles using never-frozen, nondonor ova or embryos in 2001, 4 or more embryos were transferred.[20]

Typically embryos are transferred into the uterus using a catheter. The catheter is inserted through the woman's cervix and the embryos are injected into her uterus (along with some amount of the culture fluid). This procedure does not require anesthesia. Following injection, the patient must lie still for at least one hour. While the transfer procedure is regarded as simple, different practitioners tend to achieve different outcomes.[21]

An alternative method of embryo transfer is zygote intrafallopian transfer (ZIFT). In ZIFT, the embryo is placed (via laparoscopy) directly into the fallopian tube, rather than into the uterus. In this way, it is similar to the transfer of gametes in GIFT. Some individuals opt for ZIFT on the theory that it enhances the likelihood of implantation, given that the embryo matures en route to the uterus, presumably as it would in natural conception and implantation. Additionally, many patients prefer ZIFT to GIFT because the process of fertilization and early development of the embryo may be monitored.[22] However, ZIFT remains a rare choice, accounting for 0.8 percent of all ART cycles in 2001.[23]

D. Pregnancy

Successful implantation of an embryo in the uterine lining marks the beginning of pregnancy. In 2001, 32.8 percent of the ART cycles undertaken resulted in clinical pregnancy.[24*] This

---

* This statistic is for never-frozen, nondonor ova or embryos—the most common approach in 2001.

number varied according to patient age.[25] After the inception of pregnancy, patients are carefully monitored and treated by an obstetrician. Pregnancies resulting from assisted reproduction are sometimes treated as high risk.[26] Clinicians recommend prenatal diagnosis and testing for many pregnancies resulting from assisted reproduction.

There are a number of medications and procedures that may be indicated during a pregnancy facilitated by assisted reproduction. It is typical for a patient to receive progesterone injections to support key functions necessary to pregnancy.

Multiple gestations are common among pregnancies facilitated by assisted reproductive technologies. The rate of multiple-fetus pregnancies from ART cycles using never-frozen, nondonor ova or embryos in 2001 was 36.7 percent.* For the same time period, the multiple infant birth rate in the United States was 3 percent. The extraordinarily high rate of multiple pregnancies resulting from assisted reproduction is almost entirely attributable to the transfer of multiple embryos per cycle.†

In an effort to reduce the risks of multiple pregnancy, practitioners sometimes employ a procedure termed "fetal reduction," the reduction in the number of fetuses in utero by selective abortion. Fetuses are selected for destruction based on size, position, and viability (in the clinician's judgment).[27] The clinician, using ultrasound for guidance, inserts a needle through the mother's abdomen (transabdominal multifetal reduction) through the uterine wall. The clinician then administers a lethal injection to the heart of the selected fetus—typically potassium chloride. The dead fetus's body decomposes and is resorbed. To be effective, transabdominal multife-

---

* Specifically, 29.3 percent were twins, and 7.4 percent were triplets or more. In 5.2 percent of ART pregnancies, the pregnancy ended in miscarriage where the number of fetuses was impossible to determine. (CDC Report, p. 20.) The rate of multiple-fetus pregnancies from ART cycles using never-frozen donor ova was 43.6 percent. (CDC Report, p. 50.) The rate of multiple-gestation pregnancies for frozen nondonor embryos was 26.6 percent. (Id. at 46.)

† It should be noted, however, that progress is being made toward single-embryo transfer with retention and pregnancy in about 34 percent of the transfers. *See* DeSutter, P., et al., "Single Embryo Transfer and Multiple Pregnancy Rate Reduction in IVF/ICSI: A Five Year Appraisal," *Reproductive BioMedicine Online* 6: 2003, http://www.rbmonline.com/Article/836 (accessed May 30, 2003).

tal reduction must be performed at ten to twelve weeks' gestation. In an alternative procedure, transvaginal multifetal reduction, a needle is inserted through the vagina. Transvaginal multifetal reduction must be performed between six and eight weeks gestation (eight weeks is recommended).

E. Delivery

In 2001, for never-frozen nondonor ova or embryos, the overall rate of live births per cycle[*] was 27 percent (33.4 percent live births per transfer).[†28] Among these pregnancies, 82.2 percent resulted in live births.[29] Of these resulting 21,813 live births, 35.8 percent were multiple infant births (32 percent twins and 3.8 percent triplets or more).[‡30] One 1993 Canadian study showed that nearly 25 percent of all births facilitated by ART are premature, and 30 percent of the resulting infants had low birthweight.[§31] While this low birthweight may be attributable to the high rate of multiple pregnancies, one 1987-89 French study reported that even for singleton births facilitated by ART, the rate of prematurity and low birthweight was twice that of children conceived by natural means.[32] Another study suggests that women using ART are more likely to induce labor and undergo elective caesarian section delivery.[33]

---

[*] A "cycle" is initiated when a woman begins the process of superovulation and monitoring. (CDC Report, p. 4.) Not all cycles result in successful ova collection, fertilization, transfer, pregnancy, or birth.

[†] There seems to be a negative association between cryopreservation and implantation. For all pregnancies initiated using frozen, nondonor embryos, the success rate was 20.3 percent live births per transfer (19.5 percent per thaw). (CDC Report, p. 44.) For cycles using never-frozen, donated embryos, 43.4 percent of transfers resulted in live births. (CDC Report, p. 49.) For frozen, donated embryos, the success rate was 23.5 percent per transfer. (CDC Report, p. 49.)

[‡] Of the 3,075 live births using frozen, nondonor embryos, 26.8 percent resulted in multiple births (CDC Report, p. 46). Of the 3,629 live births using never-frozen, donated embryos, 41.7 percent resulted in multiple births. (CDC Report, p. 50.) There are no such statistics for cycles using frozen, donated embryos.

[§] The U. S. national average for prematurity among children born by natural means is approximately 12 percent. (March of Dimes Survey, 2000.)

F. Disposition of Unused Embryos

As mentioned above, in many cases of ART there are in vitro embryos that remain untransferred following a successful cycle. There are five possible outcomes for such an embryo: (1) it may remain in cryostorage until transferred into the mother's uterus in a future ART cycle; (2) it may be donated to another person or couple seeking to initiate a pregnancy; (3) it may be donated for purposes of research; (4) it may remain in cryostorage indefinitely; or (5) it may be thawed and destroyed.

G. Projected Techniques/Recent Experiments

There is a range of research in the reproductive technology area that is now experimental and in some cases speculative, but still worth noting. One such area of research is "nuclear transfer," which involves transplanting the nucleus from a fertilized human egg into an enucleated fertilized human egg.* The process is similar to somatic cell nuclear transfer (or human cloning), except that the nucleus inserted into the egg comes from another fertilized egg rather than from a somatic cell of a living child or adult. The resulting child could conceivably carry genetic material from three (perhaps four) people: the male and female progenitors of the original fertilized human egg and at least the mitochondrial DNA from the donor of the egg into which the embryo's nucleus is inserted. In experiments in China in 2003, researchers reported achieving a triplet pregnancy with such embryos, though none of the fetuses survived to birth (a result they attribute to substandard obstetrical care).[34] Researchers have also begun investigating whether ovarian tissues from aborted fetuses may be developed in the lab in hopes of one day providing mature eggs suitable for IVF.† In July 2003, researchers announced that they obtained ovarian follicles from aborted fetuses aged be-

---

* Here, we use the term "fertilized human egg" to denote an egg that has been fertilized, but whose pronucleus has not yet fused with that of the fertilizing sperm. In the nucleus transfer procedure, both donor pronuclei are transferred into the recipient egg and fuse thereafter.

† Biron-Shental, T., et al., "Preliminary results of cultured human ovaries from second and third trimester fetuses," presented at the 19th Annual Meeting of the European Society of Human Reproduction and Embryology, June 29 to July 2, 2003, Madrid, Spain (www.eshre.com).

tween twenty-two and thirty-three weeks gestation, and were able to develop the follicles in culture to a secondary stage. The researchers are working to improve the culture media and prolong the culture period to completely develop the follicles as a source for human eggs.[35]

In their quest for alternative sources of gametes, researchers are working to develop human eggs and sperm from embryonic stem cells. There has already been some success coaxing embryonic stem cells from mice to develop into sperm and eggs, and some researchers project that this technology will succeed with human embryonic stem cells in "about ten years."* This would make possible the novel prospects of producing male-derived eggs or female-derived sperm, and of producing children whose biological progenitors were embryos that were disaggregated for their stem cells. There has also been an experiment that fused blastomeres from two separate embryos to produce a single (in this case, hybrid male-female) embryo.[36]

Most speculative is research aimed at engineering uterine lining tissue outside the body, for use as a diagnostic tool to study implantation. Researchers have transferred human embryos to an artificial endometrium, to which these embryos attached and began to develop. The implanted, developing embryos were grown for six days, but researchers did not attempt to cultivate them further.[37] It is not possible now to predict just how much further in vitro human embryos may someday be developed with such "uterine-like" substitutes. Another area of highly speculative research involves uterus transplants, contemplated as a means to enable women with damaged or absent uteri to bear children.[38] There has also been speculation about the prospect of implanting human embryos into specially prepared non-human animal uteruses in order to study their development, but there are as yet no reports of such experiments having taken place with any noteworthy results.

* "Stem cells can end infertility, say IVF pioneers," *NewScientist.com*, July 24, 2003, quoting Dr. Alan Trounson of the Monash Institute of Reproduction and Development in Victoria, Australia.

II. ETHICAL CONSIDERATIONS

The development and practice of assisted reproductive technologies have yielded great goods. They have relieved the suffering of many who are afflicted with infertility, helping them to conceive biologically related children. Yet these activities also raise a variety of ethical issues. Some concern the well-being of the participants in assisted reproduction: gamete donors, prospective parents, and their resulting children. Other issues arise from the expansion of control over reproduction, including current and projected possibilities for altering the biological relationships central to human procreation. Still other issues concern the use and disposition of human embryos that are incident to these new capacities and techniques.

The intersection of two key factors—patient vulnerability and novel (in some cases untested) technology—defines much of the arena of concern. First, assisted reproduction is generally practiced on patients who are experiencing great emotional strain. When it succeeds it can be a source of great joy—as it has been for tens of thousands of parents each year. But success is far from universal, especially for older patients; and even when it happens, the process and the circumstances surrounding it can be difficult to bear. Those suffering from infertility often come to practitioners of assisted reproduction after prolonged periods of failure and dismay. This vulnerability may lead some individuals to take undue risks (such as to insist on transferring an unduly large number of embryos). The occasional irresponsible clinician may even pressure patients to take such risks, for the sake of improving his reportable success rates.

Second, some assisted reproductive technologies have been used in clinical practice without prior rigorous testing in primates or studies of long-term outcomes. IVF itself was performed on at least 1,200 women before it was reported to have been performed on chimps, although it had been extensively investigated in rabbits, hamsters, and mice.[39] The same is true for ICSI. The reproductive use of ICSI was first introduced by Belgian researchers in 1992.[40] Two years later, relying on a two-study review of safety and efficacy, ASRM declared ICSI to be a "clinical" rather than "experimental" procedure. Yet the first non-human primate conceived by ICSI was born only in 1997 and the first successful ICSI procedure in mice was reported in 1995.[41] Absent long-term studies of the children conceived using ICSI or other novel procedures, it is unclear to what extent these alterations in the ART process affect the health and development of the children so conceived.[42]

Below, we survey the ethical concerns raised by ART in four specific areas: (1) the well-being of children born with the aid of ART; (2) the well-being of women in the ART process; (3) the meaning of enhanced control over procreation; and (4) the use and destruction of embryonic human life. As we proceed, two points are worth noting. First, we raise these areas of concern solely to enable us to diagnose whether the current regulatory system is adequately protecting the human goods at stake. In no way have we lost sight of the human goods *made possible* by ART—most notably, the treatment of infertility and the creation of biologically related children for couples who desire and could not otherwise have them. Second, we shall be raising three different kinds of questions: First, questions of *fact*, such as whether a certain assisted reproduction technique is safe. Second, questions of *principle*, such as the moral significance of embryo destruction incident to fertility treatment or the significance of using fetal gametes for reproductive purposes. Third, questions of *judgment*, such as what degree of risk to the carrying mother or child conceived with assisted reproduction is justified in cases where bearing such risks is the only way for individuals or couples to have a biologically related child. Connected to this last question is the issue of who should make such judgments—individuals, doctors, or society as a whole acting through public institutions. For each of these questions—questions of fact, questions of principle, and questions of judgment—both better data and more public discussion are crucial.

A. Well-Being of the Child

The central figure in the process of assisted reproduction, directly affected by every action taken but incapable of consenting to such actions, is the child born with the aid of ART. Each intervention or stage in the ART process might affect this child's health and well-being: gamete retrieval and preparation, fertilization, embryo culture, embryo transfer, pregnancy, and of course birth.[43]

The health of the child born through ART may be affected by actions taken as early as gamete retrieval and preparation. Some studies show that superovulation decreases embryo and fetal viability (compared with those in unstimulated cycles).[44] One study of embryos created during stimulated cycles revealed a high level of "developmental arrest, embryonic aneuploidy, mosaicism, apoptosis and failure of cytokinesis."[45] It is possible that lesser abnormalities, compatible with birth, make their way into the children born alive.

There have been very few comprehensive or long-term studies of the health and well-being of children born using ART, although more than 170,000 such children have been born in the United States.[46] The fact that no major investigation or public study has yet been called for in this area might suggest that there is no discernible health crisis in assisted reproduction, as does the fact that demand for ART has grown substantially and continuously since its inception. At the same time, however, our ability to know this with certainty is limited, both because of the absence of major longitudinal studies of the well-being of children born using different assisted reproduction techniques, and because the oldest person conceived through ART is only in her mid-twenties.

Some recent studies have associated various birth defects and developmental difficulties with the uses of various technologies and practices of assisted reproduction. None of these studies provide a causal link between ART and the dysfunctions observed, and some commentators have taken issue with some of the methodologies used. Nevertheless, these findings have raised some concerns. One such study concluded that children conceived by assisted reproduction are twice as likely to suffer major birth defects as children conceived without such assistance.*[47] Other recent studies have reached similar conclusions.[48] Additional studies have associated the use of

* Specifically, among the children in the study conceived by IVF, 9 percent were diagnosed with a major birth defect or defects by the age of one year. Among children conceived using ICSI, the rate was 8.6 percent. The incidence of such abnormalities among children in the study who were conceived by natural means was 4.2 percent.

assisted reproduction technologies with a higher incidence of diseases and malformations, including Beckwith-Wiedemann syndrome (BWS),* rare urological defects, retinoblastoma,[49] neural tube defects,[50] and Angelman syndrome.[51]

While many are concerned about the increased risk to children suggested by these studies, the overall incidence of such harms is low enough that infertile couples have not been deterred in their efforts to conceive using IVF or ICSI. Indeed, ART clinicians (and in some cases the authors of these studies)[52] advise their patients that such data should not dissuade them from pursuing infertility treatment.

ICSI has raised concerns among some observers largely for the very reasons that it has proven so successful as a means of fertilization: ICSI circumvents the ovum's natural barrier against sperm otherwise incapable of insemination. Some suspect that removing this barrier may permit a damaged sperm (for example, aneuploid or with damaged DNA) to fertilize an ovum, resulting in spontaneous abortion or harm to the resulting child. Some male ART patients have a gene mutation or a chromosomal deletion that renders them infertile. Yet, if a sperm can be retrieved from these patients, they may be able to conceive a child via ICSI, possibly passing along the genetic abnormality to the resulting child. For example, two-thirds of men with congenital bilateral absence of the vas deferens (rendering them unable to ejaculate) carry certain cystic fibrosis mutations.[53] ICSI may permit these men to overcome their infertility, but the resulting child will (in 50 percent of the cases) bear this genetic mutation. Similarly, another form of

---

* Researchers at Johns Hopkins University noted that among the patients listed in the 1994 Beckwith-Wiedemann registry, IVF conception was six times more common than in the general population. That is, 4.6 percent of the patients in the registry were conceived through IVF, as compared with 0.8 percent of the national population. Children with BWS have symptoms that can include an abnormally large tongue (which can cause respiratory difficulties), abdominal wall defects (including umbilical hernia and protrusion of intestine or other abdominal organs from the child's navel), low blood sugar, lethargy, poor feeding, seizures, and enlargement of organs and some tissues. BWS sufferers are predisposed to Wilms' tumor, hepatoblastoma, neuroblastoma, and other cancers. Despite their findings, JHU researchers suggested that parents should not alter their plans to use IVF. See, for example, DeBaun, M. R., et al., "Association of in vitro fertilization with Beckwith-Wiedemann syndrome and epigenetic alterations of LIT1 and H19," *American Journal of Human Genetics* 72: 156-160 (2003)

male factor infertility characterized by a very low sperm count is associated with a particular Y-chromosome deletion. The use of ICSI in such cases risks transferring this chromosome deletion to the resulting child, rendering any male child infertile, and, according to some studies, at risk for sex-chromosome aneuploidy.[54] Additional studies have associated the use of ICSI with an increased incidence in novel chromosomal abnormalities and mental developmental delays.[55]

It is a matter of concern that there have been few longitudinal studies analyzing the long-term effects of ICSI on the children born with its aid. The Belgian group that pioneered ICSI has collected a database that details neonatal outcome and congenital malformations in children conceived through ICSI.[56] But there do not seem to be any ongoing or published studies of this kind investigating the long-term effects of ICSI beyond the neonatal stage.

Many adjuncts to the fertilization and transfer process raise concerns for the health and well-being of the children born as a result.* Some have speculated that factors such as culture conditions and length of time an embryo spends in culture may affect the development of the children later born.[57] Some authorities claim that differences in salt or amino acid concentrations in the culture media can affect gene expression.[58] Additionally, one researcher notes that the process of extended culture in mice (for example, permitting extended embryo development prior to transfer) can cause imprinting problems leading to abnormal development.[59]

Still other adjuncts to fertilization and transfer may not be risk-free. Cryopreservation might affect gene expression or lead to other molecular effects such as "telomere shortening and replicative senescence, damage to plasma and nuclear membranes, and inappropriate chromatin condensation."[60] Similarly, ooplasm transfer has been linked to an unusually high rate of Turner syndrome.[61] Finally, assisted hatching (or any technique that results in manipulation of the zona pellucida) has been associated with a higher incidence of monozygotic twinning and an increased risk of twins carried in the same amniotic sac, which can lead to malformation, disparities in growth, and pregnancy complications.[62]

---

* The discussion of one such adjunct, preimplantation genetic diagnosis, will be deferred to Chapter 3.

Multiple gestations, far more common in the context of assisted reproduction than in natural conception,*[63] have a higher incidence of adverse impacts on the health of the children born.[64] Such pregnancies greatly increase the risk of prenatal death.[65] Multiple pregnancies are also more likely to lead to premature birth; and prematurity is associated with myriad health problems including serious infection, respiratory distress syndrome, and heart defects.[66] One in ten children born following high-order pregnancies dies before one year of age.[67] Children born following a multiple pregnancy are at greater risk for such disabilities as blindness, respiratory dysfunction, and brain damage.[68] Moreover, infants born following such a pregnancy tend to have an extremely low birthweight, which is itself associated with a number of health problems, including some that manifest themselves only later in life, such as hypertension, cardiac disease, stroke, and osteoporosis in middle age.[69] Interestingly, the higher incidence of low birthweight may not be limited to infants born from multiple pregnancies. According to recent studies, singletons born with the aid of ART tend to have an abnormally high incidence of prematurity and low birthweight.[70]

So-called "fetal reduction" aims to reduce the problems associated with multiple pregnancy. But fetal reduction is itself potentially associated with a number of adverse effects on the children who remain following the procedure. One study shows that following transabdominal multifetal reduction there is a miscarriage rate of 16.2 percent, and 16.5 percent of the remaining pregnancies end in premature birth.[71] The alternative method, transvaginal multifetal reduction, carries a higher risk of infection and has been associated with a higher risk of infant mortality than its counterpart.[72] It has been observed that children born following fetal reduction (by either method) tend to be premature, thus exposing them to the complications described above.[73] One study has suggested that children born following fetal reduction are more vulnerable to periventricular leukomalacia, which is characterized by brain dysfunction and developmental difficulties.[74]

---

* This higher incidence of multiples is largely due to the transfer of multiple embryos, rather than to the use of IVF. But, as we have noted, IVF also produces a higher incidence of identical twins (a result of embryo splitting), perhaps the consequence of embryo manipulation.

Taken together, the significance of these various studies is uncertain. They raise a broad range of concerns, but the scale of the research has been limited. In many cases, there are observed correlations between ART and a higher incidence of certain health problems in the resulting children. But in most studies, there is no demonstrable causal relationship between a particular facet of ART and the undesirable health effect. Infertile individuals seeking assisted reproduction may be disproportionately afflicted with heritable disorders, and these may in part account for the higher incidence of birth and developmental abnormalities in ART children compared to those conceived in vivo. The results are therefore still preliminary. The need seems clear for more data to determine what risks, if any, different assisted reproduction techniques present to the well-being of the future child. Moreover, in cases where ART is the only available means for individuals or couples to conceive a biologically related child, it is an important ethical and social question what level of increased risk can be privately justified by patients and doctors, and what level of increased risk should be publicly justified by society as a whole, especially should the society bear the costs of caring for any resulting health problems.

B. Well-Being of Women in the ART Process

Another concern is for the well-being of the women who participate directly in the process of assisted reproduction.

Aside from the discomforts and burdens of ovarian stimulation and monitoring, there are also some risks attached to hormonal stimulation. One such risk is "ovarian hyperstimulation syndrome," characterized by dramatic enlargement of the ovaries and fluid imbalances that can be (in extreme cases) life threatening.* Complications can include rupture of the ovaries, cysts, and cancers. The reported incidence of severe ovarian hyperstimulation syndrome is between 0.5 and 5.0 percent.[75] Additionally, adverse side effects of the hormones administered during superovulation have included memory loss, ne-

* Pregnancy itself increases the risks and aggravates the duration and severity of the syndrome's symptoms. Those women who donate their ova to others are at much reduced risk.

rological dysfunction, cardiac disorders, and even sudden death.[76] There do not appear to be any studies on the incidence of such side effects.[77]

Some women who become pregnant with the aid of assisted reproduction are treated as "high-risk" patients and experience a higher incidence of complications than do women with natural pregnancies. Some commentators have suggested that this is due to the age of the patients (who tend to be older than most childbearing women) and the high rate of multiple pregnancies.[78]

Multiple pregnancies are far more common following ART, owing especially to the practice of transferring multiple embryos but also to the higher incidence of spontaneous twinning with any single embryo. Multiple pregnancies pose greater risks to mothers than do singleton pregnancies. A woman carrying multiple fetuses has a greater chance of suffering from high blood pressure, anemia, or pre-eclampsia.[79] Because multiple-gestation pregnancies are generally more taxing on the mother's body, they are likelier to aggravate pre-existing medical conditions.[80] Moreover, such pregnancies expose the woman to higher risks of uterine rupture, placenta previa, or abruption.[81] One commentator noted in 1995 that the added expense growing out of complications from multiple-gestation pregnancies is one of the primary reasons private health insurance generally does not cover assisted reproduction.[82] Both professional societies and advocates for infertile patients argue that mandating insurance coverage could reduce multiple-gestation pregnancies because it would reduce financial pressure to succeed in the first attempt.[*]

C. Meaning of Enhanced Control over Procreation

The ability to initiate fertilization artificially may also profoundly affect the character of human reproduction and our attitudes toward it, as well as the relationships between parents

[*] One published study concluded that in states where IVF is covered by insurance, there are associated "decreases in the number of embryos transferred per cycle, the percentages of cycles resulting in pregnancy, and the percentage of pregnancies with three or more fetuses." Jain, T., et al., "Insurance Coverage and Outcomes of In Vitro Fertilization," *New England Journal of Medicine* 347(9): 661 (August 29, 2002).

and children and across generations. Three potential hazards or concerns seem especially worthy of note. First, ART raises novel possibilities for altering the biological relationships that are central to normal sexual reproduction, and thus for confounding the human relationships that follow from it. Through ART, it is now possible for a surrogate (or an adoptive parent) to carry and give birth to another couple's biological child; it is possible for a woman to become pregnant with an anonymous donor's sperm; it is possible for a deceased male to become a biological father after death; and it is possible to produce a child with genetic material from three progenitors. Moreover, current research might one day make it possible to use gametes from aborted fetuses, and thus make such fetuses into biological parents, and to produce eggs from male-derived embryonic stem cells or sperm from female-derived embryonic stem cells, which would in theory allow for the creation of a child with *two male* or *two female* embryonic progenitors. Second, ART raises the possibility of moving human procreation in the direction of manufacture, by introducing technical approaches or attitudes into the activity of human reproduction. And finally, ART might affect our general understanding of or attitudes about parenthood and childhood, by making sexual reproduction simply one option among many, with no special significance for how we understand the coming-to-be of the next generation.

Particular techniques raise certain specific concerns in this regard. Cryopreservation, ooplasm transfer, and the possible use of fetal oocytes directly raise concerns about the definition and identity of "father" and "mother." Cryopreservation of sperm and embryos makes posthumous parentage possible. For instance, some American soldiers have been reported to store up sperm on the eve of shipping out to a battle zone. And instances have been reported in which women have requested that their newly deceased husband's sperm be harvested via assisted sperm retrieval from the corpse and used for artificial insemination. If techniques for cryopreservation of ova are ever perfected, or if ova can be derived from adult stem cells, new opportunities for posthumous conception involving deceased women will also arise.

Ooplasm transfer raises a slightly different issue. Because donated ooplasm contains mitochondrial DNA from the donor, the resulting child receives a small genetic contribution from a third person. Moreover, because mitochondrial DNA is maternally inherited, if the resulting child is female, she will pass on to her own offspring the genetic contribution of both her mother and the female ooplasm donor.

A projected technique that raises new ethical concerns is the harvesting and use of fetal oocytes. Some researchers have posited that oocytes (or their precursors) might be harvested from aborted fetuses and used as donated ova (once they have matured in vitro) for patients who have impaired ovarian function.* The aborted fetuses would be the genetic mothers of any resulting children. If recent studies in which mouse oocytes have been derived from mouse embryonic stem cells[83] can be replicated in humans, a five-day-old embryo (the age of the mouse embryo when cells were retrieved) could also become the biological progenitor of new children.[84]

These procedures, and others like them, raise the possibility that children conceived through ART might be connected to their biological parents in fundamentally different ways than children conceived and born without artificial intervention. In some cases, children conceived with these technologies might be denied the biparental origins that human beings have always taken for granted and that have always been the foundation of familial relations and generational connections. ART techniques do not have to disrupt such relations, but they might be used in ways that confound parentage, involve more or fewer than two biological parents, or otherwise depart from the biologically grounded parent-child relation.

Fetal reduction raises its own distinct set of concerns. In this procedure, parents effectively choose to have some developing fetuses (each of which was conceived in the hope that it would be developed to term) live and some not, and they use surgical procedures to reduce the number of living fetuses in utero.

---

* It was announced in July 2003 that scientists had developed in the laboratory ovarian tissues obtained from aborted fetuses, which might one day provide mature female oocytes suitable for in vitro fertilization. (Biron-Shental, T., et al., "Preliminary results of cultured human ovaries from second and third trimester fetuses," presented at the 19th Annual Meeting of the European Society of Human Reproduction and Embryology, June 29 to July 2, 2003, Madrid, Spain [www.eshre.com].)

D. Use and Destruction of Human Embryos

Assisted reproduction usually entails the loss of human embryos, especially when superovulation is used and many ova are fertilized at once. Large numbers of embryos die at all stages of assisted reproduction (in vitro and in vivo).* An unknown number of additional embryos are discarded when it is determined that they are no longer needed or desired. Still others are donated to researchers, who use them in biomedical or scientific experiments that involve or lead to their destruction. Thousands of embryos are cryopreserved for indefinite periods of time. As previously noted, an estimated 400,000 embryos were in cryostorage in the United States as of April 2002.

Actions that result in the end of embryonic life are morally significant and require careful consideration and attention. We consider the ethical significance and current regulation of human embryo research in Chapter 5.

III. CURRENT REGULATION

The following discussion provides an overview of the current state of regulation of the biotechnologies and practices discussed above. The discussion will be broadly divided into sections treating the governmental (federal and state) and nongovernmental regulation of assisted reproduction, both direct and indirect. Each source of regulation will be described in terms of its aims, animating values, jurisdictional scope and requirements, mechanisms of regulation, and efficacy.

---

* In 2001, approximately 72 percent of all transfers failed to result in birth. It bears noting, however, that there is in the course of unassisted reproduction a very high degree of embryo loss, much of it probably due to chromosomal and genetic abnormalities. Because the causes of failure in both natural and assisted reproduction are not fully understood, it is difficult to compare the two phenomena in a meaningful way.

A. Direct Governmental Regulation of Assisted Reproduction

1. Federal Oversight.

a. Consumer protection and embryo laboratory standards. There is only one federal statute that aims at the regulation of assisted reproduction: the Fertility Clinic Success Rate and Certification Act of 1992 ("the Act").[85] The purposes of the statute and its related regulations are twofold: (1) to provide consumers with reliable and useful information about the efficacy of ART services offered by fertility clinics, and (2) to provide states with a model certification process for embryo laboratories.

(i) Success rates: Under the implementing regulations of the Act, each ART program or clinic in the United States is required to report annually to the CDC data relating to its rates of success.[86] The Act defines ART as "all treatments or procedures which include the handling of human oocytes or embryos, including in vitro fertilization, gamete intrafallopian transfer, zygote intrafallopian transfer, and such other specific technologies as the Secretary [of Health and Human Services] may include in this definition . . ."[87] An "ART program or clinic" is defined as a legal entity practicing under state law, recognizable to the consumer, that provides ART services to couples who have experienced infertility or are undergoing ART for other reasons.[88] Each ART program is required to collect and report data for each cycle of treatment initiated. For these purposes, an "ART cycle" is initiated when a woman begins taking fertility drugs or starts ovarian monitoring with the intent of creating embryos for transfer. The data that must be collected include: patient demographics; medical history and infertility diagnosis; clinical information pertaining to the ART cycle; and information on resulting pregnancies and births.

Information is presented in terms of pregnancies per cycle, live births per cycle, and live births per transfer (including never-frozen and frozen embryos from both patients and donors). The statistics are also organized according to age (younger than 35, 35 to 39, and older than 39). Programs are also required to report information on cancelled cycles, number of embryos transferred per cycle, multiple birth rates per transfer, percentage of patients with particular diagnoses, and types and frequency of ARTs used (for example, the frequency with which ICSI is used). The outcome information that ART clinics must report includes the maximum number of fetal hearts observed in ultrasound, whether there was a medically induced fetal reduction, and birth defects diagnosed for each live-born and still-born infant.

The data, reported by the Society for Assisted Reproductive Technology (SART, with whom CDC has contracted to implement the Act) are subject to external validation through an auditing process,* performed by SART's Validation Committee in conjunction with the CDC. This committee is composed of fourteen members assembled from both SART and non-SART member programs. Inspection teams of two Validation Committee members visit ten percent of the reporting clinics for each annual report. The clinics visited are randomly selected by the CDC. All live births reported by each visited clinic are validated. Additionally, twenty other variables are validated from fifty randomly selected cycles. The data collected during the on-site inspections are compiled and jointly reviewed by the Validation Committee and the CDC.

Any ART program can satisfy the federal reporting requirements by reporting its data to SART. If a clinic or program fails to comply with the requirements of the act, it is listed as "nonreporting" in the annual CDC publication that collects and analyzes the data reported. There are no other penalties for failure to report.

CDC publishes much (but not all) of the information it collects in an annual report of ART success rates. Each annual report includes three sections: (1) a national report that compiles information from all ART programs to provide an in-depth national picture of ART; (2) fertility clinic reports that provide ART success

* Until recently, no federal money was budgeted for validation. Instead, SART underwrote the costs of validation itself.

rates for each ART program that reports and verifies its data; and (3) an appendix containing a glossary of terms, an explanation of how the success rates (according to age group) were calculated, the names and addresses of reporting programs, and a list of programs not reporting data, including those who refuse to participate in the validation process discussed above.* The annual report does not include some of the information that ART clinics are required to report, such as the number of oocytes retrieved, embryos transferred, or cryopreserved; maximum number of fetal hearts observed in ultrasound; the number of fetal reductions performed; and adverse outcomes (including information relating to birth defects or low birthweight).

Have the reporting requirements of the Act been an effective means of informing and protecting consumers? Critics assert that because there are no serious penalties for noncompliance, the law is merely hortatory. Supporters of the Act respond that the stigma of being listed as "nonreporting" creates sufficient market pressure to compel the vast majority of ART programs to report the required data. Indeed, in 2000, 384 of the nation's 421 ART programs were deemed in compliance with the Act's reporting requirements.

Some critics argue that the reporting requirements could be greatly improved to provide more information for prospective patients. For example, Pamela Madsen, Executive Director of the American Infertility Association (an advocacy organization for infertile persons) has called for "improving informed consent, augmenting reporting from clinics, and delineating costs."[89] Moreover, some have observed that focusing on pregnancy success rates (per cycle) may create an incentive to transfer too many embryos per cycle, resulting in multiple pregnancies that can be extremely risky for both mother and children. One clinician has noted: "We're under pressure to have high pregnancy rates . . . the

* Macaluso, Maurizio, Division of Reproductive Health, National Center for Chronic Disease Prevention and Health Promotion, Centers for Disease Control and Prevention, written comments to the President's Council on Bioethics, May 12, 2003.

problem is we've never had any way of knowing what was the right number of embryos to transfer."[90] Finally, some have argued that "success rates" are not a reliable measure, given the ease with which they can be manipulated; clinics can artificially inflate these rates by accepting only those patients with promising prognoses, reclassifying or canceling failed cycles rather than reporting them, or transferring many embryos per cycle.[91]

(ii) Model certification program: The second function of the Act is to provide states with a model certification program for embryo laboratories. An "embryo laboratory" is defined as "a facility in which human oocytes are subject to assisted reproductive technology treatment or procedures based on manipulation of oocytes or embryos which are subject to implantation."[92] Unlike the reporting system, adoption of the model program is entirely voluntary. The model certification program is intended to provide a resource for states wishing to develop their own programs or for professional organizations seeking to develop guidelines or standards for embryo labs. States can apply to the Secretary of Health and Human Services to adopt the program and qualifying states will be required to administer the program as provided by the regulations. To date, no state has done so.

The overarching purpose of the model program is to help states to assure consistent quality control, record keeping, performance of procedures, and quality of personnel. The specific standards applied were developed in conjunction with the College of American Pathologists and ASRM, borrowing generously from the guidelines used in the voluntary certification program (discussed further below).

The final version of the program, incorporating comments received by the CDC, was published in the *Federal Register* on July 21, 1999.[93] Under the program, embryo laboratories *may* apply to their respective states for certification. Those laboratories that choose to do so are inspected and certified by states or approved accreditation organizations. Certification is valid for a two-year period. The Secretary, through the CDC, has authority to inspect any laboratory that has been certified by a state to ensure compliance with the standards. The penalty for noncompliance under the model program is revocation of certification. A key limitation of the program is that neither the Secretary nor the states may establish "any regulation, standard or requirement which has the effect of exercising supervision or control over the practice of medicine in assisted reproductive technologies."[94] Even if a state were to adopt the program, there is no requirement that laboratories apply for certification; it is entirely voluntary.

2. State Oversight.

There are a variety of state laws that bear directly on the clinical practice of assisted reproduction. The vast majority of state statutes directly concerned with assisted reproduction, however, are concerned mostly with the question of access to such services. These states have legislative directives as to whether and to what extent assisted reproduction services will be covered as insurance benefits. Other state statutes regarding assisted reproduction aim to prevent the malfeasance of rogue practitioners (for example, California criminalizes unauthorized use of sperm, ova, and embryos). Still others focus on the regulation of gamete and embryo donation (for example, California sets forth screening requirements for donated sperm). There are a host of states whose laws dictate parental rights and obligations in the context of assisted reproduction.[95] A few jurisdictions (such as New Hampshire and Pennsylvania) have statutes that provide for fairly comprehensive regulation of the practitioners and participants in ART. Many jurisdictions have statutes that bear generally on the treatment and disposition of embryos, but only a subset of these jurisdictions explicitly speaks to the treatment of embryos in the context of assisted reproduction (including Louisiana, New Mexico, and South Dakota).

New Hampshire has an "In Vitro Fertilization and Pre-embryo Transfer" statutory scheme that provides that "IVF will be performed in accordance with the rules adopted by the [state] department of Health and Human Services."[96] The state additionally specifies who may receive IVF treatment, namely, a woman who is at least twenty-one years of age, who has been medically evaluated for her "acceptability" to undergo the treatment (it is unclear what this means), and who has undergone requisite counseling.[97] New Hampshire likewise extends the medical and counseling requirement to the woman's husband.[98]

Pennsylvania also regulates ART as such, but focuses its efforts on record keeping and standards for maintenance of clinical facilities.[99] All IVF practitioners are required to submit reports and be available for inspection. The reports must include the names of the practitioners, their locations, the number of ova fertilized, the number of embryos destroyed or discarded, and the number of women "implanted with a fertilized egg."

Louisiana, New Mexico, and South Dakota, as noted, have embryo experimentation statutes that directly speak to assisted reproduction.[100] The New Mexico statute prohibits any "clinical research activit[ies] involving fetuses, live-born infants or pregnant women."[101] Clinical research "includes research involving human in vitro fertilization, but . . . shall not include human in vitro fertilization performed to treat infertility; provided that this procedure shall include provisions to insure that each living fertilized ovum, zygote or embryo is implanted in a human female recipient . . ."[102] There have been no court opinions interpreting this language, but some commentators suggest that this effectively proscribes the practice of IVF except in cases in which all embryos are transferred to the mother.[103]

South Dakota, like New Mexico, prohibits "non-therapeutic research" on embryos. In contrast to New Mexico, however, it explicitly exempts from this definition "IVF and transfer, or diagnostic tests which may assist in the future care of a child subjected to this test." Again, there are no cases interpreting this language, but it seems that this statute would not require the transfer to a uterus of all embryos created in the process of IVF.

Louisiana's regulation of ART provides the highest level of protection to human embryos of any U.S. jurisdiction. It defines the in vitro embryo as a "juridical person" with nearly all of the attendant rights and protections of infants.* It stipulates that the use of an in vitro embryo must be solely for "the support and contribution of the complete development of human in utero implantation." The production, culture, or use of human embryos for any other purpose is proscribed. An in vitro embryo is not considered the property of the clinician or the gamete donors. If the ART patients identify themselves as the embryo's progenitors, they are deemed parents according to the Louisiana Civil Code. If the ART patients do not identify themselves, the "physician shall be deemed to be the temporary guardian . . . until adoptive implantation can occur." The physician who creates the embryo through IVF is directly responsible for its safekeeping. The gamete donors owe the embryo "a high duty of care and prudent administration." They may, however, renounce their parental rights through a formal proceeding, after which the embryo shall be available for adoptive implantation. Donors may convey their parental rights to another married couple, but only if "the other couple is willing and able to receive" the embryo. Under Louisiana law, the judicial standard governing any disputes involving the embryo is "the best interests of the embryo." Thus, there can be no intentional destruction of a viable embryo.

Louisiana has also set standards for who may perform IVF and where IVF may be performed: It may be practiced only by a licensed physician in medical facilities that meet "the standards of [ASRM] and the American College of Obstetricians and Gynecologists."

Some states have enacted statutes that preclude "experimentation" on human embryos. Given the experimental nature of certain ART procedures (such as preimplantation genetic diagnosis), these statutes might be construed broadly to reach such practices. Some individuals have challenged such statutes on constitutional grounds, arguing that the operative terms are so vague as to violate the constitutional guarantee of due process.† Practitioners have argued that they have not

* Note, however, that this provision attaches only to "fertilized in vitro [ova]." La. Rev. Stat. Ann. § 9:129. Thus, embryos created by means other than fertilization (for example, embryos created by somatic cell nuclear transfer) would not be deemed juridical persons by Louisiana law.

† To prevail on a due process challenge for vagueness, the plaintiffs must show that the statute at issue is "impermissibly vague in all its applications" (*Village of Hoffman Estates v. Flipside*, 455 U.S. 489, 497 [1982]) and that

been adequately informed about which procedures could expose them to criminal liability. Courts in three jurisdictions have invalidated such statutes on these grounds.[104] One court among these three struck down the statute on the additional ground that it impermissibly infringed the plaintiff's right to choose a particular means of reproduction, noting: "It takes no great leap of logic to see that within the cluster of constitutionally protected choices that includes access to contraceptives, there must be included within that cluster the right to submit to a medical procedure that may bring about, rather than prevent, pregnancy."[105]

In short, there are very few state laws that bear directly on assisted reproduction. Most of these laws relate to the provision of insurance coverage for infertility treatment. A few state laws directly relating to ART focus on health and safety concerns; a handful of states provide modest consumer protections. Some state laws regulating embryo research may indirectly affect the practice of assisted reproduction, though the decisional law in this area is unsettled. In the main, however, assisted reproduction is regulated at the state level by the same mechanisms that apply to the practice of medicine more generally, namely, through the licensure and certification of practitioners.

B. Indirect Governmental Regulation of Assisted Reproduction

There are a number of state and federal governmental authorities that do not explicitly aim at the regulation of ART, but indirectly and incidentally provide some measure of oversight and direction.

1. Federal Oversight.

a. Safety and efficacy of products and public health. The U.S. Food and Drug Administration (FDA) is the federal agency that regulates some of the *articles* used in assisted repro-

---

"men of common intelligence must necessarily guess at its meaning and differ as to its applications" (*Baggett v. Bullitt*, 377 U.S. 360, 367 [1964]).

duction, but it does not, as a general matter, oversee the *practice* of assisted reproduction.

FDA regulates drugs, devices, and biologics that are or will be marketed for use in the United States. Its principal purpose is to ensure the safety and efficacy of products according to their approved use.[106] The FDA is also broadly authorized to adopt regulations to prevent the spread of communicable disease.[107] Additionally, it exercises regulatory authority over clinical trials of unapproved medical products subject to its regulations. The FDA does not, however, have the authority to regulate "the practice of medicine" (which is the province of the states). Thus physicians may, in the course of administering medical treatment according to acceptable standards of care, employ FDA-approved articles in a manner that is outside the scope of their approved use. This is sometimes called "off-label" use.

The FDA's jurisdiction is a product of congressional authority under the interstate commerce clause of the United States Constitution. FDA's principal powers derive from the authority conferred by the Food, Drug, and Cosmetic Act (FDCA) and the Public Health Services Act (PHSA) to regulate the introduction of certain products (and their components) into interstate commerce. Given the Supreme Court's expansive interpretation of what constitutes "interstate activity" for purposes of deciding cases involving the commerce clause, this has not proven to be a significant limitation on the FDA's authority. Nevertheless, it is conceivable that one might mount a credible constitutional challenge to FDA regulation of an activity that is wholly intrastate.

FDA regulatory mechanisms are driven by the statutory definitions provided by the FDCA and PHSA. If FDA determines that a given article falls within the broad statutory definitions of "drug," "device," or "biologic," it could exercise jurisdiction, provided the interstate nexus is satisfied. Thus, to describe the breadth and depth of FDA's authority, particularly as it relates to assisted reproduction, it is necessary to explain in some detail how these statutory definitions and related provisions function in practice.

"Drug" is defined by the FDCA in an extremely expansive way, encompassing any officially recognized article that is either (1) intended for use in the diagnosis, cure, mitigation, treatment, or prevention of disease in man, or (2) (excepting foods) intended to affect the structure or any function of the body of man. The definition also extends to anything intended for use as a component of the foregoing articles.[108] It is unlawful to introduce a "new drug"—a legal category that encompasses nearly every prescription and many non-prescription drugs—into interstate commerce without an FDA-approved New Drug Application (NDA).[109] The NDA process is onerous and expensive, requiring the sponsor to provide large amounts of information to the FDA including details regarding the composition of the drug, "the chemistry of the formulation for delivering the active ingredient, methods of manufacture and packaging, proposed labeling, and, most critically, the results of clinical studies that will support a conclusion that the drug product is safe and effective."[110] As Professor Richard Merrill points out, the FDA's proscription on distribution of unapproved drugs, combined with its demand for clinical trials as a prerequisite to new drug approval, seems to create a paradox.[111] For how can a "new drug" be tested for safety and efficacy if it cannot move in interstate commerce? Congress enabled the FDA to resolve this tension by creating a limited exemption for distribution of an "Investigational New Drug" (IND)[112]—that is, a limited approval solely for purposes of a clinical trial. Upon receipt of an IND application, FDA imposes a thirty-day waiting period during which it reviews the proposed protocols. FDA can deny or suspend an IND (called a "clinical hold") and effectively prevent clinical trials for a new drug if it finds that (1) human subjects would be exposed to unreasonable and significant risk of illness or injury or (2) the IND does not contain sufficient information required to assess the risks to subjects of the proposed study.

Pursuant to Section 351 of the PHSA, the FDA has the authority to regulate "biological products," defined as "any virus, therapeutic serum, toxin, anti-toxin, vaccine, blood, blood component or derivative, allergenic product or analogous product, applicable to the prevention, treatment or cure of diseases or injuries to humans."[113] This is, on its face, a very broad definition, particularly in light of the somewhat ambiguous phrase "analogous product." Under

Section 351, it is unlawful to introduce any biological product into interstate commerce without an approved biologics license application (BLA).[114] The BLA process is much akin to the NDA process in that applicants are required to demonstrate that the biological product is "safe, pure, and potent," and manufactured in a facility meeting certain specifications.[115] The data in support of the application must be developed through clinical and nonclinical studies. The same regulations governing preclinical testing and clinical testing of new drugs in the IND context[116] govern these activities in the BLA process as well. Indeed, the definition of "biological product" falls within the statutory definition of "drug" in the FDCA. However, if a biologic is licensed under Section 351, it need not be approved under the parallel FDCA provisions.[117]

Pursuant to its authority to regulate biological products, FDA's Center for Biologics Evaluation and Research (CBER) has also undertaken regulation of cellular and gene-therapy products. Researchers developing gene-therapy products must receive an IND before studying gene-therapy products in humans and must meet FDA requirements for safety and efficacy before such products can be approved for marketing. The regulation of such activities is discussed extensively in Chapter 5.

Section 361 of the PHSA empowers the FDA to issue regulations to prevent the spread of communicable diseases.[118] Under this authority, CBER has issued or proposed regulations for Human Cellular and Tissue-Based Products (HCT/Ps), which include a variety of medical products derived from the human body and used for replacement, reproductive, or therapeutic purposes, such as semen, ova, and embryos used for reproductive purposes.[*119] Sperm, ova, and embryos were originally exempted from this definition, but were later added out of concern for the transmission of disease. In 1997, the FDA released a general plan for the comprehensive regulation of HCT/Ps. In 1998, the FDA pub-

[*] If HCT/Ps were "drugs," requiring FDA approval, premarket approval would be effectively required for all HCT/Ps before any could be distributed to human beings (including for clinical trials). This would effectively put all tissue banks (including blood and sperm banks) and clinicians working with the products of such banks out of business.

lished three proposed rules that would require: (1) registration for facilities working with reproductive tissue; (2) screening for communicable disease; and (3) adherence to FDA good tissue practices for "minimally processed or manipulated" tissues transplanted from one person to another for their normal structural functions.[120] The first rule is now final; the latter two are pending.*

Owners and operators of establishments or persons engaged in the recovery, screening, testing, processing, storage, or distribution of HCT/Ps must register with the FDA and list those human cells, tissues, and cellular and tissue-based products with CBER.† However, there are several important exceptions to these registration requirements. Specifically, registration is not required if (1) an establishment removes HCT/Ps from an individual and implants such HCT/Ps into the same individual during the same surgical procedure; (2) an establishment does not recover, screen, test, process, label, package, or distribute, but only receives or stores HCT/Ps solely for implantation, transplantation, infusion, or transfer within the facility; or (3) an establishment only recovers reproductive cells or tissue and immediately transfers them into a sexually intimate partner of the cell or tissue donor.[121]

Like the statutory definition of "drug" and "biological product" discussed above, "device" is defined in a similarly expansive manner, covering any "instrument, apparatus, implement, machine, contrivance, implant, in vitro reagent, or other similar related article, including any component" that is officially recognized, intended for the diagnosis, treatment, cure, mitigation, or prevention of disease in man,

---

* These tissues would not, however, be subject to the onerous requirements for premarket approval. "Minimal manipulation" was defined as "processing that does not alter the relevant biological characteristics and, thus potentially, the function or integrity of the cells or tissues." (63 Fed. Reg. 26,748 [May 14, 1998].) "More than minimally manipulated" tissues and cells that are (1) combined with non-cellular or non-tissue components, (2) labeled or promoted for purposes other than their normal functions, or (3) have systemic effect (except in cases of autologous use, transplantation into a first-degree blood relative or reproductive use) would require FDA's more stringent premarket review and approval described above.

† As of February 2004 the effective date of these regulations had been delayed.

or intended to affect the structure and function of the body of man, "and which does not achieve its primary intended purpose through chemical action within or on the body of man . . . and which is not dependent upon being metabolized for achievement of its primary intended purpose."[122] Devices are categorized according to the risk of harm associated with their use.[123] Those devices that present a low safety risk are designated as Class I or II. Devices that present the greatest risk, such as those used to sustain or support life, or those that are implanted in the human body, are designated as Class III. All new devices are subject to a process known as "premarket notification" (PMN), in which the FDA engages in a preliminary evaluation of safety and efficacy, and determines whether the proposed device is substantially equivalent to a product that is already on the market. Other devices (particularly those presenting a greater safety risk) are subject to the more onerous "premarket approval" (PMA) process, which is akin to the NDA procedure, requiring a much more rigorous demonstration of safety and efficacy. The timing and schedule of the PMA process for new devices is highly complex, and beyond the scope of the present inquiry.

FDA has a number of means at its disposal to enforce the foregoing regulations under the PHSA and FDCA. FDA has authority to conduct inspections to determine compliance with these requirements.[124] Approved BLAs or NDAs can be revoked (subject to an adversarial hearing).[125] License revocation is used to address concerns about the marketability of a given product in general (perhaps based on the FDA's reassessment of the relative risks and benefits of the given product). Additionally, the FDA has the power to recall or seize previously approved products.[*126] Unlike license revocation, recall and seizure powers are invoked to address concerns about a *given subset* of marketed products (for example, a defective batch). Finally, the FDA can pursue criminal prosecution as an additional mechanism of enforcement.[127]

---

[*] Technically, the FDA has only the *formal* authority to recall previously approved devices. Manufacturers and distributors are likely in practice, however, to accede to requests for voluntary recall of drugs and biological products, so as to avoid forcible seizure of such articles by the FDA.

How do the above regulations of drugs, devices, and biologics affect the practice of assisted reproduction? First, to the extent that articles used in ART meet the statutory definition of drug, device, or biologic, they must satisfy the relevant FDA requirements for marketing.* This is, however, principally a regulatory mechanism applicable to the manufacturers of these articles—rather than the clinicians who use them following their approval. Once an article is approved, the FDA surrenders much of its regulatory control. Clinicians treating infertile patients are regarded as engaged in the practice of medicine, which has long been acknowledged as beyond the regulatory reach of the FDA:

> The physician may, as part of the practice of medicine, lawfully prescribe a different dosage for his patient, or may otherwise vary the conditions of use from those approved in the package insert, without informing or obtaining the approval of the Food and Drug Administration. . . . [T]he Act does not require a physician to file an investigational new drug plan before prescribing an approved drug for unapproved use or submit . . . data concerning the therapeutic results and adverse reactions.[128]

Further, federal courts have held that a licensed physician, in treating a patient, can prescribe a lawful drug for a non-FDA approved purpose.[129] If the FDA wants to control (or influence) off-label use of approved products it would likely impose some new labeling requirement warning users of the dangers animating its concern. Again, any such action would influence the manufacturer more than the clinician administering these articles in the practice of medicine. Theoretically, if the FDA were concerned that the risks of widespread off-label use utterly outweighed the benefits of the approved use, it could withdraw its approval. But this is not often done.

The FDA's regulations for reproductive tissues, if and when they are finalized (in the case of the screening and good tissue practice provisions) and officially implemented,

* Indeed, there are specific regulations governing devices used in ART. *See* 21 C.F.R. § 884.6100 et seq.

may have some impact on assisted reproduction. The regulations currently in effect require certain owners and operators of facilities that work with reproductive tissues to register and list such tissues with CBER. However, many fertility clinics seem to be exempt from these requirements, as discussed above.

In the main, the FDA has abstained from regulating the field of assisted reproduction. This is understandable, given that some of the activities in assisted reproduction fall under the aegis of the practice of medicine, which the FDA has not sought to regulate. Given that FDA's authority is largely driven by the statutory definitions of "articles" under its purview, extension of this authority to the context of assisted reproduction would require some strange recategorization of certain aspects of human procreation. For example, in order to acquire jurisdiction under current law, it might be necessary for the FDA to construe an embryo that might be transferred into a uterus as a "drug," "biological product," or "device." What would safety and efficacy mean in such a context? Finally, the FDA may have been historically hesitant to assert jurisdiction over assisted reproduction because of the nature of the regulatory mechanisms themselves. The categorization and approval mechanisms through which FDA exercises much of its authority are not graduated or flexible. Thus, when FDA asserts jurisdiction over an article by defining it as a "new drug" subject to the relevant approval requirements, it becomes immediately unlawful to distribute it. FDA's unwillingness to regulate assisted reproduction under the FDCA may be partly due to a concern that to do so would effectively shut down the entire practice of assisted reproduction.

There are, however, some notable exceptions to the FDA's reluctance to step into the arena of assisted reproduction. Already mentioned is the regulation, through HCT/P registration requirements, of entities that collect, process, or distribute sperm, ova, and embryos as reproductive tissue. A more controversial example is the FDA's recent pronouncements on cloning for reproduction.* Here, the

* Inclusion of this example is not meant to imply that practitioners of assisted reproduction or their patients approve of cloning to produce children.

FDA has invoked its authority by asserting that the implantation of a cloned embryo into a woman's uterus is tantamount to the administration of an unapproved new drug, requiring an IND.[130] Because of safety concerns, FDA declared that it would withhold approval of any such IND.* To date, no IND has been submitted. It bears noting that the animating principles of FDA's regulation in this context are, as usual, safety and efficacy. A former head of CBER, Katherine Zoon, told a congressional committee that if concerns over safety were properly addressed, FDA would not likely reject an IND for cloning for reproduction.[131]

Finally, the FDA has also ventured into the field of assisted reproduction to halt the practice of ooplasm transfer. In 2001, FDA asserted that clinicians at St. Barnabas Hospital in Livingston, New Jersey, were required to submit an IND before performing further procedures involving ooplasm transfer, on the grounds that it is a form of gene-transfer research, as the procedure results in the transfer of mitochondrial DNA. This sent a shock wave through the ART community, and most if not all practitioners halted the procedure altogether rather than submit to the IND process.

These examples serve to illustrate the contours and limits of FDA's authority in the context of assisted reproduction. First, it is clear that the FDA will act if it perceives a sufficiently grave harm that can be formulated in terms of FDA's mandate—safety and efficacy, and the prevention of communicable disease. However, to assert jurisdiction, FDA must sometimes engage in definitional contortions. By most lights, for example, human embryos are not "drugs." Finally, these examples suggest that the line between clinical experimentation and the practice of medicine is not always easy to draw. As a general rule, clinicians can, without FDA oversight, employ novel and untested interventions on patients in the course of treatment, provided that the articles involved have been previously approved for their originally intended purpose.

---

* The FDA has released no further statements on the subject of cloning since 2001. It is not clear whether the agency still subscribes to these jurisdictional and legal theories.

b. Quality assurance and control in clinical laboratories. Another federal authority that indirectly affects assisted reproduction arises from the Clinical Laboratory Improvement Amendments of 1988 (CLIA).[132] This statute (and regulations issued thereunder by the Centers for Medicare and Medicaid Services, or CMS) requires laboratories engaged in the "examination of materials derived from the human body for the purpose of providing information for the diagnosis, prevention, or treatment of any disease or impairment" to meet certain quality requirements. Specifically, CLIA requires that such laboratories must satisfy requirements relating to quality assurance, personnel qualifications and responsibilities, record keeping, quality control, and the like. Moreover, such labs must submit to inspections (announced or unannounced). Failure to comply can result in revocation of certification and inclusion in a published list of sanctioned laboratories. States can opt out of CLIA if they have their own certification program that is equally or more rigorous.

CLIA does not apply to assisted reproduction laboratory facilities as such. Rather, it applies to andrology and endocrinology diagnostic tests (such as semen and blood-hormone analysis) in such laboratories. These tests are *not covered* by CLIA when undertaken as an adjunct to the delivery of assisted reproduction services. This creates what some consider to be a confusing regulatory atmosphere. The American Board of Bioanalysis (ABB) (which advocates on behalf of clinical laboratory directors) brought a lawsuit in 1999 to compel Health and Human Services (HHS) to apply CLIA to all ART embryo laboratories. The case was dismissed on the grounds that the ABB lacked standing to sue. The Court agreed with HHS's contention that the Department should be allotted more time to consider the question of CLIA's application.

c. Regulation of unfair trade practices. The Federal Trade Commission (FTC) is charged with providing safeguards against anti-competitive behavior and promoting truth in advertising in interstate commerce. FTC thus has the authority to investigate deceptive claims in advertising by health care providers, including fertility clinics (for example, claims of pregnancy success rates).

2. State Oversight.

a. Regulation of the practice of medicine. To describe the current regulation of assisted reproduction fully and fairly, it is necessary to treat in some detail the regulation of the practice of medicine more generally. The bulk of external governmental regulation of assisted reproduction is entirely indirect, and is subsumed in this more general context. The following requirements, pertinent to the entire practice of medicine, apply also to the practice of assisted reproduction. Despite the fact that they are not specifically addressed to the practice of reproductive medicine, these requirements are generally cited by practitioners of ART in support of the proposition that the field is subject to close regulatory scrutiny.

(i) Informed consent: One of the core principles of ethical medical practice, supported also by legal standards, is the requirement that patients provide their informed consent to medical treatments and procedures. While informed consent is necessary in all medical contexts, it is required under the federal human-subject research regulations and, in most states, is explicitly called for by the state's patient's-rights laws.[133] The doctrine of informed consent has also been long recognized in case law through recognition that treatment without consent constitutes a battery. Even outside of the human-subject research context, most hospitals require written informed consent when complicated or risky procedures or treatments are being administered (for example, chemotherapy treatments or surgeries). This is also true when experimental procedures are being utilized for treatment. Under such circumstances, the informed consent form is commonly drafted in accordance with the human-subject research requirements.

All physicians providing infertility treatment or working in the field of assisted reproduction are bound by this standard and must ensure that their patients give informed consent to any intervention.

(ii) Licensure: The practice of medicine is regulated under state licensing statutes. States regulate the practice of medicine pursuant to their authority to defend the health, safety, and general welfare of the community (the so-called "police power"). Each state has enacted a medical practice act governing the practice of medicine. The model Medical Practice Act (set forth by the Federation of State Medical Boards) defines the practice of medicine quite broadly.*

Persons practicing medicine must be licensed by the state to do so and are subject to the state's Medical Practice Act and the regulations promulgated by the licensure board. Licensure boards oversee the initial and continuing licensure of physicians practicing in the state. These boards are also responsible for disciplining physicians who render incompetent or unprofessional care in violation of applicable regulations and standards. The Federation of State Medical Boards, in cooperation with the National Board of Medical Examiners,

* The Model Medical Practice Act defines "practice of medicine" as: "advertising, holding out to the public or representing in any manner that one is authorized to practice medicine in the jurisdiction; offering or undertaking to prescribe, order, give or administer any drug or medicine for the use of any other person; offering or undertaking to prevent or to diagnose, correct or treat in any manner or by any means, methods, or devices any disease, illness, pain, wound, fracture, infirmity, defect or abnormal physical or mental condition of any person, including the management of pregnancy and parturition; offering or undertaking to perform any surgical operation upon any person; rendering a written or otherwise documented medical opinion concerning the diagnosis or treatment of a patient or the actual rendering of treatment to a patient within a state by a physician located outside the state as a result of transmission of individual patient data by electronic or other means from within a state to such physician or his or her agent; rendering a determination of medical necessity or a decision affecting the diagnosis or treatment of a patient; and using the designation Doctor, Doctor of Medicine, Doctor of Osteopathy, Physician, Surgeon, Physician and Surgeon, Dr., M.D., D.O. or any combination thereof in the conduct of any occupation or profession pertaining to the prevention, diagnosis or treatment of human disease or condition unless such a designation additionally contains the description of another branch of the healing arts for which one holds a valid license in the jurisdiction."

creates and administers the required United States Medical Licensing Examination (USMLE).

Physicians engaged in the field of reproductive medicine must be licensed by their state as a condition of practicing. This is the chief mechanism of regulation for the practice of assisted reproduction.

(iii) Registration with DEA: All physicians, including those working in the field of reproductive medicine, are required by the Controlled Substances Act[134] to register with the United States Drug Enforcement Agency (DEA) if they will be prescribing or dispensing controlled substances. The Controlled Substances Act is a federal criminal statute. DEA registration permits physicians to possess and dispense (prescribe) controlled substances and certain listed chemicals to patients and research subjects to the extent authorized by their registration and in conformity with the Controlled Substances Act and related regulations. There are state law counterparts to the Controlled Substances Act that may impose additional requirements on physicians beyond the federal law.

(iv) Hospital credentialing: Any practitioner seeking to practice in the field of assisted reproduction at a hospital is required to apply for medical staff privileges. The process for obtaining privileges is often referred to as "credentialing" because it is a method of ensuring that a physician has the appropriate credentials prior to granting permission to practice at a hospital. The credentialing process is set forth in a hospital's medical staff bylaws. At a minimum, initial credentialing includes a lengthy application process including proof and verification of medical education, USMLE scores, residency training, all past employment, criminal background checks, and professional recommendations. The hospital's governing board must approve all credentialing appointments and reappointments (which by Joint Commission on Accreditation of Healthcare Organizations [JCAHO] accreditation standards must be every two years at a minimum), as the hospital is generally considered legally responsible for the acts of its medical staff.

(v) Board certification: In an effort to ensure that a hospital has only physicians practicing good medicine and providing the appropriate "standard of care," many hospitals now require Board certification in order for a physician to obtain clinical privileges in a specialty or to be granted privileges to perform certain procedures (for example, to practice in the field of assisted reproduction). A hospital's medical staff bylaws establish this requirement, which is enforced through the credentialing appointment and reappointment process.

(vi) National Practitioners Data Bank: The Health Care Quality and Improvement Act[135] enacted in 1986, among other things, established the National Practitioners Data Bank. This is a national, centralized source of information on physician disciplinary actions related to professional competence or conduct and medical malpractice and settlements. State licensing boards and all licensed hospitals are required to report disciplinary actions to the Data Bank. Hospitals have a statutory duty to request information from the Data Bank upon credentialing a new physician for clinical privileges to practice at the hospital and, at a minimum, every two years for every medical staff member and privileged physician. The Data Bank is not accessible to the public, and is accessible to plaintiff attorneys in only very limited circumstances. This national mechanism helps to prevent a physician found by one state licensing board to be practicing below standard or violating professional standards from continuing to practice medicine legally by moving to another state.

(vii) Facility licensure: JCAHO is a private accrediting body whose standards are voluntary and do not have the force of law. However, the Medicare regulations provide that a hospital's compliance with JCAHO standards is "deemed compliance" with Medicare's conditions of participation—a requirement for all hospitals participating in the Medicare program (that is, receiving any reimbursement from the government for the provision of health care).[136] As a result, virtually all hospitals in the United States with more than twenty-five beds are JCAHO accredited. These detailed standards cover hospital policy, procedures, and operations with respect to several areas, including, for example, clinical practice. Facilities delivering health care are regulated by the state within which they are located. Most states have specific standards applicable to licensure of hospitals, clinics, free-standing surgical centers, and other facilities where health care is provided. Note, however, that most states do not require a doctor's office to be licensed as a health care facility.

(viii) Malpractice insurance coverage: As part of the credentialing process, hospitals require physicians to meet certain clinical standards in order to obtain and maintain appropriate malpractice insurance. Carriers are increasingly requiring hospitals through contract to mandate specialty training and board certification in order to maintain insurability for certain types of procedures and treatments. Additionally, many states require practicing physicians to maintain minimum levels of malpractice insurance coverage as a condition of licensure.

(ix) Disciplinary proceedings by state licensure board: In cases of suspected unprofessional behavior or substandard care, the Board may investigate, hold a hearing, and discipline physicians. Disciplinary actions may include suspension or revocation of licensure. Such actions are reported to the National Practitioners Data Bank.

In sum, practitioners in the field of assisted reproduction—like all other physicians—must be: licensed by their states; registered with the DEA (if they are prescribing or dispensing controlled substances); appropriately credentialed (if they are to practice in a hospital); Board certified (if their hospitals require it); subject to the reporting requirements of the National

Practitioners Data Bank (if they are disciplined); insured for malpractice (if their hospitals or states require it); and subject to disciplinary proceedings by the state licensure board (if appropriate). Also, like any other physicians, those engaged in the practice of reproductive medicine must ensure that their patients provide informed consent to all medical treatments or interventions.

b. Litigation as regulation. Another crucial mechanism for the regulation of the practice of medicine is litigation. The most common litigation arising out of the context of assisted reproduction relates to the custody or disposition of untransferred embryos and the rights and obligations of people standing in direct relation to these embryos. Courts are currently struggling with how to handle such cases, and they draw on concepts from family law, constitutional law, and contract or informed consent law to resolve the disputes. Several courts have encouraged clinics to assist couples in planning and recording their preferences for future embryo disposition if death, divorce, or other unforeseen circumstances arise. Some courts have said such documents should be enforced if the couple later disagrees about embryo disposition.

In *Davis v. Davis*,[137] the Tennessee Supreme Court took a slightly more nuanced approach. The case involved a divorce-related custody dispute over the disposition of a couple's cryopreserved embryos. The husband sought custody of the embryos so that he could destroy them. The wife sought custody in order to convey them to another couple seeking to become pregnant.[*] The Court began by noting that the embryos in question should not be regarded legally as property or people, but rather as occupying an interim category of "special respect."[138] It then provided an analytical framework for resolving such disputes:

> [The Court should first look] to the preferences of the progenitors [of the embryos]. If their wishes cannot be ascertained, or if there is dispute, then

[*] Earlier in the divorce proceeding, the wife argued that she wanted custody so that she could transfer the embryos to her own uterus in an effort to become pregnant.

> their prior agreement concerning disposition should be carried out. If no prior agreement exists, then the relative interests of the parties in using or not using the [embryos] must be weighed. Ordinarily, the party wishing to avoid procreation should prevail, assuming that the other party has a reasonable probability of achieving parenthood by means other than the use of the [embryos] in question. If no other reasonable alternatives exist, then the argument in favor of using the [embryos] to achieve pregnancy should be considered. However, if the party seeking control of the [embryos] intends merely to donate them to another couple, the objecting party obviously has the greater interest and should prevail.
>
> But the rule does not contemplate the creation of an automatic veto, and . . . we would not wish to be interpreted as so holding.[139]

Applying this rule to the facts presented, the Court awarded custody to Mr. Davis, the husband.

Medical malpractice litigation is the primary tool available to patients who have been harmed by a physician in the delivery of medical services. To sustain a claim for medical malpractice, an injured patient must demonstrate that the defendant breached a duty owed to the patient and that this breach resulted in harm. A physician breaches his duty to a patient when he provides services that fall below the recognized "standard of care." Standard of care is defined with respect to all applicable benchmarks, including licensure standards, specialty protocols and standards, and professional codes. The standard of care has been formulated as "professional competence and care customary in similar communities among physicians engaged in the particular field of practice." This duty attaches once the physician-patient relationship is formed.

IVF is considered a specialty for purposes of the standard of care. However, courts are sometimes reluctant to entertain claims for harms in this context, to the extent that the harms alleged are to persons not yet born. Moreover, it is often difficult for claimants to demonstrate that the actions of the clinician proximately caused the harm alleged. For example, when an effort at assisted reproduction fails it can be difficult to prove that the cause of such failure was the result of the clinician's negligence rather that the underlying infertility.

Another tort theory on which injured parties might rely in the context of assisted reproduction is wrongful conversion. This theory has been invoked to sue individuals who have destroyed in vitro embryos without the patients' consent. In one case, *Del Zio v. Presbyterian Hospital*, a couple sued a hospital and its chief of obstetrics and gynecology for $1.5 million for deliberately destroying the couple's in vitro embryos prior to implantation. In addition to wrongful conversion, the couple alleged intentional infliction of emotional distress. The jury awarded $50,000 to the wife for emotional distress, and the husband received nominal damages. The jury rejected the couple's claim for wrongful conversion.[140]

Suits may also be filed for prenatal and even preconception injuries to the unborn child. Many states permit such suits only if the child is born alive. Other states permit such suits only if the child was "viable" at the time of injury. Suits on behalf of children born through assisted reproduction can be brought as "wrongful death" actions if the child is stillborn or born alive but dies soon thereafter. A majority of states permit the administrator of the estate of an unborn child to recover damages.

C. Nongovernmental Regulation

1. Safety, Efficacy, and Privacy.

The key sources of nongovernmental guidance and oversight for the practice of assisted reproduction are the standards propounded by ASRM, published in conjunction with its sister organization, SART. SART clinics must agree to adhere to these guidelines as a condition of membership. SART additionally requires certification of its members' embryo labs by the College of American Pathologists, JCAHO, or the New York State Tissue Bank program. Moreover, SART requires its members to comply with the reporting provisions of the federal Fertility Clinic Success Rate and Certification Act. According to

SART's website, 95 percent of the nation's assisted reproduction clinics are SART members.

ASRM provides guidance by means of published statements, opinions, and guidelines issued by its practice and ethics committees. The chief values ASRM seeks to promote through its opinions and guidelines are safety (of ART participants), efficacy (of techniques and procedures), and privacy (of ART patients). According to ASRM, these documents are framed in a variety of ways:

> Some, like the Practice Committee's "Guidelines for Gamete and Embryo Donation," take the form of a list of considerations to be made or steps to be followed, while others take the form of a survey or review of research on a particular medical topic, i.e., "Aging and Infertility in Women." Ethics Committee documents are usually framed as a discussion of issues, sometimes leading to a particular conclusion and other times recommending a number of approaches based on different circumstances that can arise.[141]

The *practice* guidance documents provide direction as to minimal standards for IVF (such as personnel requirements, laboratory requirements, quality assurance, and control standards). Specific examples of subjects covered by such documents include guidelines for gamete and embryo donation,[142] ICSI,[143] informed consent,[144] induction of ovarian follicle development and ovulation with exogenous gonadatropins,[145] number of embryos transferred,[146] and preimplantation genetic diagnosis.[147] Practice committees also evaluate novel procedures. These committees review the existing literature on randomized clinical trials. If two peer-reviewed published studies show that the risk-benefit ratio is acceptable, the procedure is elevated from "experimental" to "practice." ICSI has been elevated to practice status in this way, as have PGD and blastocyst transfer.

The *ethical* guidelines published by ASRM address a number of subjects including advertising,[148] informed consent,[149] and disposition of abandoned embryos.[150] Most are framed in terms of discussions that merely highlight concerns rather than prescribe or proscribe specific courses of conduct among members. However, as ASRM's then-president, Dr. Sandra Carson, pointed out in her presentation to the President's Council on Bioethics in March 2003, ASRM "actively discourages" some procedures on ethical grounds. She gave the examples of PGD for elective sex selection, oocyte donation after natural menopause,* posthumous reproduction in absence of advance directives, and cloning for reproduction. Compliance of ART practitioners with the ethical guidelines, as with the practice guidelines, is entirely voluntary.

In conjunction with the College of American Pathologists, ASRM has adopted a Reproductive Laboratory Accreditation Program (RLAP). RLAP requires accredited laboratories working with infertility programs to meet minimum standards, submit to on-site inspections (every three years), and complete proficiency testing surveys for evaluating performance. The process is expensive and time consuming.

As mentioned above, in 2003 ASRM and RAND published a study estimating the number of embryos in cryopreservation at 400,000 in 2002. ASRM also collects information on congenital abnormalities of IVF and ICSI births, but, according to Dr. Carson, this process is non-rigorous and the data are inadequate.† During her presentation, she noted that to undertake a comprehensive and effective study on the association of ART with birth defects would be extremely expensive. It would require neonatalogists, epidemiologists, statisticians, and child development specialists. ASRM has no current plans to undertake such a study.

ASRM committee opinions are advisory and are not formulated as "commandments." ASRM's system of professional self-regulation is voluntary and there appear to be no penalties for or consequences of noncompliance. SART membership has a number of requirements and conditions, but membership itself is voluntary.

Recently ASRM, in conjunction with the Genetics and Public Policy Center of Johns Hopkins University and the American

* This guideline is currently being re-evaluated.

† In her March 7, 2003, presentation to the President's Council on Bioethics, Dr. Carson said: "[SART, ASRM, and CDC do] collect [data relating to] congenital anomalies of IVF and ICSI births. However, it is a non-rigorous collection. The data that we do collect we feel is inadequate to come with a truly scientific evidence based review of the birth defect risks. It's a start, but it's not the best we can do."

Academy of Pediatrics, has undertaken a comprehensive review of all published materials relating to the health effects of ART on children conceived with its aid. A report analyzing this information is scheduled to be released in 2004. Additionally, the American Infertility Association (a national patient's advocacy group for the infertile) recently announced that it plans to collaborate with the RAND Corporation to study the health and welfare of children conceived by IVF. The study (which will be called "Footprints: The IVF Children's Health Study") will collect general health information from such children (on a voluntary basis) for their first three years of life. Data to be collected will include information relating to birthweight, multiple gestations, birth defects, surgical procedures, and developmental milestones. The study will include a control sample of children conceived with the aid of intrauterine insemination (IUI). The study will be supervised by a scientific advisory committee, including representatives of the American Infertility Association and RAND, reproductive endocrinologists, patient advocates, mental health professionals, epidemiologists, pediatricians, and the like.[151]

2. Safeguarding Professional Integrity and Promoting the Ethical Practice of Medicine.

There are numerous professional medical associations that have specific codes of practice or guidelines to which its members agree to adhere. The most notable example is the American Medical Association (AMA) Code of Ethics. This code consists of the Principles of Medical Ethics, which are adopted by the AMA's House of Delegates, and the Current Opinions of the Council on Ethical and Judicial Affairs, which interpret the principles. The AMA's Code of Ethics is widely disseminated and has provided the most commonly cited standard for courts, legislatures, administrative agencies, medical boards, and other peer review entities. Most medical societies, and virtually all state medical societies, accept the code as the profession's code.

The AMA has a specific code regarding assisted reproductive technology,[152] which states four main principles: (1) The medical profession should continue to develop technical and ethical guidelines including educational materials on clinic-specific success rates. (2) All fertility labs should participate in credible professional accreditation and should voluntarily adhere to ethical standards. Physicians should report unethical behavior. (3) Patients should be fully informed of all aspects of ART, and payment based on clinical outcome is unacceptable. (4) Physicians practicing ART should, in any marketing materials, accurately describe available services, success rates, fee structures, and payment obligations.

The American Board of Obstetrics and Gynecology (ABOG) certifies obstetricians and gynecologists in the United States, and is one of twenty-four specialty boards recognized by the American Board of Medical Specialties. New certificates and maintenance of certification issued by the ABOG are valid for six years.

ABOG has a Division of Reproductive Endocrinology and Infertility. A reproductive endocrinologist is a sub-specialist in obstetrics and gynecology trained to manage complex problems relating to reproductive endocrinology and infertility. The stated objectives of this Division are to promote health care in this field, help maintain professional standards, and establish standards and procedures for candidates for this specialization.

The American Academy of Pediatrics (AAP) also has stated positions that relate to the practice of assisted reproduction, albeit in an attenuated way. AAP does not consider an in vitro embryo a "person" or a pediatric patient. However, one AAP statement entitled "Ethical considerations in Fetal Therapy"[153] indicates that with recent advances in prenatal medicine, the pregnant woman and her fetus are increasingly viewed as two treatable patients.

IV. CONCLUSION

How well do the current regulatory institutions and activities address the various ethical concerns noted above? The current regulatory landscape is a patchwork, with authority divided among numerous sources of oversight. A first question might be whether such a system of regulation, involving multiple authorities, is well-suited to address the concerns. To the extent that the harms are sufficiently grave and commonly recognized, a uniform system might be preferable to this patchwork one. On the other hand, to the extent that the ethical concerns reflect matters of personal morality and autonomy, a system of diverse or decentralized regulation might be preferable.

The current system of regulation of assisted reproduction is characterized not only by diverse authorities but also by the diversity of the regulatory mechanisms brought to bear on practitioners and participants. Such mechanisms fall at every point on the regulatory spectrum, from criminal enforcement by the federal government to hortatory and merely aspirational statements of policy by professional organizations.

The objectives of current direct federal oversight of ART are consumer protection and quality assurance for embryo laboratories. While these are important goals, they do not aim directly at most of the ethical concerns described above, including the health and safety of women and children whose lives are touched by ART. There is some federal record keeping by the CDC regarding the practice of assisted reproduction, focusing predominantly on pregnancy success rates at different clinics. The CDC also collects some information regarding the health effects of ART on women and children, but this information has not, as yet, been publicly disseminated, nor is the CDC legally required to publish it.

The objectives of analogous state regulation vary widely, and include ensuring access to infertility services; policing irresponsible clinicians; providing standards for donors of human tissue; defining parental rights and obligations; protecting embryonic human life; ensuring the quality of ART practitioners; and protecting consumers of ART. Although some of these state regulations do, in fact, aim at the ethical concerns animating this inquiry, there is a lack of uniformity among states, with many states providing little regulation or none at all.

Indirect federal oversight of assisted reproduction aims principally at the safety and efficacy of products for their approved uses and the defense of the public against communicable disease (FDA). However, the FDA mainly regulates manufacturers and developers of products, and it does not reach off-label uses in the practice of medicine. Moreover, because the FDA's authority is based largely on the definitions of the articles it regulates, reaching ART seems to require some questionable redefinition of aspects of human procreation (for example, declaring the human embryo transferred to a uterus to be a "drug" or "biological product"). Finally, FDA lacks the mandate and institutional competence to make decisions about moral and ethical concerns akin to those at the heart of this inquiry; even securing the health and well-being of the children born as a result of using ART is not within FDA's jurisdiction.

The application of CLIA, ensuring quality control in diagnostic clinical laboratories, is minor in the context of ART labs—applying only to andrological and endocrinological diagnostic activities when performed for the sake of themselves; CLIA is inapplicable when these tests are performed as an adjunct to the provision of ART services. The FTC's oversight of truth in advertising and competition may promote better informed consent by ART patients. But it does not go so far as to govern the sorts of risks to which these individuals may be exposed.

The regulation of the practice of medicine by the states aims at the safety of some ART participants, but seems to neglect the health and well-being of the children produced through ART, and it offers no guidance concerning the proper treatment of embryonic human life. Another mechanism of indirect regulation, namely, the tort system, is driven by a concern for the rights and interests of injured parties. The definitions of duty, breach, causation, and injury in the context of assisted reproduction make this a problematic source of regulation. While the tort system does regulate assisted reproduction in ways that implicate the ethical concerns raised above, an adversarial process that reduces questions of procreation to theories of torts, contracts, or even family law may not be adequate to or fitting for the profound human goods at stake.

Nongovernmental regulation by ASRM is chiefly focused on the safety, efficacy, and privacy of participants in the ART process. ASRM provides practice guidelines and ethical opinions to promote these values. The enforceability of these guidelines, however, is weak. Indeed, one might argue that the standards are merely hortatory and aspirational—evidenced by the fact that one prominent member of SART openly advertises a service that ASRM "actively discourages" on ethical grounds (PGD for elective sex selection). As a substantive matter, the guidelines provide very few direct, affirmative protections for the well-being of the children who result from ART, relying instead on their prospective parents to safeguard their interests. This is certainly the norm in most situations involving the delivery of medical care to children. In such cases, however, the controlling criterion is the best interests of the patient, namely, the sick child. By contrast, in ART, the patient is the (often) infertile individual or individuals and it is their interests that are considered controlling. It is not necessarily the case that the best interests of the ART patient and the resulting children are co-extensive. Thus, using the interests of the patient as a proxy for those of the children later born is potentially problematic. The ASRM guidelines make no allowance for any potential conflict of interest in this regard.

ASRM's animating ethical principles of safety, efficacy, and privacy are neutral toward other relevant values. They do not address other concerns occasioned by the growing control over procreation conferred by the new capacities discussed above. Nevertheless, ASRM's ongoing effort to review all existing literature on the health effects of ART on children signals an increased concern and arguably a new focus on this subject.

Finally, indirect regulation by professional medical associations aims generally at the well-being of patients in the physician's care. Yet the AMA's guidelines relating to ART do not seem calculated to meet the ethical concerns raised above. The same could be said of ABOG's guidelines. The AAP guidelines do seem to suggest that the child later born and the mother may both be patients and thus entitled to all the attendant duties and obligations of care. Such guidelines do not, however, seem to reflect a concern for the use and destruction of in vitro human embryos.

All of the foregoing professional society guidelines have limited mechanisms of enforcement and rely primarily on the good will of practitioners. For many of the ethical matters of concern to this Council, beginning with the well-being of children, existing procedures for monitoring, data collection, or investigation are not adequate.

ENDNOTES

[1] Centers for Disease Control and Prevention (CDC), *2001 Assisted Reproductive Technology Success Rates, National Summary and Fertility Clinic Reports*, Atlanta, Georgia: Government Printing Office, 2003, p. 14.

[2] *Ibid.*, p. 71.

[3] *Ibid.*, p. 71.

[4] *Ibid.*, p. 71.

[5] *Ibid.*, p. 37.

[6] *Ibid.*, p. 39.

[7] Depypere, H., et al., "Intracellular pH Changes During Zona Drilling," *Fertility and Sterility* 61: 319 (1994).

[8] Catt, J., et al., "Subzonal Insertion of Multiple Sperm Is a Treatment for Male Factor Infertility," *Fertility and Sterility* 61: 123 (1994).

[9] Barritt, J., et al., "Cytoplasmic Transfer in Assisted Reproduction," *Human Reproduction Update* 7: 428-435 (2001).

[10] Edwards, R., et al., "Destruction of Cryopreserved Embryos: UK Law Dictated the Destruction of 5000 Cryopreserved Human Embryos," *Human Reproduction* 12: 3 (1997).

[11] Hoffman, D., et al., "Cryopreserved Embryos in the United States and Their Availability for Research," *Fertility and Sterility* 79: 1063-1069 (2003).

[12] CDC Report, *op. cit.*, p. 45.

[13] *Ibid.*, p. 45.

[14] Hoffman, D., et al., *op. cit.*

[15] Van Voorhis, B., et al., "The Efficacy and Cost Effectiveness of Embryo Cryopreservation Compared with Other Assisted Reproductive Techniques," *Fertility and Sterility* 64: 647 (1995).

[16] Gardner, D. K., et al., "Culture and Transfer of Human Blastocysts Increases Implantation Rates and Reduces the Need for Multiple Embryo Transfers," Presentation at the October 1997 annual meeting of the American Society for Reproductive Medicine, Cincinnati, Ohio.

[17] Scott, R., et al., "Embryo Quality and Pregnancy Rates in Patients Attempting Pregnancy Through In Vitro Fertilization," *Fertility and Sterility* 55: 426 (1991).

[18] American Society for Reproductive Medicine, Practice Committee Report, "The Role of Assisted Hatching in IVF: A Review of the Literature," August 2000, http://www.asrm.org/Media/Practice/assistedhatching.pdf (June 4, 2003).

[19] CDC Report, *op. cit.*, p. 71.

[20] *Ibid.*, p. 34.

[21] *See generally,* CDC Report, *op. cit.*, p.74 et seq.

[22] New York State Task Force on Life and the Law, *Assisted Reproductive Technologies: Analysis and Recommendations for Public Policy*, New York: New York, 1998, p. 63.

[23] CDC Report, *op. cit.*, p. 37.

[24] *Ibid.*, p. 17.

[25] *Ibid.*, p. 71.

[26] NYSTF Report, *op. cit.*, p. 69.

[27] *See,* for example, NYSTF Report, *op cit.* p. 71 (citing R.L. Berkowitz, et al., "First-Trimester Transabdominal Multifetal Pregnancy Reduction: A Report of Two Hundred Completed Cases," *American Journal of Obstetrics and Gynecology* 169: 17, 18 [1993]; R. Maymon, et al., "First Trimester Embryo Reduction: A Medical Solution to an Iatrogenic Problem," *Human Reproduction* 10: 668 [1995]).

[28] CDC Report, *op. cit.*, p. 17.

[29] *Ibid.*, p. 19.

[30] *Ibid.*, p. 20.

[31] McElrath, T., et al., "Fertility Therapy and the Risk of Very Low Birth Weight," *Obstetrics and Gynecology* 90: 600 (1997); Mullen, M., "Medically Assisted Reproductive Technologies: A Review," *Research Studies of the Royal Commission on New Reproductive Technologies* 9: 47 (1993).

[32] Rufat, P., et al., "Task Force Report on the Outcome of Pregnancies and Children Conceived by In Vitro Fertilization (France: 1987 to 1989)," *Fertility and Sterility* 61: 324 (1994).

[33] NYSTF Report, *op. cit.*, p. 70.

[34] Zhang, J., et al., "Pregnancy derived from human nuclear transfer," presented at the 59th annual meeting of the American Society for Reproductive Medicine, October 11-15, 2003, San Antonio, Texas.

[35] Biron-Shental, T., et al., "Preliminary Results of Cultured Human Ovaries from Second and Third Trimester Fetuses," 19th annual meeting of the European Society of Human Reproduction and Embryology Final Program (June 30, 2003), p. 50.

[36] Gleicher, N., "Blastomere Transplantation as a Possible Treatment," 19th annual meeting of the European Society of Human Reproduction and Embryology Final Program (July 1, 2003), p. 93.

[37] *See* interview with Dr. Helen Liu at the 57th annual meeting of ASRM, Orlando Florida, October 22-24, 2001 (available online at http://www.obgyn.net/displaytranscript.

asp?page=/avtranscripts/asrm2001-liu); *see also*, press release: "Highlights from the 57th Annual Meeting of ASRM: Engineering Uterine Lining Tissue Outside the Uterus" (October 22, 2001); *see also,* Paula Moyer, "Engineered Endometrial Tissue May Provide New Infertility Therapies," *Reuters Health Medical News*, October 24, 2001.

[38] *See* Racho El-Akouri, R., "Normal Pregnancies Achieved in Transplanted Murine Uteri after Long-Term Cold Preservation," 19th annual meeting of the European Society of Human Reproduction and Embryology Final Program (July 2, 2003), p. 120; *see also*, Rick Weiss, "Saudi Surgeons Perform Human Uterus Transplant," *Washington Post*, March 7, 2002, Page A08.

[39] *See* Edwards, R., et al., "Current Status of In-Vitro Fertilisation and Implantation of Human Embryos," *Lancet* 2: 1265-1269 (1983); and Gould, K., "Ovum Recovery and In Vitro Fertilization in the Chimpanzee," *Fertility and Sterility* 40: 378-383 (1983).

[40] Van Steirteghem, A., et al., "High Fertilization and Implantation Rates After Intracytoplasmic Sperm Injection," *Human Reproduction* 8: 1061-1066 (1993).

[41] Hewitson, L., et al., "Unique Checkpoints During the First Cell Cycle of Fertilization After Intracytoplasmic Sperm Injection in Rhesus Monkeys," *Nature Medicine* 5: 431-433 (1999); Kimura, Y., et al., "Intracytoplasmic Sperm Injection in the Mouse," *Biology of Reproduction* 52: 709-720 (1995).

[42] Schatten, G., "Safeguarding ART," *Nature Cell Biology & Nature Medicine* S19—S22 (2002).

[43] *Ibid.*

[44] Winston, R., et al., "Are We Ignoring Potential Dangers of In Vitro Fertilization and Related Treatments?" *Nature Cell Biology & Nature Medicine* S14-S18 (2002).

[45] *Ibid.*

[46] American Society for Reproductive Medicine press release, "Highlights from ASRM 2002: The 58th Annual Meeting of the American Society for Reproductive Medicine, October 12-17, 2002—Seattle, Washington; 170,000 Babies Born in USA from ART since 1985: Success Rate More Than Doubled in That Time," October 14, 2002, http://www.asrm.org/Media/Press/170000babies.html (June 1, 2003).

[47] Hansen, M., et al., "The Risk of Major Birth Defects After Intracytoplasmic Sperm Injection and In Vitro Fertilization," *The New England Journal of Medicine* 346: 725 (2002).

[48] Bonduelle, M., et al., "Neonatal Data on a Cohort of 2889 Infants Born After ISCI (1991-1999) and of 2995 Infants Born After IVF (1983-1999)," *Human Reproduction* 17: 671 (2002); *see also* Bergh, T., et al., "Deliveries and Children Born After In-Vitro Fertilisation in Sweden 1982-1985," *Lancet* 354: 1579-1585 (1999).

[49] Moll, A., et al., "Incidence of Retinoblastoma in Children Born After In-Vitro Fertilisation," *Lancet* 361: 309-310 (2003).

[50] Bergh, T., et al., *op. cit.*

[51] Mestel, R., "Some Studies See Ills for In Vitro Children: Evidence of Increases in Eye Cancer and Mental Retardation Needs to be Verified," *Los Angeles Times*, January 24, 2003, Page A1.

[52] Johns Hopkins Medical Institutions press release, "In Vitro Fertilization May Be Linked to Bladder Defects," March 18, 2003, http://www.hopkinsmedicine.org/press/2003/March/030318A.htm (April 28, 2003), quoting the study's senior author, John P. Gearhart, M.D., "These defects are extremely rare, and our preliminary findings should not alone discourage couples from undergoing IVF."

[53] Josserand, R. N., et al., "Cystic Fibrosis phenotype evaluation and paternity outcome in 50 males with congenital bilateral absence of vas deferens," *Human Reproduction* 16: 2093-2097 (2001); Robert F., et al., "Relation between the anatomical genital phenotype and cystic fibrosis transmembrane conductance regulator gene mutations in the absence of the vas deferens," *Fertility and Sterility* 77: 889-896 (2002).

[54] Oates, R. D., et al., "Clinical characterization of 42 oligospermic or azoospermic men with microdeletion of the AZFc region of the Y chromosome, and of 18 children conceived via ICSI," *Human Reproduction* 17: 2813-2824 (2002).

[55] Hansen, M., et al., *op. cit.*; Bonduelle, M., et al., *op. cit.*

[56] Winston, R. et al., *op. cit.*

[57] Mestel, R., *op. cit.*; *see also*, Winston, R. et al., "Are We Ignoring Potential Dangers of In Vitro Fertilization and Related Treatments?" *Nature Cell Biology* 4 (S1), S14-S18 (2002), *Nature Medicine* 8 (S1), S14-S18 (2002) *op. cit.* (citing Kwong, W.Y., et al., *Development* 127, 4195-4202 [2000]).

[58] *See* Winston, R. et al., *op. cit.* (citing Ho, Y., et al., *Molecular Reproduction and Development* 41(2): 232-238 [1995]; Niemann, H., et al, *Theriogenology* 53: 21-34 [2000]).

[59] Winston, R., et al., *op. cit.* (citing Doherty, A.S., et al., *Biological Reproduction* 62: 1526-1535 (2000); Khosla, S., et al., *Human Reproduction Update* 7: 419-27 [2001]).

[60] Winston, R., et al., *op. cit.*

[61] Schatten, G., "Safeguarding ART," *op. cit.*

[62] Slotnick, R., et al., "Monoamniotic Twinning and Zona Manipulation: A Survey of U.S. IVF Centers Correlating Zona Manipulation Procedures and High-Risk Twinning Frequency," *Journal of Assisted Reproduction and Genetics* 13: 381 (1996).

[63] CDC Report, *op. cit.*, p. 20; Wilcox, L., et al., "Assisted Reproductive Technologies: Estimates of Their Contribution to Multiple Births and Newborn Hospital Days in the United States," *Fertility and Sterility* 65: 361 (1996).

[64] CDC Report, *op. cit.*, p. 20.

[65] American Society for Reproductive Medicine, "Patient Fact Sheet: Complications of Multiple Gestation," August 2001, http://www.asrm.org/Patients/FactSheets/complications-multi.pdf (June 3, 2003).

[66] Haning, R., et al., "Effects of Fetal Number and Multifetal Reduction on Length of In Vitro Fertilization Pregnancies," *Obstetrics and Gynecology* 87: 964-966 (1996).

[67] Martin, J., et al., "Triplet Births: Trends and Outcomes, 1971-1994," *Vital and Health Statistics. Series 21, Data from the National Vital Statistics System* 21: 1-20 (1997).

68 NYSTF Report, *op. cit.*, p. 74.

69 Barker, D., "The Wellcome Foundation Lecture, 1994: The Fetal Origins of Adult Disease," *Proceedings of the Royal Society of London, Series B, Biological Sciences* 262: 37-43 (1995).

70 Helmerhorst, F., et al., "Perinatal Outcome of Singletons and Twins after Assisted Conception: A Systematic Review of Controlled Studies," *British Medical Journal*, doi:10.1136/bmj.37957.560278.EE (published January 23, 2004); Schieve, L., et al., "Low and Very Low Birth Weight in Infants Conceived with Use of Assisted Reproductive Technology," *The New England Journal of Medicine* 346: 731-737 (2002).

71 Evans, M., et al., "Efficacy of Transabdominal Multifetal Pregnancy Reduction: Collaborative Experience Among the World's Largest Centers," *Obstetrics and Gynecology* 82: 61 (1993).

72 NYSTF Report, *op. cit.*, p. 71.

73 Haning, R., et al., *op. cit.*; Lee, J., et al., "Obstetric Outcomes of Twin Pregnancy after Multifetal Pregnancy Reduction (MFPR) Are Affected by Initial Number of the Fetuses," presentation at the Annual Meeting of the American Society for Reproductive Medicine, October 18-22, 1997, Cincinnati, Ohio.

74 Geva, E., et al., "Multifetal Pregnancy Reduction: A Possible Risk Factor for Periventricular Leukomalacia in Premature Newborn," presentation at the annual meeting of the American Society for Reproductive Medicine, October 18-22, 1997, Cincinnati, Ohio.

75 Delvigne, A., et al., "Systematic Review of Data Concerning Etiopathology of Ovarian Hyperstimulation Syndrome," *International Journal of Fertility and Women's Medicine* 47: 211-226 (2002).

76 American Society for Reproductive Medicine, Practice Committee Report, "Induction of Ovarian Follicle Development and Ovulation with Exogenous Gonadotropins," 1998, http://www.asrm.org/Media/Practice/ovulation.html (June 2, 2003); Millican, L., testimony before the Senate Health, Education, Labor, and Pensions Committee, April 24, 2002.

77 Millican, *op. cit.*

78 Verlaenen, H., et al., "Singleton Pregnancy After In Vitro Fertilization: Expectations and Outcome," *Obstetrics and Gynecology* 86: 906 (1995).

79 NYSTF Report, *op. cit.*, p. 70.

80 *Ibid.*

81 *Ibid.*

82 Collins, J., "A Couple with Infertility," *Journal of the American Medical Association* 274: 1159 (1995).

83 Hübner, K., et al., "Derivation of Oocytes from Mouse Embryonic Stem Cells," *Science* 300: 1251-1256 (2003).

[84] Biron-Shental, T., et al., "Preliminary results of cultured human ovaries from second and third trimester fetuses," presented at the 19th Annual Meeting of the European Society of Human Reproduction and Embryology, June 29 to July 2, 2003, Madrid, Spain (www.eshre.com).

[85] Pub. L. No. 102-493, 106 Stat. 3146, codified at 42 U.S.C. § 263a-1 et seq.

[86] 42 U.S.C. § 263a-1(a).

[87] 42 U.S.C. § 263a-7(1).

[88] 65 Fed. Reg. 53,312 (September 1, 2000).

[89] Madsen, P., American Infertility Association, letter to the President's Council on Bioethics, September 30, 2003; *see also* Madsen's public comments at the January 16, 2004, meeting of the President's Council on Bioethics, Washington, D.C., available at www.bioethics.gov.

[90] Quoted in Shannon Brownlee, "Designer Babies," *Washington Monthly*, March 1, 2002.

[91] *See*, Schulman, Joseph D., "What's Your Success Rate?: Understanding IVF Pregnancy Statistics: Part I," published by The Genetics and IVF Institute (available at http://www.givf.com/success.cfm).

[92] 42 U.S.C. § 263a-7(2).

[93] 64 Fed. Reg. 39,374-01 (July 21, 1999).

[94] 42 U.S.C. § 263a-2(i).

[95] *See*, for example, Fla. Stat. Ann. § 742.11 et seq.; La Rev. Stat. Ann. 9:126; Va. Code Ann. § 20-156 et seq.; Wash. Rev. Code Ann. 26.26.700 et seq.

[96] N.H. Rev. Stat. § 168-B:13.

[97] *Ibid.*

[98] *Ibid.*

[99] 18 Pa. Cons. Stat. Ann. § 3213(e).

[100] N.M. Stat. Ann. § 24-9A-1 et seq.; La. Rev. Stat. Ann. 9:121 et seq.; S.D. Codified Laws § 34-14-17.

[101] N.M. Stat. Ann. § 24-9A-5.

[102] N.M. Stat. Ann. § 24-9A-1.

[103] Reilly, C., "Constitutional Limits on New Mexico's In Vitro Fertilization Law," *New Mexico Law Review* 24: 125-144 (1994).

[104] *See generally*, *Lifchez v. Hartigan*, 735 F. Supp. 1361 (N.D. Il. 1990); *Margaret S. v. Edwards*, 794 F. 2d 994 (5th Cir. 1986); *Jane L. v. Bangerter*, 102 F. 3d 1112 (10th Cir. 1996).

[105] *Lifchez v. Hartigan*, 735 F. Supp 1361, 1377 (N.D. Il. 1990).

[106] *See generally*, 21 U.S.C. § 301 et seq. ("Federal Food, Drug and Cosmetic Act"); 42 U.S.C. § 201 et seq. ("Public Health Services Act").

[107] 42 U.S.C. § 264 (known as "Section 361" of the Public Health Services Act).

[108] 21 U.S.C. § 321(g)(1).

[109] 21 U.S.C. § 355(a).

[110] Merrill, R., "Human Tissues and Reproductive Cloning: New Technologies Challenge FDA," *Houston Journal Health Law and Policy* 3: 1-86 (2002), citing 21 U.S.C. § 355(b). The specific FDA protections for human subjects involved in clinical trials are discussed extensively in Chapter 3.

[111] *Ibid.*

[112] 21 U.S.C. § 355(i).

[113] 42 U.S.C. § 262(i).

[114] 42 U.S.C. § 262(a)(1)(A).

[115] 42 U.S.C. § 262(a)(C).

[116] 21 C.F.R. § 601.2.

[117] 42 U.S.C. § 262(j).

[118] 42 U.S.C. § 264.

[119] 63 Fed. Reg. 26,744 (May 14, 1998).

[120] *Id.*

[121] 21 C.F.R. § 1271.15.

[122] 21 U.S.C. § 321(h).

[123] 21 U.S.C. § 360c.

[124] 42 U.S.C. § 262(c).

[125] 42 U.S.C. § 262(a)(2)(A) and 21 U.S.C. § 355(f).

[126] 42 U.S.C. § 262(d).

[127] 42 U.S.C. § 262(f) and 21 U.S.C. §§ 332, 333, and 334.

[128] 37 Fed. Reg. 16,503 (1972).

[129] *United States v. Evers*, 643 F. 2d. 1043 (5th Cir. 1981). *See also*, *United States v. Evers*, 453 F. Supp. 1141 (M.D. Ala. 1978) (stating that Congress did not intend for the FDA to interfere with the practice of medicine).

[130] For an exhaustive analysis of the FDA's exercise of jurisdiction in the context of human cloning, *see* Merrill, R., *op. cit.*

[131] Zoon, K., testimony before the Subcommittee on Oversight and Investigations of the Committee on Energy and Commerce, House of Representatives, March 28, 2001; *see also*, Merrill, R., *op. cit.*

[132] 42 U.S.C. § 263a.

[133] *See,* for example, Mass. Gen. Laws Ann. ch.111 § 70E.

[134] 21 U.S.C. § 801 et. seq.

[135] 42 U.S.C. §§ 11101-11152.

[136] *See* 42 U.S.C. §§ 1395x(e), 1395bb.

[137] 842 S.W.2d 588 (Tenn. 1992).

[138] *Id.* at 597.

[139] *Id.* at 604.

[140] *Del Zio v. Presbyterian Hospital*, 74 Civ. 3588 (S.D.N.Y. April 12, 1978).

[141] Rebar, R., American Society for Reproductive Medicine, written comments to the President's Council on Bioethics, April 15, 2003.

[142] *See*, for example, "2002 Guidelines for Gamete and Embryo Donation: A Practice Committee Report," *Fertility and Sterility*, 77(6), Suppl. 5 (June 2002).

[143] "Does Intracytoplasmic Sperm Injection (ICSI) Carry Inherent Genetic Risks?" *ASRM Practice Committee Report* (November 2000).

[144] "Elements to be Considered in Obtaining Informed Consent for ART," *ASRM Practice Committee Report* (1998).

[145] "Induction of Ovarian Follicle Development and Ovulation with Exogenous Gonadotropins," *ASRM Practice Committee Report* (1998).

[146] "Guidelines on Number of Embryos Transferred," *ASRM Practice Committee Report* (November 1999).

[147] "Preimplantation Genetic Diagnosis," *ASRM Practice Committee Report* (April 2001).

[148] "Guidelines for Advertising by ART Programs," *ASRM Practice Committee Report* (October 1999).

[149] "Informed Consent and the Use of Gametes and Embryos for Research," *ASRM Ethics Committee* (1997).

[150] "Disposition of Abandoned Embryos," *ASRM Ethics Committee Report* (July 1996).

[151] March 2, 2004, letter from Pamela Madsen, Executive Director of the American Infertility Association, to O. Carter Snead, General Counsel, the President's Council on Bioethics.

[152] American Medical Association, *Ethical Conduct in Assisted Reproductive Technology*, July 22, 2002, http://www.ama-assn.org/ama/pub/category/8418.html (accessed June 3, 2003).

[153] American Academy of Pediatrics, *Fetal Therapy—Ethical Considerations*, May 1999, http://www.aap.org/policy/re9817.html (accessed June 3, 2003).

3

Screening and Selection for Genetic Conditions and Traits

The ability to screen developing human life for chromosomal abnormalities and genetic disorders has been ours for some time. Individuals and doctors have for many years been able to test fetuses in utero, either through the genetic analysis of cells obtained from amniotic fluid by amniocentesis (in the second trimester) or through genetic analysis of chorionic villus samples obtained from the placenta by biopsy (in the first trimester). The "selection" that follows such testing is achieved by means of abortion; it amounts to "selecting against" a developing fetus with a diagnosed genetic disease or other unwanted trait (for example, maleness or femaleness).

More recently, however, innovations in assisted reproduction and molecular genetics have yielded new ways to test early-stage embryos in vitro for genetic markers and characteristics. After such testing only those embryos with the desired genetic characteristics are transferred to initiate a pregnancy. By comparison with the older form of screening, this approach is more "positively" selective; it amounts more to "choosing in" rather than merely to "weeding out." Methods to test or screen eggs and sperm before fertilization are also being developed, and at least one type of sperm sorting—sorting by the presence of X or Y chromosomes—is already in use in several clinical trials. These two new techniques for testing early-stage embryos—preimplantation genetic diagnosis (PGD) and sperm sorting—are the subjects of the following discussion.

I. USES AND TECHNIQUES

A. Preimplantation Genetic Diagnosis of Embryos

PGD is a technique that permits clinicians to analyze embryos in vitro for certain genetic (or chromosomal) traits or markers and to select accordingly for purposes of transfer. The early embryo (six to eight cells) is biopsied by removal of one or two cells, and the sample cell(s) is then examined for the presence or absence of the markers of interest. PGD is practiced in approximately fifty clinics worldwide, the majority of them located in the United States. PGD was first used in 1989 as an adjunct to in vitro fertilization (IVF) for treating infertility. Official statistics do not tell us how many children have been conceived following PGD. Estimates vary widely; one recent report suggested that "more than 1,000 babies have been born worldwide."[1]

PGD was initially used for sex identification to avoid transfer of embryos with X-linked genetic diseases, such as Lesch Nyhan syndrome, hemophilia, and X-linked mental retardation.[2] PGD is now most commonly used to detect aneuploidies (that is, an abnormal number of chromosomes, for example, trisomies and monosomies).[3] Some aneuploidies prevent the embryo from implanting, whereas others are associated with disorders such as Down syndrome and Turner syndrome. PGD is used also to detect monogenic diseases such as cystic fibrosis and Tay-Sachs disease. More recently PGD has been used to select embryos that would be compatible tissue donors for older siblings in need of transplants.[4] In still other cases PGD has been used for elective (non-medical) sex selection.[5] Today at least one-third of individuals who use PGD are otherwise fertile, and this number may increase as the potential uses of PGD expand.[6]

At present, PGD can identify genetic markers that correlate with (or suggest a predisposition for) more than one hundred diseases, including illnesses that become manifest much later in life, such as early-onset Alzheimer disease.[7] As genomic knowledge increases and more genes that correlate with diseases are identified, the applications for PGD will likely increase. In principle any known gene and its variants can be tested for, and with improved methods for amplifying genetic screening on small samples, it may some day be possible to test the single cell removed from the embryo for hundreds of genetic markers. Dr. Francis Collins, director of the National Human Genome Research Institute, recently speculated that within five to seven years the major contributing genes for diabetes, heart disease, cancer, mental illness, Parkinson disease, stroke, and asthma will be identified.[8] Many couples with family histories of these diseases may be drawn to PGD, even in the absence of infertility. Moreover, if genetic associations with other, non-medical conditions are identified, PGD might one day be used to screen for positive traits and characteristics such as height, leanness, or temperament.[*]

PGD is a multi-step process requiring considerable technical skill and expertise in the fields of genetics and reproductive medicine. Because the testing is performed on early embryos in vitro, individuals electing to use PGD must undergo all of the phases of IVF described in Chapter 2.[†] Typically, embryo biopsy is performed three days after fertilization when the embryo is at the six- to eight-cell stage. The researcher makes a small hole in the zona pellucida (using a sharp pipette, acidic solution, or laser), and then inserts a suction pipette into the opening and removes one or two cells ("blastomeres"). Some researchers wait until the embryo reaches the blastocyst stage (approximately five to six days after fertilization, when the given embryo has grown to approximately one hundred cells) to undertake this biopsy. The procedure is technically less demanding at this stage and more cells can be removed and analyzed. Researchers who biopsy blastocysts remove approximately ten cells from the trophectoderm (the blastocyst's outer

---

[*] During his presentation to the Council in December 2002, Dr. Collins speculated that one such application of PGD would be to screen for genetic markers correlated with higher IQ levels. While he expressed skepticism that such tests would be effective or reliable, he did think the demand for such tests would be high.

[†] ICSI is the preferred technique for insemination in this context. PGD following ICSI yields the most accurate results, because there are no excess sperm imbedded in the zona pellucida of the fertilized ovum that might contaminate or otherwise affect the accuracy of the analysis of the biopsied cells.

ring of cells that are the precursors of the fetal portion of the placenta).

Once collected, the blastomeres or trophectoderm cells can be analyzed by a variety of means depending on the purpose of the test. PGD for detection of monogenic diseases is performed using a technique called "polymerase chain reaction" (PCR). Sex identity and chromosomal abnormalities are detected using a technique called fluorescence in situ hybridization (FISH). PCR allows clinicians to amplify sections of the DNA sequence, providing them with enough DNA to detect specific gene mutations. In FISH, labeled markers bind to chromosomes, permitting the researcher to observe and enumerate such chromosomes.

In all these procedures, timing is critical. The clinician must complete the analysis before the embryo develops beyond the stage at which it can be successfully transferred. If the biopsy is performed on Day 3, the practitioner has approximately forty-eight hours in which to complete the analysis, verify results, and discuss options with the patient or patients.

The error rate for PGD has been estimated between 1 and 10 percent, depending on the assay used.[9] Several technical difficulties may compromise accuracy. Working with so few cells—in many cases only one or two—leaves little room for technical error. PCR can be problematic. In some instances, for example, one allele fails to amplify to a detectable level. This phenomenon, called "allele dropout," can lead to misdiagnosis. Contamination of the PGD sample can also lead to misdiagnosis. Technical difficulties associated with FISH may also affect accuracy of diagnosis. Following the transfer of the selected embryos and the initiation of pregnancy, clinicians routinely follow up with chorionic villus sampling and amniocentesis to confirm the results of PGD.

B. Genetic Analysis of Gametes

As well as testing early embryos, researchers are also trying to test and screen gametes (ova and sperm) before fertilization.

1. Preimplantation Genetic Diagnosis of Ova.

As an alternative to embryonic PGD, clinicians can now perform a similar analysis on the developing oocyte, by testing DNA from the polar bodies—nucleus-containing protrusions that are ultimately shed from the maturing oocyte.[10] As with cells obtained from embryo biopsy, PCR or FISH can be used to test for, respectively, monogenic diseases or chromosomal abnormalities (most aneuploidies are maternally derived). The utility of polar body analysis is limited, however, in that it reveals only the maternal contribution to the child's genotype.

2. Sperm Selection.

Another form of gamete screening is sperm sorting. A number of techniques are now under study, all of them aimed at controlling the sexes of the children ultimately conceived from these gametes. Most techniques to sort sperm have proven unreliable. These have included albumin gradients, percoll gradients, sephadex columns, and modified swim-up techniques. One technique currently in clinical trials—commercially called Microsort—has proven more successful. It exploits the difference in total DNA content between X-chromosome (female-producing) sperm and Y-chromosome (male-producing) sperm. The researcher collects the sperm sample and stains it with a fluorescent dye, bisbenzimide, which binds to the DNA in each sperm. A female-producing sperm shines brighter because it has 2.8 percent more DNA than the androgenic sperm, owing to the larger size of the X-chromosome. Using fluorescence-based separating equipment, the researcher sorts the sperm into X-bearing and Y-bearing preparations. The appropriate preparation is selected according to the couple's preference and used to inseminate the woman. The latest statistics report a 90 percent success rate for conceiving female children and 72 percent success for conceiving male children.

II. ETHICAL CONSIDERATIONS

PGD, when effective, enables parents to avoid the deep grief and hardship that accompany the birth of a child with dreaded and incurable diseases such as cystic fibrosis and Tay-Sachs. And by screening out embryos with genetic abnormalities before a pregnancy begins, it prevents many women from having to decide whether to abort an abnormal fetus. Yet PGD also raises a number of ethical concerns, similar to but extending beyond the concerns attached to assisted reproduction itself.

A. IVF-Related Concerns

IVF, and typically intracytoplasmic sperm injection (ICSI), are essential to the practice of PGD. Thus, all of the ethical concerns attending these practices of assisted reproduction (discussed in Chapter 2) are likewise concerns here. But the prospect of genetic selection creates a further reason, beyond infertility, to seek and make use of assisted reproductive technologies. In what follows we shall confine our attention to *new* issues raised by genetic selection (though some of these issues may overlap those raised by the established practice of prenatal diagnosis).

B. Well-Being of Children

PGD typically requires the removal of one or two cells from a six- to eight-cell embryo. It is not known whether this embryo biopsy affects the development of the child later born.[11] PGD has entered clinical practice after only limited trial experience. No comprehensive studies have been published on the effects of PGD on the physical well-being of those involved. Some prospective studies are currently underway in Europe, but it is unclear how well-funded or comprehensive they will be.

C. Increased Control over the Characteristics of Children

PGD gives prospective parents the capacity to screen and select for specific genetic traits in their children. For now, that capacity is limited. Technical limitations on the number of embryos that can be produced in a single PGD cycle and on the number of tests that can be performed on a single blastomere severely restrict the number of characteristics for which practitioners can now test. Similarly, the complexity of the relationship between identifiable single genes and phenotypic characteristics will complicate the development of genetic tests for many traits and characteristics of interest (for example, where traits have polygenic contributions or result from complex gene-environmental interactions). Moreover, one cannot select for genes that are not brought to the embryos by their genetic progenitors; efforts at positive selection will be limited. Thus, the capacity to use PGD to select for a "superior genotype"—a "designer baby"—is in our estimation *not* on the horizon.*

The present, more modest, applications of PGD—screening for severe medical conditions, screening for genetic predispositions or risk factors for a given disease, elective sex selection, and selection with an eye to creating a matching tissue donor—do give rise to ethical concerns about possible impacts on children and families. PGD used for these purposes might in some cases treat the resulting child as a means to the parents' ends. This concern would be amplified should the reasons for embryo screening move from "medical" purposes to non-medical or enhancement purposes, from preventing the birth of a diseased child to trying to "maximize" a child's genotype for desired characteristics. (This line is, admittedly, hard to draw.)† Because the prospective child is deliberately selected on qualitative, genetic grounds out of a pool of possible embryonic siblings, PGD risks normalizing the idea that a child's particular genetic make-up is quite properly a province of parental reproductive choice, or the idea that entrance into the world depends on meeting certain genetic criteria. Even if the prospective parents are guided by their own sense of what would be a good or healthy baby, their selection may in some cases serve their own interests more than the child's (as in the

* For an extensive discussion of the reasons why so-called "designer babies" do not seem to us at all scientifically plausible in the foreseeable future, see the Council's 2003 report, *Beyond Therapy: Biotechnology and the Pursuit of Happiness,* especially pp. 37-40.

† The difficulty of distinguishing between therapy and non-medical treatment is demonstrated with the following example: In July 2003, an Australian couple screened their embryos to guarantee a child with perfect hearing. It is the first time an embryo was screened to guard against a non-life-threatening condition. (*The Age*, July 10, 2003.) For a more extensive discussion of this subject, see the Council's 2003 report, *Beyond Therapy: Biotechnology and the Pursuit of Happiness*, Chapter 2, "Better Children," especially pp. 27-70.

case, for example, of a deaf couple using PGD in an effort to produce a deaf child). The new technologies, even when used only to screen out and eliminate the sick or "deficient," may change parents' attitudes toward their children, increasing both the desire to control and the tacit expectation of certain qualities—an attitude that might intensify as PGD becomes more sophisticated. Children who are selected on non-medical grounds—such as elective sex selection or trait selection—may experience increased pressures to meet parental expectations.

The use of PGD to identify a prospective child as a tissue donor match (currently a very rare practice) poses an additional ethical concern: the deliberate creation and selection of a particular child as a means for the benefit of another.* It is, of course, likely that in most families such children would be loved by their parents and by the siblings who would benefit directly from their tissue donation. But even here there is a dramatic shift in how the new PGD-selected donor-child is conceived and regarded by the parents and family. Is it proper to assign to an unconceived child the burden of being a savior of a sibling, and then give that child life on condition that he or she fulfill that role?

A closely related ethical concern is that this sort of selection could reduce the scope of reproductive choice. As the aggregate effect of parental choices reshapes society's understanding of "normal" or "acceptable" phenotypes, parents might feel social pressure to undergo PGD, as many pregnant women now are pressured to undergo amniocentesis. In addition, parents might feel pressured to use PGD for financial reasons; it is conceivable that HMOs or health plans that cover IVF might someday require PGD for selection against certain potentially costly diseases.

Some see these ethical concerns as unjustified or premature. They believe that expanding our control over human reproduction is an extension of the parental responsibility to care for one's offspring, and that PGD will be used almost exclusively to prevent the births of diseased children. They argue

---

* In August 1997, Adam Nash was born after being screened to ensure he would be a correct tissue match, and therefore could serve as a bone-marrow donor, for his older sister who suffered from Fanconi anemia. (*Genomics and Genetics Weekly,* February 14, 2003.)

that the prospect of using PGD for "enhancement" purposes is unlikely, since the burdens of undergoing IVF and PGD would outweigh the limited possibility of selecting an embryo that is genetically superior. The possibility of so selecting will be limited both by the genetic complexity of human traits like intelligence, and by the vast number of embryos that would be required in order to make the choice for a "better" genetic baby a meaningful one.

Whether and to what extent either the concerns or the reassurances about PGD are justified is in many cases an empirical question, surely worth considering and monitoring.

D. PGD for Late-Onset Disease

PGD can be used not only to identify abnormalities that would lead to certain and immediate diseases (like Tay-Sachs or Down syndrome), but can also be used to identify an increased susceptibility to particular diseases later in life. Is PGD justified to avoid the birth of a child who will be likely to live "only" thirty years? Is it justified to avoid the birth of a child who is especially susceptible to a late-onset disease like breast cancer or Alzheimer disease? Questions like these will need to be confronted as the ability to make biological and genetic predictions about unimplanted embryos continues to grow.

E. Eugenics and Inequality

For some critics, PGD calls to mind the specter of "eugenics"; it is seen as a technology that facilitates the selection of "better" children. Some worry that as PGD becomes more widespread, it will serve to further stigmatize the disabled and promote the notion that some lives are not worth living or are better off prevented in the first place. This is in a sense nothing new—amniocentesis and prenatal diagnosis are common and have already raised similar concerns. What is novel about PGD, though, is that it can be used to select "for" desirable traits, not just "against" markers for disease.

Other commentators worry that widespread use of PGD (so long as it is not covered by insurance or subsidized by taxpayers) could widen and worsen the gap between the "haves" and the "have-nots" in society, as access to PGD, like access to IVF itself, is restricted to those who can afford it. Furthermore, techniques that permit parents to screen and select their children's genetic make-up might produce a new kind of inequality between parents and children. Such techniques would allow parents not simply to give life to their offspring, but to choose (or try to choose) what *kind* of offspring they have. Of course, through education and upbringing parents have always had an enormous influence on the lives of their children, but inasmuch as the consequences of genetic screening and selection are imposed before birth and are biologically permanent, the inegalitarian effects of the new technology are novel and potentially significant. Biology is not destiny, but one's genetic make-up is surely crucial to one's life; if selected deliberately in advance by others, it might shape or limit a child's self-understanding and sense of future possibilities. The ability to affect the genetic make-up of the next generation may also exacerbate the tendency to assign too much importance to genetic make-up, and so may promote an excessively reductionist view of human life. These new practices may lend undue credence to the notion that human characteristics and conditions are simply or predominantly genetically determined—a too-narrow understanding of human freedom, agency, and experience, and a simplistic understanding of human biology.

F. Parents and Children

The introduction of rigorous genetic screening into childbearing might set a new standard for what counts as an acceptable birth. The attitude of parents toward their child may be subtly shifted from unconditional acceptance toward critical scrutiny: the very first act of parenting could become not the unreserved welcoming of an arriving child, but the judging of his or her fitness, while still an embryo, to become one's child, all by the standards of contemporary genetic screening. Moreover, as the screening technology itself is further refined, becoming better able to pick out serious but not life-threatening genetic conditions (from dwarfism and deafness to dyslexia and asthma) and then to distinguish genetic markers for desirable traits, the standards for what constitutes an acceptable birth may grow more exacting.

III. REGULATION

There is now no direct regulation of either PGD or sperm sorting as such. There are, however, sources of regulation, described below, that touch or might conceivably touch these practices to some extent.

A. Federal Regulation

CLIA, the Clinical Laboratory Improvement Amendments, which as previously noted regulates laboratories that perform diagnostic tests for health assessment on human specimens, does not apply to tests performed in the context of IVF including PGD. Because these are the contexts in which PGD and related techniques for selection are practiced, CLIA is inapplicable. If, in the future, CLIA were deemed applicable to PGD and related activities, it would function to ensure quality assurance and control, as described in Chapter 2.

Similarly, the FDA has a limited role in the regulation of PGD and related activities. The FDA governs any articles that may be used in these activities, ensuring that they are safe and effective for their intended uses. Specifically, the FDA regulates (as devices) any test kits that are manufactured and sold for purposes of genetic testing. However, it seems that there are today no such kits for PGD or the related activities discussed above. Most labs use assays that they develop themselves.

To the extent that PGD and related activities occur in the research setting, they may be subject to the human-subjects protections discussed in Chapter 5 (Institutional Review Board [IRB] approval, informed consent, etc.). That is, under certain circumstances, the donors of embryos or reproductive tissue for such experiments would be considered "human subjects" and protected accordingly. But insofar as PGD is regarded as part of standard medical practice, no such oversight would obtain.

B. State Laws

There are currently no state laws that directly govern PGD or related practices. Some statutes that govern embryo research may touch these activities, as discussed in Chapter 5. In the main, however, there is no significant state regulation.

C. Tort Litigation

As in the case of standard assisted reproduction, individuals can use litigation as a means of regulating the practice of PGD and related activities. To prevail on a theory of malpractice, a plaintiff would have to demonstrate that a clinician owed a duty to the plaintiff, which the clinician breached resulting in injury. The viability of tort claims as an effective regulatory mechanism remains to be seen, though one might imagine the difficulties inherent in demonstrating causation and harm.

There seem to be only two reported cases in which malpractice suits have been brought against practitioners of PGD for negligence and fraud. In one of the cases, *Paretta v. Medical Offices for Human Reproduction*,[12] a couple sued an IVF clinician for medical malpractice for his failure to perform PGD on an embryo to test for cystic fibrosis, when he knew that the ova donor was a carrier for the disease. The defendant moved for summary judgment (that is, a ruling from the court that, in light of undisputed material facts, the defendant is entitled to judgment in his favor as a matter of law). The court held that a right of recovery did not exist for the child's birth with cystic fibrosis or for the parents for emotional distress, because to rule otherwise would "give children conceived with technology more rights and expectations than those conceived without such assistance." However, the court ruled that a right of recovery did exist for the monetary expenses incurred for the infant's treatment and care. Remaining questions such as whether the clinician was grossly negligent or fraudulent "in failing to prevent the patient and her husband from bearing a child, conceived through in-vitro fertilization, that had cystic fibrosis" involved disputes of important facts that could not be resolved in the context of a motion for summary judgment. The court refused to rule out, however, the possibility that, if successful, the plaintiffs might ultimately be entitled to monetary losses resulting from the mother's decision to stay home to provide special care to the sick child.

D. Professional Self-Regulation

The chief sources of guidance and regulation for the practice of PGD and related activities the guidelines propounded by professional societies. The American Society for Reproductive Medicine (ASRM) provides guidance to clinicians who practice PGD and related activities. Its practice committee has published extensive guidelines on the practice of PGD, indicating that it should be treated as a clinical (rather than experimental) procedure.* Thus, it may be practiced without oversight by an institutional review board (IRB) or the substantial equivalent. Additionally, the ethics committee of ASRM has published a report entitled "Sex Selection and PGD"[13] that deems sex selection in this context as ethically acceptable for medical indications, but discourages purely elective use on the grounds that it might promote gender discrimination and other harms. It is not clear what is meant by the injunction to "actively discourage" this use, but at the time of this writing there are Society for Assisted Reproductive Technology (SART) member clinics that advertise the use of PGD for elective sex selection, even though SART requires, as a condition for membership, adherence to ASRM guidelines, including ethics opinions.

A related ASRM ethics opinion, entitled "Preconception Gender Selection for Nonmedical Reasons,"[14] deals with sperm sorting for sex selection. It discusses the same ethical concerns as in "Sex Selection and PGD" but reasons to a different conclusion, namely, that such practices (achieved through techniques such as Microsort) are ethically acceptable for couples seeking "gender variety in their family, i.e., only to have a child of the gender opposite an existing child or children,"† [15] provided couples understand the risks and affirm that they will accept a child of the opposite sex, should the procedure fail. ASRM notes, however, that the techniques for preconception sex selection are experimental, and should be treated accordingly. The American College of Obstetricians and Gynecolo-

---

* This is in contrast to the ethical opinion of the American Academy of Pediatrics (1994), which deems PGD an "experimental" procedure.

† The ASRM ethics committee report further advised that "[i]f the social, psychological, and demographic effects of those uses of preconception gender selection have been found acceptable, then other nonmedical uses of preconception selection might be considered."

gists echoes the views of ASRM, declaring PGD for sex selection acceptable if it is for medical indications, but rejects as unethical its use for purely elective purposes.

The American Medical Association's Code of Medical Ethics explicitly states that it is "unethical to engage in selection on the basis of non-disease related characteristics or traits." None of these opinions have more than hortatory power. In the absence of public policy governing the permissible uses of the sex selection of children, it is likely that a small number of medical specialists will continue to engage in and perhaps normalize this practice.

The American College of Medical Genetics provides voluntary guidelines for quality control and quality assurance of laboratories performing genetic testing. It does not, however, regulate PGD or related activities as such.

IV. CONCLUSION

While its use is now limited, the advent of PGD is significant. PGD represents the first fusion of genomics and assisted reproduction and the first reproductive technology that allows would-be parents to screen and select the genetic characteristics of their potential offspring, to a limited but growing degree. It is striking that this new capacity arrived with little fanfare—entering into routine practice essentially unmonitored, unstudied, and unregulated. There is now no governmental body, state or federal, monitoring or regulating PGD.* There are no regulatory efforts to address the well-being of children born after PGD or to assess the risks presented to them by embryo biopsy. There are practice guidelines issued by professional societies on the use of PGD for elective sex selection, but these

* When used as an adjunct to assisted reproduction, PGD is regulated within the larger regulatory framework applicable to that domain (discussed in Chapter 2). When used for purely research purposes, the regulation of PGD is subsumed under the framework for regulating embryo research (discussed in Chapter 5). But PGD is not regulated or monitored in any way or by any public authority that addresses what is novel or distinct about the practice itself: screening and selecting the genetic characteristics of offspring (when they are still embryos).

are statements of principle rather than enforced standards.* There are also neither governmental nor nongovernmental guidelines regarding the boundary between using PGD in efforts to produce a disease-free child and using it in efforts to select genetic traits that go "beyond therapy"—that is, traits that are useful to older siblings or simply desirable to the would-be parent.

* There is demographic evidence that choosing the sex of children is increasing in the United States—largely by using sonography and abortion. No governmental or private institution to the best of our knowledge is monitoring such uses or such demographic effects.

ENDNOTES

[1] Genetics and Public Policy Center, "Preimplantation Genetic Diagnosis: A Discussion of Challenges, Concerns, and Preliminary Policy Options Related to the Genetic Testing of Human Embryos," Washington, D.C. (2004).

[2] American Society for Reproductive Medicine, Practice Committee Report, "Preimplantation Genetic Diagnosis," June 2001, http://www.asrm.org/Media/ Practice/preimplantation.pdf (accessed June 3, 2003).

[3] International Center for Technology Assessment, written comments to the President's Council on Bioethics, May 2003.

[4] Pennings, G., et al., "Ethical consideration on preimplantation genetic diagnosis for HLA typing to match a future child as a donor of haematopoietic stem cells to a sibling," *Human Reproduction* 17: 534-538 (2002).

[5] American Society for Reproductive Medicine, Ethics Committee Report, "Sex selection and preimplantation genetic diagnosis," *Fertility and Sterility* 72: 595-598 (1999).

[6] Schatten, G., presentation at the December 13, 2002, meeting of the President's Council on Bioethics, Washington, D.C., available at www.bioethics.gov.

[7] Verlinsky, Y., et al., "Preimplantation diagnosis for early-onset Alzheimer disease caused by V717L mutation," *Journal of the American Medical Association* 287: 1018-1021 (2002).

[8] Collins, F., presentation at the December 13, 2002, meeting of the President's Council on Bioethics, Washington, D.C., available at www.bioethics.gov.

[9] ASRM Patient Education Committee, "Patient Fact Sheet: Preimplantation Genetic Diagnosis," December 1996, http://www.asrm.org/Patients/FactSheets/PGD-Fact.pdf (accessed September 9, 2003).

[10] Munne, S., et al., "First Pregnancies after Polar Body Biopsy for Testing of Chromosome Translocations," presentation at the ASRM annual meeting, Boston, Massachusetts, November 2-6, 1996; Smith, S., et al., "Birth after Polar Body Biopsy Using Acidified Tyrode's Medium Followed by ICSI," presentation at the ASRM annual meeting, Cincinnati, Ohio, October 18-22, 1997.

[11] Schatten, G., "Safeguarding ART," *op. cit.*

[12] No. 122555/00, 2003 WL 1922819 (N.Y. Supp.) (slip opinion).

[13] Ethics Committee of the American Society for Reproductive Medicine, "Sex Selection and PGD," *Fertility and Sterility* 72: 595-598 (1999).

[14] ASRM Ethics Committee Report, "Preconception Gender Selection for Nonmedical Reasons," May 2001, pp. 861-864.

[15] *Ibid.*, p. 863.

4

Modification of Traits and Characteristics

Advances in molecular biology and increases in genomic knowledge have begun to raise the possibility that scientists may one day be able not merely to screen and select embryos (or gametes) for particular traits and characteristics, but also to modify and engineer them. Should this capacity arrive, it would greatly increase our control over the genetic make-up of future generations and alter the relationships between parents and their engineered children. Such a capacity could, in principle be used both to treat genetic abnormalities and to try to engineer desired enhancements.

For now, and for the foreseeable future, such a prospect is purely speculative. The following chapter attempts to assess the state of the science in this area, as well as the ethical, social, and regulatory questions such a capacity would present to us, *if it ever came to be*.

I. TECHNIQUES AND PRACTICES

Currently, genetic modification of human embryos is purely hypothetical. There seem to be two techniques with the potential—not yet realized—to make this possibility a reality. The first would be the direct genetic modification of developing embryos through gene-transfer (insertion of genetic material in cells to repair or replace defective genes, to add new genetic information, or to regulate expression of resident genes). The second would indirectly achieve and would amount to the prospective genetic modification of an embryo (not yet conceived) by changing the genes in the progenitor's gametes. Both are discussed below.

Gene-transfer is the process by which a DNA sequence containing a functional gene (or part of a gene or another regulatory genetic element) is inserted into cells, resulting in the expression (or silencing) of a gene product. This transfer is achieved by means of a "vector"—usually a modified virus that penetrates the targeted cells and introduces the new genetic information in a stable way. There are two broad categories of gene-transfer, defined according to which cells are modified. "Somatic gene-transfer" is the delivery of genes (or other genetic elements) to the differentiated cells of the body (or even totipotent stem cells). Here the effects of genetic modification are limited to the individual who receives the new DNA sequence. By contrast "germ-line gene-transfer" refers to a delivery of genes that affect the reproductive cells, thus causing a genetic modification that is heritable.[*]

Somatic gene-transfer for humans is now being developed for therapeutic purposes ("gene-therapy"), in an effort to correct genetic abnormalities or cure genetic diseases.[†] The first such effort was undertaken by researchers at the National Institutes of Health (NIH) in 1990 to treat patients with severe combined immunodeficiency syndrome (SCIDS).[1] Currently, there are more than 500 gene-transfer research protocols under development,[2] all of them limited to genetic modification of somatic cells. While some people have suggested that germ-line gene-transfer might be a useful means of preventing the

---

[*] Some commentators prefer the term "inheritable genetic modification" rather than "germ-line modification," because there are means of effecting heritable genetic change that do not involve gene-transfer into the reproductive cells. Such alternatives include ooplasm transfer or ovum nuclear transplantation, both of which can result in inheritance of the mitochondrial DNA from the donor of the ooplasm or ovum.

[†] Many gene-transfer studies are aimed at multigenic disease, diseases that are caused by mixed genetic-environmental favors, and even totally environmental disorders such as infectious diseases.

transmission of genetic abnormalities to offspring, there are currently no protocols for such treatment in humans.

Several experimental methods of germ-line modification are, however, being studied in animals, and not only for the treatment of genetic disease. One method, using mouse embryos, employs gene-transfer into the fertilized ovum. This has the effect of modifying all of the cells of the developing embryo, including the reproductive cells. In research to date, the resulting offspring expressed the new genetic information in variable ways—many of which have resulted in harmful abnormalities.[3] Those offspring that express the new genetic materials in the desired manner are bred to produce a line of mice containing the new genetic characteristic. This approach has succeeded also in primates.[4] An alternative method, currently in the very early stages of development, effects inheritable genetic modification by inserting an artificial chromosome that carries new genetic information into the reproductive cells of the recipient animal.[5]

Two principal obstacles to the safe and effective use of gene-transfer (in children or adults) are the difficulty of controlling, first, the exact locations in the host DNA into which new genetic information is inserted and, second, the extent to which the new genes are expressed in the right cells at the correct developmental time (without inducing other unwanted gene expression or altered regulation of resident genes). Unintended and unforeseen genetic expression has been responsible for the development of leukemia in children participating in clinical trials investigating gene-transfer for SCIDS.[*6] These difficulties would likely worsen in attempts to modify the germ-line. The practitioner must contend not only with difficulties of placement and function of the new gene in the recipient, he must also try to anticipate and control these effects for the future generations who will inherit the genetic change. It would be difficult to study this approach in a scientifically rigorous way, given that the full results might not be known for decades. For these reasons, deliberate germ-line gene-transfer in human beings is risky, and unintentional germ-line modification is a danger to be avoided.

---

[*] It bears noting that most of the children treated in these studies are well and apparently normal up to four years or more after treatment. Most of the treated children have not (as yet) shown any problems.

The problem of controlling placement and gene expression might perhaps be greater in the hypothetical case of genetic modification of embryos. There are now no effective means of ensuring the appropriate distribution, levels, or timing of expression of an inserted gene in an embryo. The risks of germ-line gene modification in this context would be profound.

II. ETHICAL CONSIDERATIONS

Many of the ethical concerns raised by the potential new capacities to modify and engineer specific traits or characteristics in developing human beings are much the same as those discussed in Chapter 3. They relate to effects on procreation and family, attitudes toward children, possible effects on human capacities, and potential new types of inequality. However, this new ability would bring with it certain unique concerns and augment some concerns previously discussed. These special problems are discussed briefly below—both those connected to the safety of these techniques, and the ethical and social concerns that such technologies might raise if direct genetic modification were one day to become possible.

A. Safety of Embryonic Genetic Modification

There are today no safe and effective means of genetic modification of early embryos. For reasons described above, the effects of direct gene-transfer into an embryo are unpredictable—there is no reliable way to control the insertion, function, and heritability of the new genetic information.* There is

* Newman, S., Department of Cell Biology and Anatomy, New York Medical College, written comments submitted to the President's Council on Bioethics, April 2003. He writes: "Laboratory experience shows that insertion of foreign DNA into inopportune sites in an embryo's chromosomes can lead to extensive perturbation of development. For example, the disruption of a normal gene by insertion of foreign DNA in a mouse caused abnormal circling behavior when present in one copy, lack of eye development, lack of development of the semicircular canals of the inner ear and anomalies of the olfactory epithelium (the tissue that mediates the sense of smell), when mice were inbred so that mutation appeared in the homozygous form (that is, on both copies of the relevant chromosome). Another such 'insertional mutagenesis' event led to a strain of mice that exhibited limb, brain and craniofacial malformations, as well as displacement of the heart to the right side

no reliable way to guarantee that the gene will express itself in the intended way or to prevent the gene from expressing itself (or triggering other genetic expressions) in an adverse manner. Prospective genetic modification of offspring by germ-line gene-transfer to the gonads of the parents (or to isolated ovum and sperm) is equally, if not more, problematic, given that the effects of the gene insertion are even more attenuated (by the vagaries of sexual recombination) and thus less controllable. This problem is aggravated by the fact that harms resulting from germ-line gene modification may not be apparent for generations. There is widespread agreement in the scientific community that genetic modification of human embryos or gametes, with the intent of producing a child, is not now safe or ethical.

B. Sources of Disquiet Regarding Genetic Modification

The possible creation of children with specific and deliberately chosen genetic characteristics—at present wholly speculative—raises many of the same ethical concerns as genetic screening and selection, but is distinct in some noteworthy respects. A child who is *designed* to certain specifications might be viewed as more of an artifact—or more answerable to the will of his or her parents—than a child who is merely *selected* for his or her existing characteristics. In this way, genetic modification of developing human beings, should it become feasible, might have even broader and more significant

---

of the chest, in the homozygous state. Each of these developmental anomaly syndromes were previously unknown. From current, or even anticipated models for the relationship between genes and organismal forms and functions, the prediction of complex phenotypes on the basis of knowledge of the gene sequence inserted or disrupted is likely to remain elusive. . . . During [embryonic] development, [gene alteration] is much more complicated [than in a developed individual]. Tissues and organs are taking form during this period, and the activity of genes is anything but modular. During development many, if not most, gene products can have multiple effects on the architecture of organs and the wiring of the nervous system, including the brain. Individuals produced by developmental intervention (particularly as it comes to extend beyond the single gene, to chromosomes or groups of chromosomes) could turn out to be 'experimental artifacts,' in the sense that their bodies and mentalities could be quite different from those of anyone generated by natural processes using standard starting materials (including by IVF)."

consequences: turning procreation into a form of manufacture; promoting a new eugenics, where parents and society seek only the "best" children; allowing individuals or society to alter the native human capacities of offspring in a direct way, and perhaps to engineer novel capacities not hitherto present in human beings; and binding the next generation to a genetic fate that suits the will of the present one.

It bears repeating that "designer babies" and "super babies" are not at all likely in the foreseeable future, and that even the introduction into embryos of any specific genes, with the aim of particular modest improvements, is not now feasible or safe. At present, therefore, these broader ethical and social concerns are wholly speculative.*

III. CURRENT REGULATION

There is currently no regulation specifically governing attempts at genetic modification of gametes or early embryos. Yet the extensive federal regulations on gene-transfer research—undertaken for the purpose of gene-therapy of existing individuals—are broad enough to cover any such activities. There is no state regulation of genetic modification. There have been instances of individuals using tort litigation as a means of bringing regulatory pressure to bear on the practice of genetic modification, but this is relatively new.

A. Federal Regulation of Gene-Transfer Research

There are two principal sources of federal oversight and regulation of gene-transfer research: NIH and the Food and Drug Administration (FDA). The long and complicated history of the roles played by these institutions in the regulation of gene-transfer research need not be recited here, but the result of that history is that FDA has chief responsibility for ensuring that not only all gene-transfer products but also all *gene-*

---

* In an earlier report, *Beyond Therapy: Biotechnology and the Pursuit of Happiness,* the Council discussed in great detail the reasons why this prospect is unlikely (see especially pp. 37-40). (The President's Council on Bioethics, *Beyond Therapy: Biotechnology and the Pursuit of Happiness,* Washington, D.C.: Government Printing Office, 2003.)

transfer research protocols are safe and effective. NIH, by contrast, provides more limited oversight through its Recombinant DNA Advisory Committee (RAC). The RAC considers the ethical implications of—and offers advice to the NIH director about—novel gene-transfer research protocols that have some funding connection with NIH.

1. FDA Oversight.

No gene-therapy products are currently approved for general use in human beings. Accordingly, any transfer to a human subject of products that introduce genetic material into the body to replace faulty or missing genetic material (or to alter the regulation of resident genes) for the treatment or cure of disease constitutes a gene-transfer clinical trial, requiring prior submission of an investigational new drug (IND) application to the FDA.* "Gene-therapy products" include biologically based articles, such as a subject's own cells that have been extracted and modified outside the body prior to re-transfer into the human subject, or articles (natural or synthetic) that are directly transferred to the human subject with the intention of genetically altering his or her cells.

The FDA has asserted authority over gene-transfer technologies, regarding them as a type of drug or biologic, under the federal Food, Drug, and Cosmetic Act (FDCA) and Public Health Service Act (PHSA). The FDA claimed this authority as early as 1984, when it issued a policy statement noting that "nucleic acids used for human gene-transfer research trials will be subject to the same requirements as other biological drugs."[7] Since that time, the FDA has provided guidance to the research community through a series of informational publications. One such guidance document, issued in 1998, gave comprehensive direction regarding technical and safety requirements.[8] It included advice on matters such as preclinical safety data, molecular sequence of gene vectors, characteriza-

* Because all gene-therapy is currently understood as experimental, recipients of gene-therapy are considered human subjects with all the attendant protections of the Common Rule and FDA safeguards. An embryo, however, is not a "human subject" for purposes of these protections, though parents (certainly the mothers) would qualify as subjects in the context of ex utero gene modification. Human subjects protections reach embryos once they are implanted in vivo, as discussed in Chapter 5.

tion of cell lines used in vectors, and the long-term monitoring of the health of human subjects.[9]

The most comprehensive articulation of FDA's legal authority to regulate in this area came in the form of a *Federal Register* notice in 1993.[10] It defined gene-therapy products as those articles that "contain genetic materials administered to modify or manipulate the expression of genetic material or to alter the biological properties of living cells."[11] Such products are subject to the licensing, false labeling, and misbranding provisions for biologics (under PHSA[12]) and drugs (under the FDCA).* In the case of gene-transfer, the product in question will fall into one or both categories, depending on whether it is of synthetic or biological origin. The biological products that are the source materials for gene-transfer are also subject to the aforementioned licensing requirements. The FDA additionally claims jurisdiction to regulate gene-therapy products pursuant to its authority to prevent the interstate spread of communicable disease under Section 361 of the PHSA.

Because gene-therapy products are regarded as biologics or drugs or both, manufacturers and developers of gene therapies who wish to introduce technologies for general use must apply for premarket approval in the form of biologics license applications (BLAs), in the cases of biologics, or new drug applications (NDAs), in the cases of drugs.[13] To qualify for such licenses, manufacturers of gene-therapy products must provide the FDA with voluminous information. In addition, the FDA requires such manufacturers to test the gene-therapy products in human subjects in clinical trials, which may be initiated only after the issuance of an IND. An IND requires the sponsor to explain to the FDA the nature of the study, the risks to the human subjects, the relevant human-subject protections in place (including institutional review board [IRB] approval), and the data supporting the study.[14]

As discussed in Chapter 2, the FDA has, on one occasion, prominently exercised its authority over gene-therapy products in the context of assisted reproduction. Upon learning of the efforts of clinicians at St. Barnabas Hospital in Livingston, New Jersey, to perform ooplasm transfer, the FDA asserted its authority on the grounds that such activities constituted unau-

---

* As discussed in Chapter 2, an article may be regulated both as a drug and a biologic, if it satisfies both definitions—which are very expansive.

thorized clinical trials in gene-transfer. Thus, the FDA informed St. Barnabas that it must halt all such activity and submit an IND before proceeding further.

Since the death in 1999 of Jesse Gelsinger, a young man participating in a gene-transfer clinical trial for treatment of ornithine transcarbamylase deficiency (OTC), FDA has increased its oversight of gene-transfer trials. It has instituted the "Gene Therapy Trial Monitoring Program," whereby sponsors of clinical trials are required to designate independent monitors who are supervised by the FDA. Additionally, the FDA issued a "Dear Sponsor" letter to all IND sponsors requesting that they include detailed information in their IND applications regarding products used in the manufacture and testing of gene-therapy products and evidence of quality-control mechanisms. Additionally, FDA officially promised to advise NIH's Office of Biotechnology Activities (the parent office of the RAC) of any alterations in gene-transfer research protocols. In January 2003, the FDA ordered a temporary halt to all gene-transfer research trials using retroviral vectors and blood stem cells.

As of 2000, FDA was overseeing more than 200 gene-transfer research clinical trials.[15] None involve germ-line gene modification, which in the FDA's view cannot now be undertaken in a manner safe and effective enough to satisfy the IND requirement. Indeed, any gene-transfer research protocol that carries a serious risk even of inadvertent germ-line modification is unlikely to meet IND requirements. From a legal perspective, however, the proscription of germ-line modification does *not* exist for the benefit of the unconceived embryo, since the FDA has no clear legal authority to consider the safety of future generations. Rather, the FDA's justification for treating germ-line therapy with such caution is framed in terms of safety, efficacy, and the protection of human subjects in clinical trials (not including the embryos, who are not considered legal subjects).*

---

* It may be the case, however, that the FDA does consider potential danger to the embryo in setting policy, even if its strict legal jurisdiction gives it no authority or grounds to do so.

2. NIH/RAC Oversight.

NIH is a "major funder of human gene-transfer research and the basic science that underpins it."[16] As such, it shares with FDA some responsibility for oversight of gene-transfer research. Any project funded by NIH, or conducted at an institution that receives NIH funding, is subject to NIH review. NIH also accepts and reviews protocols from researchers who voluntarily submit them, regardless of the funding source. The approval process itself considers the ethical, scientific, and safety dimensions of each protocol. The document that governs this process is the "NIH Guidelines for Research Involving Recombinant DNA Molecules," which provides the standards researchers must meet to ensure safety and safe handling of the articles used and derived in such research. The NIH Guidelines additionally provide the requirements for institutional oversight by the Institutional Biosafety Committees (IBC) and the RAC. The NIH Guidelines also provide extensive guidance to researchers on the standards and procedures for the conduct of their clinical trials.[17]

Researchers submit their materials to NIH's Office of Biotechnology Affairs (OBA). These materials include a cover letter that, among other things, identifies the IBCs and IRB at the proposed clinical trial site and acknowledges that no research participant will be enrolled until RAC review is complete and IBC, IRB, and other regulatory approvals have been obtained; a scientific abstract; non-technical abstract; the proposed clinical protocol, including tables, figures, and relevant manuscripts; the proposed informed consent forms; and the curriculum vitae of the principal investigator. Additionally, researchers must respond to a series of questions listed in the NIH Guidelines about the objective and rationale of the proposed project, and questions relating to informed consent and privacy (this is commonly referred to as "Appendix M"). An important characteristic of NIH oversight is that the materials submitted to OBA are generally considered to be in the public domain. This is a key difference from the FDA, which by law must safeguard proprietary information from public access.

Once it has received the aforementioned information, OBA forwards the application for preliminary consideration by the RAC. The RAC is a panel of experts—including scientists, physicians, lawyers, ethicists, and laypersons—that advises the NIH director and the OBA on recombinant DNA research. In addition to reviewing specific research proposals involving gene-transfer, the RAC recommends changes to the NIH Guidelines. While the RAC has no formal authority to accept or reject research proposals, submission to the RAC is a compulsory aspect of the NIH review process. Thus, the RAC's current refusal to "entertain proposals for germ-line alterations"[18] effectively ensures that no such protocols will receive NIH funding.

Following its review of a given proposal, the RAC determines whether the protocol "raises important scientific, safety, medical, ethical, or social issues that warrant in-depth discussion at the RAC's quarterly public meeting."[19] Any protocols that present "unique applications of gene transfer research, the use of new or otherwise salient vector or gene delivery systems, special clinical concerns, or important social or ethical issues"[20] are singled out for further review and public discussion.

If the RAC selects a protocol for further review, the researcher must make a brief presentation at a RAC meeting and take questions about the protocol from RAC members and, possibly, outside experts. This process is open to the public. Following the presentation, the RAC makes a recommendation to the NIH director and the OBA regarding things that the researcher "should carefully consider . . . as part of optimizing the safe and ethical conduct of the trial." The recommendations are memorialized in a letter that is sent to the researcher, the institutional IRB and IBC overseeing the protocol, and the FDA.

Within twenty days of enrolling and obtaining consent from the first research subject, the researcher must submit to the OBA a number of items, including a copy of the informed consent form approved by the IRB, a copy of the protocol approved by the IBC and IRB, a copy of final IBC approval from the clinical trial site, a copy of final IRB approval, the applicable NIH grant numbers, the FDA IND number, and the date of the initiation of the trial. Additionally, the researcher must provide a "brief written report that includes . . . (1) how the investigator(s) responded to each of the RAC's recommendations on the protocol (if applicable); and (2) any modifications to the protocol as required by FDA."[21] During the course of the clinical trial, researchers have an ongoing obligation to inform OBA, the IRBs, IBCs, FDA, and the sponsoring NIH institutions within fifteen days of serious unexpected adverse events that might be associated with the gene-transfer project. If such adverse events involve death or risk of death, this must be reported within seven days. Additionally, researchers must provide OBA with an annual report.

B. Tort Litigation as a Regulatory Mechanism

In addition to the federal system of oversight described above, individuals have recently begun to use tort litigation as a way to regulate those engaged in gene-transfer research. Because there have been no instances of human embryonic gene-transfer, there are no decisional authorities that address the viability of a claim on behalf of a person for harm done in the course of such a protocol. Still, it may be useful briefly to discuss the extant decisional authority bearing on legal claims available to an individual harmed during a clinical trial.

Claimants in clinical-trial cases have sued researchers for negligence in the conduct of the clinical trial. Such a claim requires the plaintiff to demonstrate that the researcher owed a duty of care to the subject, which he breached, resulting in cognizable injury. The question of whether a duty is owed by a researcher in this context has been the subject of some debate. Most courts that have considered the issue have found that a duty exists, by virtue of the special relationship between researcher and subject, the quasi-contract formed by the informed-consent agreement, or implied by the federal guidelines for human-subject protections. The standard of care owed under these circumstances—a question analytically separate from *whether* a duty exists—has also been the subject of some discussion. Most courts addressing the question have held that the standards for informed consent set forth by the Common Rule and FDA's human-subject protections constitute the relevant standard of care, the breach of which may be considered actionable. Two courts have gone farther: one holding that the researcher must disclose any conflicts of interest,[22] and another holding that parents are legally incapable of subjecting their children to *any* risks in nontherapeutic research.*[23] In addition to the standards for informed consent in the federal guidelines, some commentators have suggested that courts should import medical malpractice jurisprudence to determine the standard of care. They argue that the researcher owes the subject "implementation of knowledge, skill and care ordinarily possessed and employed by members of the profession in good standing."[24] Deviation from this standard, under this analysis, would constitute actionable breach. Claimants could prove the contours of this standard of care through the introduction of extrinsic evidence at trial, as through expert witness testimony. This might be problematic in the gene-transfer context; it is such a new technique that "custom" might be hard to establish.

To recover, the claimant must also demonstrate that the researcher's breach caused the relevant injury. Again, this might be difficult for gene-transfer research, given the complexity and novelty of the procedure. Moreover, even if the claimant could show that, but for the researcher's conduct, the harm would not have occurred, the court may not be willing, on grounds of public policy, to impose liability. Courts have sometimes been hesitant to impose such liability on researchers for fear that to do so would have a chilling effect on scientific experimentation that is socially beneficial.[25]

Proving harm might also be very difficult in the context of gene-transfer research, particularly when the individual harmed is unborn when the harm occurs or, as in the case of germ-line gene-transfer, unconceived. Courts have been hesitant to impose liability on harm to future generations.[26]

In addition to negligence claims, individuals can bring actions for assault and battery on the theory that their informed consent was defective or not meaningful.

C. Nongovernmental Regulation

Various professional societies have issued statements offering guidance and reflection on the ethics of genetic engineering and gene-transfer. For example, the American Medical As-

* The *Grimes* Court seems to qualify this view somewhat later, stating that parents may not authorize the exposure of their children to more than minimal risk in studies that offer no prospect of benefit to such children. This view more closely tracks the federal guidelines.

sociation (AMA) has issued ethics opinions on each of these subjects. The AMA's statement on genetic engineering makes it clear that if and when this practice becomes ready for clinical application, the AMA standards on clinical investigation, medical practice, and informed consent apply. Moreover, the AMA holds the following: genetic engineering should be conducted safely, no dangerous viruses should be employed, and the safety and effectiveness of any such procedures should be evaluated very closely.[27]

The AMA's statement on gene-transfer asserts that there should be no germ-line modification at this time because of the "welfare of future generations and its association with risks and potential for unpredictable and irreversible results." Nontherapeutic applications of gene-transfer are "contrary to the ethical traditions of medicine and against the egalitarian values of society." Such uses of gene-transfer can be undertaken only if the following three conditions are satisfied: (1) there is a clear and meaningful benefit to the affected person, (2) there is no "trade off" with other characteristics or traits, and (3) "all citizens would have equal access to the technology, irrespective of income or other socioeconomic characteristics."[28]

IV. CONCLUSION

The ability to modify human traits and characteristics at the beginning of life is not on the immediate horizon. Gene-transfer, though still experimental, may be perfected sooner than artificial chromosomes and similar high-tech approaches. Federal regulation of research (NIH) and clinical trials (FDA) is fairly strong in this area, and tort litigation may provide additional strength to ensure the safety of such experiments and techniques. The regulations are chiefly aimed at the safety of human subjects and at the safety and efficacy of the gene-therapy products themselves. While it does not have formal approval authority, the NIH's RAC publicly discusses and explores the ethical concerns implicated by innovations in this area. But such deliberation tends to focus on safety issues, not on the broader ethical issues relating to the character of human procreation or the significance of increasing the genetic control of parents over offspring. The states have not been actively legislating in this area.

ENDNOTES

[1] Blaese, R., et al., "T Lymphocyte-Directed Gene Therapy for ADA-SCID: Initial Trial Results After Four Years," *Science* 270: 475-480 (1995).

[2] NIH Recombinant DNA Advisory Committee, "Human Gene Transfer Protocols," February 2003, http://www4.od.nih.gov/oba/rac/PROTOCOL.pdf (accessed May 27, 2003).

[3] Newman, S., "Human Developmental Modification: Prospects and Perils," statement submitted to the President's Council on Bioethics by The Council for Responsible Genetics (April 2003).

[4] Chan, A., et al., "Transgenic Monkeys Produced by Retroviral Gene Transform into Mature Oocytes," *Science* 291: 309-312 (2001).

[5] Larin, Z., et al., "Advances in Human Artificial Chromosome Technology," *Trends in Genetics* 18: 313-319 (2002).

[6] Collins, F., presentation at the December 13, 2002, meeting of the President's Council on Bioethics, Washington, D.C., available at www.bioethics.gov.

[7] 49 Fed. Reg. 50,878-01 (December 31, 1984).

[8] Food and Drug Administration, "Guidance for Industry: Guidance for Human Somatic Cell Therapy and Gene Therapy," March 1998, http://www.fda.gov/cber/gdlns/somgene.pdf (accessed June 4, 2003).

[9] *Ibid.*

[10] 58 Fed. Reg. 53,248-01 (October 14, 1993).

[11] 58 Fed. Reg. 53,249 (October 14, 1993).

[12] 42 U.S.C. § 262(a).

[13] Public Health Service Act § 351(a), 42 U.S.C. 262(a).

[14] 21 C.F.R. Part 312.

[15] Food and Drug Administration, "Human Gene Therapy and the Role of the Food and Drug Association," September 2000, http://www.fda.gov/cber/infosheets/genezh.htm (accessed May 13, 2003).

[16] NIH Recombinant DNA Advisory Committee, "Frequently Asked Questions: Recombinant DNA and Gene Transfer," September 9, 2002, http://www4.od.nih.gov/oba/RAC/RAC_FAQs.htm (accessed May 13, 2003).

[17] National Institutes of Health, "NIH Guidelines for Research Involving Recombinant DNA Molecules (NIH Guidelines)," April 2002, Appendix M.

[18] *Ibid.*

[19] NIH Recombinant DNA Advisory Committee, "Frequently Asked Questions," *op. cit.*

[20] *Ibid.*

[21] *Ibid.*

[22] *Moore v. Regents of the University of California*, 793 P.2d 479, 486 (Ca. 1990).

[23] *Grimes v. Kennedy Krieger Institute, Inc.*, 782 A.2d 807, 846 (Md. 2001).

[24] Keeton, W., et al., *Prosser and Keeton on the Law of Torts* §32 at 187 (5th ed., 1984).

[25] *Enright v. Eli Lilly*, 570 N.E.2d 198 (N.Y. 1991).

[26] *Id.,* at 201-204.

[27] Council on Ethical and Judicial Affairs, American Medical Association. Opinion 2.13, "Genetic Engineering." In: *Code of Medical Ethics: Current Opinions with Annotations*. Chicago, Illinois: American Medical Association, 2002.

[28] Council on Ethical and Judicial Affairs, American Medical Association. Opinion 2.11, "Gene Therapy." In: *Code of Medical Ethics: Current Opinions with Annotations*. Chicago, Illinois: American Medical Association, 2002.

5

Research Involving In Vitro Human Embryos

The biotechnologies of human reproduction are inextricably entangled with research that uses or involves early-stage human embryos. Such research provides the experimental groundwork for many of the techniques of assisted reproduction, and it relies on assisted reproduction techniques to produce the ex vivo embryos it uses when it studies disease models and seeks treatments and cures for the sick. Thus, a comprehensive understanding of the current practices, ethical issues, and regulation of reproductive biotechnology requires a consideration of human embryo research.

Before entering the discussion, however, we need to define its scope. Many activities could reasonably be deemed "human embryo research," based on the purpose and nature of the activity. If construed broadly, "embryo research" might include novel or experimental in utero or ex utero interventions for therapeutic purposes, intended to benefit mother, embryo, or both. This might include novel assisted reproductive technologies, preimplantation genetic diagnosis, and embryonic gene-transfer—subjects discussed elsewhere in this document. Or "embryo research" might be construed to include research performed on aborted fetuses, fetal tissue, or non-living embryos or embryonic tissue. We opt for a narrower definition, in keeping with our focus on the current regulation of those biotechnologies that touch on human reproduction. We will therefore limit ourselves, in what follows, to considering basic research on early-stage ex utero living embryos not intended for transfer into a woman's uterus.

I. TECHNIQUES AND PRACTICES

A. Present Applications of Human Embryo Research

Much of basic embryo research is aimed at improving infertility treatment. Additional research protocols involving human embryos seek general knowledge about early embryonic development, including morphology, biochemical and biophysical properties, and genetic expression. Some embryo researchers seek to enhance basic knowledge about the origins of birth defects. Others seek the development of contraceptives. Still others study cell division in early embryos looking for clues relevant to understanding cancer development and metastasis (particularly cancers affecting reproductive organs). Embryo research is also undertaken to increase understanding of somatic cell nuclear transfer and parthenogenesis. Finally, embryos are used for deriving and studying human embryonic stem cells.

B. Sources of Embryos

Researchers typically procure embryos for research purposes from assisted reproduction clinics—generally, embryos that remain following completion of in vitro fertilization (IVF) treatment and that are no longer wanted for transfer by those who produced them (so-called "spare" embryos). Such researchers submit requests to clinics for embryos that have been explicitly donated for research. As mentioned in Chapter 2, the recent study by the American Society for Reproductive Medicine (ASRM) and RAND on the number of cryopreserved embryos in the United States found that of the nearly 400,000 embryos currently in cryostorage, only 2.8 percent (roughly 11,000) have been designated for donation to research. At the outset of fertility treatment, couples designate what should be done with their embryos in the event of their deaths, divorce, or abandonment. After couples have completed their treatment, they are approached by researchers who make specific requests for embryo donations. Typically, these are researchers who have pre-existing relationships with the assisted reproductive technologies (ART) clinic. In some cases the couple's fertility specialist may also be the principal researcher requesting donation.

Less often, embryos are created expressly for research. In July 2001, the Jones Institute in Norfolk, Virginia, publicized the fact that its scientists had created more than one hundred embryos in this manner from the gametes of volunteer donors. (Subsequent reports suggest this program has been stopped.) There are no reliable data on the number of researchers now producing embryos solely for research or the number of embryos that have been produced solely for research.

C. Projected Techniques/Recent Experiments

While most embryo research is conducted with embryos produced through IVF using sperm and ova, a range of recent developments in experimental embryology is noteworthy. In July 2003, it was announced that male human cells had been transplanted into a three-day-old female human embryo. Researchers grew the resulting human embryo hybrid (dubbed a "she-male" in the press) for six days before destroying it.[1] The purpose of the experiment, according to the head of the research team that conducted it, was to show that cells from a sibling might be transplanted into an embryo in order to prevent the development of certain genetic diseases.[2] This experiment was conducted in the United States, with embryos that were donated specifically for the purpose of such experimentation.

Advanced techniques in embryological experimentation have also allowed researchers to create "hybrid" cloned embryos made from human and animal cells. For instance, in August and September of 2003 it was announced that cloned embryos had been created by fusing human skin cells with enucleated eggs from rabbits[3] and by fusing female human cells with enucleated oocytes from cows.[4]

Researchers in South Korea recently produced 30 cloned human embryos (via somatic cell nuclear transfer using the egg donors' own cumulus cells), grew them to the blastocyst stage (five to six days), and successfully derived a pluripotent embryonic human stem cell line from them.[5] This marks the first verified successful cloning of human embryos, and their successful growth to the stage at which embryonic stem cells may be obtained. Although the researchers who accomplished this express no interest in using their technique for procreative purposes, the cloned embryos they produced were cultivated past the developmental stage at which in vitro embryos are typically transferred to a woman's uterus in an effort to produce a child.

II. ETHICAL CONSIDERATIONS

The ethical questions connected with embryo research have been discussed in detail in two previous Council reports: *Human Cloning and Human Dignity* (July 2002) and *Monitoring Stem Cell Research* (January 2004). We present here the briefest outline of the relevant issues; readers seeking further elaboration should consult Chapter 6 of the cloning report and Chapter 3 of the stem cell report.

First, human embryo research has the potential to do great good, both for infertile couples seeking to conceive children and for countless sick and suffering patients whose diseases or disabilities might be cured or ameliorated by regenerative medicine that made use of embryonic stem cells. Although the promise of such research for human therapies remains speculative, many researchers believe it will offer great benefits to perhaps millions of patients.

The chief ethical concerns raised by the practice of human embryo research arise from the fact that such research generally necessitates the use and destruction of human embryos. Many people regard embryos as human beings at the earliest stage of life, and thus worthy of the same respect and protections that we afford all human persons. Even among many who do not assign human embryos the moral standing of "full persons," intentional destruction of developing human life is a cause for some ethical disquiet. To regard developing human life as a mere means—even a means to a noble end, such as the alleviation of suffering—presents a moral problem with potentially serious consequences for society as a whole. It might lead to the coarsening of sensibilities in the general culture. It might make respect for human life conditional on the possession of certain capacities, and thus open the door to moral hazards both in research and beyond.

The creation of human embryos solely for research raises additional concerns. Unlike in assisted reproduction, where each embryo is created with a view to conceiving a live-born child, embryos produced solely for research are treated purely instrumentally. They become a "natural resource" for gaining scientific and medical knowledge and, in the process, the techniques of assisted reproduction are severed entirely from the aspiration to produce a human child.

Other ethical hazards include the potential for embryos to be commercialized and the danger that couples undergoing fertility treatment might be subtly or overtly pressured to donate embryos to research against their will. The first concern focuses not so much on the destruction of embryos but on their treatment in the marketplace and the laboratory; the second concern focuses on the treatment of persons involved in creating such embryos—namely, gamete donors and fertility patients. These concerns have been expressed by individuals on all sides of the debate about the moral standing of human embryos.

III. REGULATION

A. Federal Law

The federal regulation of human embryo research has a long and complicated history, and public policy debate on embryo research has centered largely on the question of federal funding, not the regulation of embryo research as such. In the 1970s, the regulations governing the protection of human subjects involved in federally funded research provided that "no application or proposal involving human *in vitro* fertilization may be funded by the Department* [until it] has been reviewed by the Ethics Advisory Board (EAB) and the Board has rendered advice as to its acceptability from an ethical standpoint."[6] In 1979, the EAB concluded that federal funding of IVF research was ethically acceptable, subject to certain conditions.† The secretary of the Department of HEW did not act on this recommendation; the EAB was dissolved in 1980. No subsequent EAB was appointed thereafter. The result was a de facto moratorium on federal funding for embryo research until 1993. Acting on the advice of newly elected President Clinton, Congress passed the National Institutes of Health (NIH) Revitalization Act of 1993, nullifying the requirement that there be an EAB review before an application can be federally funded. Thereafter, NIH Director Harold Varmus convened an advisory panel to consider which types of embryo research, as an ethical matter, should be entitled to federal funding. The NIH Human Embryo Research Panel issued a report in 1994 concluding that certain kinds of embryo research were acceptable for federal funding, others might be acceptable under certain specified conditions, and still others were unacceptable.‡ One of the most controversial aspects of the NIH Panel's conclusions was a qualified endorsement of the creation of embryos solely for purposes of research.§ The Embryo Research Panel submitted its conclusions to the Advisory Committee, which then forwarded them to the NIH director. Before the director could act on the recommendations, however, President Clinton directed NIH not to approve funds for the creation of human embryos solely for research purposes. Director Varmus ac-

---

* The Department of Health, Education, and Welfare (DHEW), now called the Department of Health and Human Services (HHS).

† These conditions included: informed consent for the use of gametes, the research had to be important and "not reasonably attainable by other means," and that embryos must not be maintained outside the body beyond fourteen days after fertilization. (DHEW EAB 1979, 106, 107.)

‡ The specific conclusions of the NIH Embryo Research Panel are discussed further, below.

§ "The Panel believes that the use of oocytes fertilized expressly for research should be allowed only under two conditions. The first condition is when the research by its very nature cannot otherwise be validly conducted. The second condition . . . is when a compelling case can be made that this is necessary for the validity of a study that is potentially of outstanding scientific and therapeutic value." (Report of the Human Embryo Research Panel, September 1994, pp. 44-45.)

cepted the remaining recommendations and began to plan for their implementation as a predicate to the funding of embryo research.

Before NIH had the opportunity to approve any proposals for embryo research protocols, however, Congress implemented a statutory ban on federal funding that remains in effect. According to the Dickey-Wicker Amendment to the Department of Health and Human Services (HHS) appropriations bill for fiscal year 1996,[7] which has been re-enacted each year since, no federal funds may be used for the following: the creation of a human embryo or embryos for research purposes, or research in which a human embryo or embryos are destroyed, discarded, or knowingly subjected to risk of injury or death greater than that allowed for research on fetuses in utero "under 45 C.F.R. 46.208(a)(2) and section 498b of the Public Health Service Act (42 U.S.C. 289g[b])."[*] The first referenced statute provides that no fetus in utero can be involved as a subject in any activity covered by Subpart B of Part 46 of Title 45 (federal human subjects protections, described below) unless the risk to the fetus imposed by the research is minimal and the purpose of the activity is the development of important biomedical knowledge which could not be obtained by other means. The second statute (section 498b of the Public Health Service Act) requires that the research risk standard be the same for fetuses that are intended to be aborted and fetuses that are intended to be carried to term. "Human embryo" is defined broadly as "any organism, not protected as a human-subject under 45 C.F.R. 46 . . . that is derived by fertilization, parthenogenesis, cloning, or any other means from one or more human gametes or human diploid cells."

In light of the legislative restriction on federal funding, in 1998 NIH sought a legal opinion from the HHS Office of the General Counsel on whether NIH funds may be used for research using embryonic stem cells. HHS concluded that the Dickey-Wicker Amendment did not prohibit the federal fund-

[*] A minor technical matter: 45 C.F.R. § 46.208 no longer exists, although the Dickey-Wicker reference to it exists as recently as the Fiscal Year 2003 Consolidated Appropriations Resolution (P.L. 108-07, signed February 20, 2003) and in NIH's March 18, 2003, explanation of the appropriations resolution (Notice NOT-OD-03-035). 45 C.F.R. § 46.208(a)(2) is currently expressed at 45 C.F.R. § 46.204(b).

ing of research "utilizing" (as opposed to deriving) human embryonic stem cells taken from embryos that have *already* been destroyed using private funding. However, before HHS allocated any funding for such research, the newly elected Bush administration initiated a review of the former administration's policy for the federal funding of embryonic stem cell research and halted the consideration of research proposals.

On August 9, 2001, President Bush announced his decision to allow federal funds to be used for research on existing human embryonic stem cell lines, so long as the following conditions were met: (1) the derivation process had been initiated prior to August 9, 2001, thus creating no public incentive for future embryo destruction; (2) the embryo from which the stem cell line was derived had already been destroyed and thus had no potential for further development. In addition, the President established the following additional criteria in order for a stem cell line to be eligible for federal funding: the stem cells must have been derived from an embryo that was initially created for reproductive purposes and no longer needed for these purposes, informed consent must have been obtained for the donation of the embryo, and no financial inducements had been provided for donation of the embryo. Because of President Bush's statement, on November 7, 2001, the NIH rescinded a November 21, 2000, guidance on NIH-funded stem cell research insofar as that guidance applied to research on stem cells derived from human embryos.* As part of the implementation of this funding policy, the NIH has created a Human Embryonic Stem Cell Registry that lists the human embryonic stem cell lines that meet the eligibility criteria.†

There are currently no federal laws or regulations directly applicable to the use of embryos in privately funded research.

---

* The guidance was issued following a decision by NIH that the Dickey-Wicker amendment did not prohibit federally funded research *preceding* or *following* the destruction of human embryos. Thus, NIH concluded that it could fund research projects on human embryonic stem cell lines that had been previously derived. The November 21, 2000, guidance remains effective with respect to NIH funding of research using germ cells derived from fetal tissue.

† The registry is available at escr.nih.gov. For a more complete discussion of the federal legislation and policy developments pertaining to stem cell research, see the Council's report, *Monitoring Stem Cell Research* (January 2004), especially Chapter 2, available at www.bioethics.gov.

The FDA does not regulate human embryo research unless it is aimed at the development of a "product" subject to its approval.

Embryo research using cloned human embryos—embryos created by somatic cell nuclear transfer—has been the subject of separate legislative activity. On July 31, 2001, and again on February 27, 2003, the House of Representatives passed a bill that would ban the creation of cloned human embryos for any purpose. It would also make illegal the shipment or receipt "for any purpose of an embryo produced by human cloning or any product derived from such embryo." If enacted, this bill would prohibit research on cloned human embryos and on stem cells extracted from such embryos. As of this writing, the Senate has not acted on the bill.

In addition to specific federal legislation directly addressed to embryo research, there are a number of other federal activities that, less directly, do or might touch embryo research.

1. Secretary's Advisory Council on Human Research Protections (SACHRP).

The charter of SACHRP, which recently replaced the National Human Research Protections Advisory Committee, requires SACHRP to "provide advice relating to the responsible conduct of research involving human subjects" with special emphasis on various special populations, including embryos. Thus, for purposes of the charter of this federal advisory committee, human embryos are human subjects.

2. Human-Subjects Protections.

Entities and individuals that conduct human subjects research are regulated under federal regulations, as well as by the policies and procedures of the institutions at which federally funded research is conducted. (Ex vivo embryos, however, are not considered "human subjects" for these purposes.) There are several regulatory structures that form the basis of the federal government's jurisdiction over human subjects research. The two major sources of regulation are the Office of Human Research Protections (OHRP) and the Food and Drug Administration (FDA), both housed in HHS. Additionally, NIH, a main source of funding for research, has regulations and policies that must be followed to the extent a research project (or institution) is funded by the NIH. HHS regulations, at 45 C.F.R. Part 46, govern federally funded or supported research on human subjects. Subpart A of the regulations, known as the "Common Rule," has been adopted and separately codified by fourteen agencies other than HHS.* Subparts B, C, and D govern research on vulnerable populations: specifically, Subpart B governs research on pregnant women, human fetuses, and neonates; Subpart C governs research on prisoners; and Subpart D governs research on children. OHRP is the office that is charged with developing guidelines interpreting the Common Rule and enforcing its requirements. OHRP determination letters are issued to institutions determined by OHRP to be out of compliance with HHS regulations and provide an additional source of guidance regarding the meaning of the regulations and the government's enforcement focus.

The Common Rule applies to "all research involving human subjects conducted, supported or otherwise subject to regulation by any Federal Department or Agency" that has adopted

---

* The FDA has never officially adopted the Common Rule. But FDA regulations governing research on human subjects include requirements that are functionally identical to the Common Rule. Unlike the Common Rule, however, the FDA's requirements for human subjects research apply *regardless* of whether the research is federally funded, *provided that* the prospective product being studied in the clinical investigation is subject to FDA regulation generally (21 C.F.R. §§ 50.1, 56.101). Even clinical investigations that are exempt from the IND requirements (for example, where the results will not be submitted to the FDA and the investigation does not increase the risks to the subjects) must nonetheless be conducted in accordance with FDA's IRB oversight and informed consent requirements. It is important to note, however, that FDA regulations governing clinical investigations do not apply to the off-label use of an investigational drug or device in the practice of medicine. (*See* 21 C.F.R. § 312.2(d) [expressly carving out the off-label use of drugs in the practice of medicine]; 812.2(a) [limiting the applicability of Part 812 to clinical investigations to determine the safety and efficacy of a device].)

The FDA requirements for IRB oversight and informed consent are similar to those under the Common Rule. One distinction is noticeable. Whereas the Common Rule provides for IRB waiver of informed consent for certain types of minimal risk research (*see* 45 C.F.R. § 46.116), waiver of informed consent is limited under FDA regulations to emergency use of an investigational drug or device or research intended to be conducted in an emergency setting, because the use of an investigational device or drug is automatically considered to present at least a minimal risk to the subjects (*see* 21 C.F.R. §§ 50.23, 50.24).

its provisions. As a practical matter, the reach of the Common Rule extends beyond federally funded or supported human subjects research to cover all research done at institutions that receive any federal funding. All institutions receiving federal funds to conduct human subjects research are required to enter into an "assurance" with the federal government, under which the institution promises to abide by applicable federal regulations and ethical principles in the conduct of *all* human subjects research undertaken at the institution.* The terms of an assurance often apply the ethical principles outlined in the Belmont Report[8] and the requirements of the Common Rule, including Subparts B, C, and D, to all research conducted at the institution, regardless of the funding source.

In addition to being limited to institutions that receive federal funds, the scope of the Common Rule's requirements are further limited by the definition of human subjects research and the regulatory exemptions within the Common Rule that expressly exclude certain types of research from its requirements.[9] For example, research that involves the collection or study of existing data—for example, a retrospective chart review—will not be subject to the Common Rule's requirements if the sources of data are publicly available or the investigator records the data in such a manner that the subjects cannot be identified, directly or through a code linked to the subjects.[10] If human subjects research falls within one of the six categories of exempt research, there is no requirement for institutional review board (IRB) review, approval, and continued oversight of the research; nor is there a federal requirement for obtaining the written informed consent of the subject.

---

* Historically, there were several forms of assurances, depending on the sort of project involved, and the terms of each assurance would vary depending upon its negotiation. Recently, OHRP instituted the "Federalwide Assurance," a uniform assurance document that is now required (as of December 31, 2003) for all institutions receiving federal research funds, regardless of what kind of assurance the institution was previously operating under. Although many institutions conducting research receive some form of federal funding requiring them to execute a Federalwide Assurance, there are institutions or other private companies that conduct research solely with private funds and that will therefore not be required to execute an assurance. Although these privately funded research entities may be governed by FDA or state law requirements, or both, they will not be subject to the requirements of 45 C.F.R. § 46.

One of the main protections of human subjects afforded by the Common Rule is the requirement that human subjects research be reviewed, approved, and monitored by an IRB, an independent ethical body constituted in accordance with the requirements of 45 C.F.R. 46.107. An IRB may approve only such research as meets the criteria in 45 C.F.R. 46.111, and any additional applicable requirements for the special populations governed by Subparts B, C, and D. Specifically, to approve research on human subjects under 45 C.F.R. 46.111, an IRB must conclude that a number of safeguards relating to risks to the subjects, selection of subjects, informed consent, monitoring of subjects, and privacy, are satisfied.* Research approved by an IRB is also subject to continuing review, at intervals appropriate to the degree of risk presented by the study, but at least once a year.[11] OHRP has issued detailed guidance regarding the continuing review process, specifying when it should occur and what materials should be reviewed.[12]

The NIH guidelines on human subjects do not directly cover ex utero embryos, but may touch other participants in such research. For purposes of 45 C.F.R. 46, a "human subject" is a living individual about whom an investigator conducting research obtains (1) data through intervention or interaction with the individual, or (2) identifiable private information. If the identity of the embryo donor(s) can be readily ascertained by the investigator—either because the research is conducted in vivo or because donor identifiers are associated with the embryo—the donor(s) could be "human subjects" within the meaning of 45 C.F.R. 46. Ex utero embryos, as such, have never been treated as "human subjects" for purposes of this section.

---

* The IRB must conclude that risks to subjects are minimized; risks to subjects are reasonable in relation to anticipated benefits, if any, and the importance of the knowledge that may reasonably be expected to result; selection of subjects is equitable (for example, no one population bears the burden of research without direct benefit; adult subjects should be used for research where possible before children are enrolled, etc.); informed consent will be sought from each prospective subject or the subject's legally authorized representative, in accordance with and to the extent required by 45 C.F.R. § 46.116; informed consent will be appropriately documented, in accordance with and to the extent required by 45 C.F.R. § 46.117; when appropriate, the research plan makes adequate provision for monitoring the data collected to ensure the safety of subjects; and when appropriate, there are adequate provisions to protect the privacy of subjects and to maintain the confidentiality of data.

Embryos inside a woman's uterus are covered by the protections under the Common Rule applicable to research on pregnant women and fetuses.* Pregnant women or fetuses may only be involved in research if the following conditions are met: (1) where scientifically appropriate, preclinical studies and clinical studies have been conducted and provide data for assessing potential risks to pregnant women and fetuses; (2) the risk to the fetus is caused solely by interventions or procedures that hold out the prospect of direct benefit to the woman or the fetus; or, if there is no prospect of direct benefit, the risk to the fetus is not greater than minimal and the purpose of the research is the development of important biomedical knowledge that cannot be obtained by any other means; (3) any risk is the least possible for achieving the objectives of the research; (4) the research holds out the prospect of direct benefit to the pregnant woman, the prospect of a direct benefit both to the pregnant woman and the fetus, or no prospect of benefit for the woman nor the fetus when risk to the fetus is not greater than minimal and the purpose of the research is the development of important biomedical knowledge that cannot be obtained by any other means and the woman's informed consent is obtained; (5) if the research holds out the prospect of direct benefit solely to the fetus and the informed consent of the pregnant woman and the father is obtained, except that the father's consent need not be obtained if he is unable to consent because of unavailability, incompetence, or temporary incapacity or the pregnancy resulted from rape or incest; (6) each individual providing consent to the research is fully informed regarding the reasonably foreseeable impact of the research on the fetus or the neonate; (7) if the pregnant individual is a child, as that term is defined under title 45 C.F.R. 46.402(a), assent and permission are obtained in accord with the provisions of Subpart D of the regulations governing re-

* The regulation provides protection for "fetuses," defined as "the product of conception from implantation until delivery." This legal definition differs from the standard medical definition, which uses the term "embryo" to name the product of conception from the time of fertilization up to eight weeks (well after implantation, which usually occurs before the end of the first week). Thus, if the research is conducted in vivo post-implantation, what might be considered research on an "embryo" by most scientists could be considered research on a "fetus" for purposes of 45 C.F.R. § 46 (and therefore subject to Subpart B).

search on children; (8) no inducements, monetary or otherwise, will be offered to terminate a pregnancy; (9) the individuals engaged in the research will have no part in any decisions as to the timing, method, or procedures used to terminate a pregnancy; and (10) the individuals engaged in the research will have no part in determining the viability of a neonate.

B. State Law

States are the principal sources for the direct regulation of embryo research. State laws vary widely in their application and content. Some states, in an effort to disincentivize abortion, regulate research on aborted fetuses and embryos,* matters beyond the scope of this document. Additionally, many states define "embryo research" broadly so as to reach experimental practices such as cryopreservation, preimplantation genetic diagnosis, and perhaps gene-transfer. Such statutes are discussed in the parts of this document that address those specific subjects. The following discussion will focus only on regulations that may govern direct research on early-stage in vitro embryos not intended for transfer, and where the aim of the research is to further scientific knowledge and medicine in a general way (unrelated to the specific embryos themselves).

A number of states have regulations potentially applicable to research on in vitro embryos. New Hampshire expressly permits research on in vitro embryos up to fourteen days of development, but prohibits implantation of these embryos once they undergo such experimentation. Additional states also prohibit research on in vitro embryos to various extents.† For example, Pennsylvania proscribes any type of "nontherapeutic experimentation" or "nontherapeutic medical procedure" upon any "unborn child," defined as "an individual organism of the species homo sapiens from fertilization until live birth."[13] Most of these states proscribe such research if not

---

* See, for example, Arizona, Arkansas, California, Florida, Indiana, Kentucky, Missouri, Nebraska, Ohio, Oklahoma, Tennessee, and Wyoming.

† See, for example, Louisiana, Michigan, Minnesota, New Hampshire, New Mexico, Pennsylvania, and South Dakota. Some states, including Maine, Massachusetts, North Dakota, and Rhode Island, prohibit research on embryos or fetuses "before or after expulsion from the mother's womb." It is unclear whether these statutes govern research on in vitro embryos.

beneficial to the embryo itself. For example, Michigan prohibits research on live human embryos, fetuses, or neonates, if such research substantially jeopardizes the subject's life or health.[14] Illinois, New Mexico, and Utah have statutes that proscribe research on fetuses that might be construed to reach in vitro embryos.

Recently there has been a groundswell of legislation introduced at the state level in response to developments in embryonic stem cell research and human cloning. In Massachusetts, efforts are currently under way to amend the fetal research statute (which now prohibits experimentation on embryos and fetuses unless it is incidental to the study of the human fetus while it is in its mother's womb) to exempt embryos from its definition of "fetus." California has recently passed legislation that expressly permits and encourages research involving the derivation of human embryonic stem cells—including research involving the creation and use of cloned embryos. A law recently passed in New Jersey similarly declares that research "involving the derivation and use of human embryonic stem cells and human embryonic germ cells" is permitted, including "somatic cell nuclear transplantation."[15] A related New Jersey law purports to outlaw "cloning," defined as "replication of a human individual by cultivating a cell with genetic material through the egg, embryo, fetal, and newborn stages into a new human individual."[16] This would seem to be the most permissive of all such state laws that proscribe cloning for reproductive purposes while permitting cloning for biomedical research. Most such laws (like the federal bill recently proposed by Senators Orrin Hatch, Dianne Feinstein, and Arlen Specter[17]) prohibit the transfer of a cloned embryo to a woman's uterus. The New Jersey law, by contrast, defines "cloning" in a way that seems to allow the transfer of a cloned embryo to a woman's uterus, as well as the cultivation of the cloned embryo up to the "newborn" stage.

It bears noting that some of the above-mentioned embryo research statutes have come under judicial scrutiny. Statutes in Illinois, Louisiana, and Utah have been held to be unconstitutionally vague, on the grounds that "experimentation" is not defined clearly enough for practitioners to understand that certain of their activities may be criminal. One court in Illinois went further, striking down a portion of an older statute on the grounds that it could reach certain practices and techniques of assisted reproduction, thus infringing upon a woman's constitutional right to make reproductive decisions.

C. Professional Self-Regulation

A number of professional organizations and societies have published guidelines and opinions on human embryo research. These are substantially similar to the guidelines proposed by the 1994 NIH Human Embryo Research Panel (discussed elsewhere in this chapter and summarized below). Two that are worth noting are statements from ASRM and the American Academy of Pediatrics (AAP).

ASRM's 1994 report, entitled "Research on Pre-embryos: Justifications and Limits," notes what it considers the great benefits of embryo research, and concludes that it is a permissible activity. ASRM further concludes that it is not "prudent at this time" to maintain embryos in vitro beyond fourteen days. The opinion does not seem to take a position on the creation of embryos expressly for research.

ASRM offers guidelines for the donation of embryos in two ethics opinions: "Donating Spare Embryos for Embryonic Stem Cell Research"[18] and "Informed Consent and the Use of Gametes and Embryos."[19] These guidelines specify the importance of making sure that potential embryo donors understand the risks and benefits, as well as the purpose and nature of the research and its potential commercial value (and their own lack of entitlement to such value). Additionally, couples are to be told that their decision does not affect their status as patients, that no research embryos will be transferred, and that they may change their minds at any point up until the protocol begins. ASRM advises that clinics should have a policy on privacy and confidentiality. Both members of a couple seeking treatment must agree on donation to research—if they disagree, then no embryos shall be donated. Final consent (confirming the couple's initially stated preferences for embryo disposition) is to be obtained only after the couple has decided not to continue storing their embryos. ASRM's opinion on the disposition of "abandoned" embryos precludes the use of such embryos in research. An embryo is deemed "abandoned" if the couple "has not given written instruction for disposition, has not been in contact with the program for a substantial period of time, and has not provided a current address and telephone number." ASRM notes that it is preferable (though not mandatory) that an individual other than the couple's fertility specialist be the person who requests donation for research. ASRM concludes that there should be no buying and selling of embryos, though reasonable fees (defined by the contracting parties) may be paid for efforts and costs incurred.

The AAP issued a statement on human embryo research in September 2001 concluding that embryonic stem cell research is sufficiently valuable that it should be funded by NIH and regulated by HHS. The Academy took the position that federally funded embryo research should be approved by IRBs subject to the following conditions (which are similar to those set out by a panel of the NIH in the late 1990s):

- The embryos are already frozen and are no longer clinically needed.
- There is a clear separation in the donor decision process between the decision by the donors to create embryos for infertility treatment and the decision to donate frozen embryos for research purposes after they are no longer clinically needed.
- The decision to donate is strictly voluntary and without monetary inducements.
- The physician responsible for fertility treatments is not to be the person performing the research on the same frozen embryos, and there should be no monetary relationship, that is, transfer of funds in the research project to the physician responsible for the fertility treatments.
- There are to be no personal identifiers associated with the embryos used for research.
- There are to be no restrictions placed by the donor on the type of research performed.

- The research performed on these frozen embryos can be of no direct benefit to the original donors.
- The embryo research does not involve research in reproductive cloning, transferring an altered embryo to a woman's uterus, or use of a human embryo in combination with other human or animal embryos.

The Academy also provided guidelines for informed consent. Specifically, informed consent should advise donors that:

- All identifiers associated with the frozen embryos will be removed.
- The donors will not receive any future information regarding subsequent testing or research on these embryos.
- Cells or tissue developed from the embryos may be used at some future time for human transplantation research.
- Cells or tissues derived from the embryos may be kept indefinitely.
- The donated frozen embryos may be of commercial value, but the donors will not receive any financial or other benefits from any such commercial development.
- The research performed on these frozen embryos is not intended to provide direct medical benefit to the donor.
- The research will not involve the transfer of these embryos to a woman's uterus or involve reproductive cloning or combination of the embryo with any other embryo of human or animal origin.

The American Medical Association (AMA) has similarly issued guidance on human embryo research, supporting the conclusions of the 1994 NIH Human Embryo Research Panel and recommending the creation of a RAC-like body to provide oversight for experiments that involve cloned embryos or cloning techniques. Additionally, the AMA has signaled its support for federal funding of research using early-stage human embryos.

While its conclusions do not have the force of law and were never fully adopted, the principles articulated by the NIH Embryo Research Panel in 1994 have been widely echoed in the policies and ethical opinions of a number of professional societies and organizations. Thus, it is worthwhile to summarize briefly the key conclusions of the Embryo Research Panel. The Panel agreed that federal funding of embryo research in certain areas is permissible for three reasons: (1) the scientific promise of such research is significant; (2) the embryo does not, in the Panel's view, enjoy the same moral status as a person; and (3) the absence of federal funding (and thus oversight) leads to a status quo in which there is no consistent scientific or ethical review of research protocols.[20]

The Panel identified and distinguished the categories of research that should receive funding. The first category was research deemed by the Panel to be "acceptable for federal funding," provided it was conducted in accordance with certain guidelines. These guidelines included requirements that the research be conducted by qualified researchers, according to a valid research design, under the direction of an IRB, with a minimum number of embryos necessary, and with adequate informed consent. Additionally, the Panel advised that there should be no purchase or sale of gametes or embryos (though reasonable compensation for expenses and efforts should be permitted), and there should be equitable selection of gamete and embryo donors to prevent discrimination. Finally, the Panel noted that, subject to certain exceptions, embryos should not be maintained in vitro for more than fourteen days following fertilization.

Types of research deemed "acceptable for funding" include research aimed at improving the outcome of pregnancy and research on the process of fertilization, the genetics of embryonic development, the effects of cryopreservation on the development of oocytes, preimplantation genetic diagnosis, embryonic stem cells (using excess IVF embryos with appropriate informed consent), and oocyte nuclear transfer (in protocols where there is no transfer to a uterus or functional equivalent).

Within the category of "acceptable research," the Panel singled out a subcategory of projects that was acceptable to them for federal funding, but deserving "very careful scrutiny" during the ad hoc review process (recommended by the Panel for research protocols). Such projects include research involving existing embryos where "one of the progenitors received monetary compensation,"* and "projects of outstanding merit requiring fertilization of ova as part of the protocol." As we noted earlier, this latter recommendation was quite controversial and was not accepted by the Clinton administration.

The Panel identified a second category, namely, research "that warrants additional review." Such research would be presumptively ineligible for federal funding, but this presumption could be overcome by a showing of outstanding merit, and following "explicit consideration of the ethical issues and social consequences." Research in this category includes cloning by blastomere separation or blastocyst splitting (without transfer), "research between the appearance of the primitive streak and the beginning of closure of the neural tube" (occurring between days 17 and 21 of embryonic development), research using fetal oocytes for fertilization or parthenogenesis (without transfer), research on oocyte nuclear transfer (with subsequent transfer to a woman's uterus), and embryonic stem cell research involving embryos fertilized exclusively for such research.

The third and final category of research identified by the Panel was projects "considered unacceptable for funding." These projects were deemed unacceptable on ethical grounds, including concerns for adverse effects on the well-being of children, women, and men involved in such research; the "special respect" due to the in vitro embryo; concern for "public sensitivities on highly controversial research proposals"; and "concern for the meaning of humanness, parenthood, and the succession of generations."[21] Research that is "unacceptable for federal funding" included the cloning of embryos via blastomere separation or blastocyst splitting (with transfer to a woman's uterus); preimplantation genetic diagnosis (PGD) for non-medically indicated sex selection; development of human-animal chimeras (with or without transfer); cross-species

---

* The Panel concluded that federal funding is acceptable only for research involving embryos acquired by these means prior to September 1994.

fertilization (except for clinical protocols exploring "the ability of sperm to penetrate eggs"); research involving transfer of parthenotes to a woman's uterus; and research involving the transfer of human embryos into nonhuman animals, or "for extrauterine or abdominal pregnancy."[22]

IV. CONCLUSION

There has been significant policy debate and direct legislative action on the question of federal funding for embryo research—culminating in the current policy of funding research that employs a limited number of specifically eligible embryonic stem cell lines. There is no federal regulation of research on in vitro embryos when such research is privately funded and supported. States have widely varying approaches to the subject, ranging from active support and endorsement, to silence (and thus permission), to prohibition of such research. The private sector's practices on this point seem to reflect the principles articulated by the NIH Human Embryo Research Panel in 1994, namely, that the embryo is entitled to "special respect," but may be used and destroyed in "worthwhile" research protocols. Additionally, there seems to be some agreement among scientific professional societies that embryos should not be cultivated beyond fourteen days' development—a limit that has been proposed by a number of bodies, both governmental and nongovernmental.

ENDNOTES

[1] Gleicher, N., et al., "Blastomere transplantation as a possible treatment," presented at the 19th Annual Meeting of the European Society of Human Reproduction and Embryology, June 29 to July 2, 2003, Madrid, Spain (www.eshre.com).

[2] "Sex Cells," *ScienCentral News,* July 29, 2003, quoting Dr. Norbert Gleicher, founder of the Center for Human Reproduction.

[3] Chen, Y. et al., "Embryonic stem cells generated by transfer of human somatic nuclei into rabbit oocytes," *Cell Research* 12:251-264 (2003), reporting on experiments in Shanghai Second Medical University in China, in which human cells were fused with empty rabbit oocytes.

[4] "First human clone embryo ready for implantation," *NewScientist.com*, September 15, 2003, reporting that fertility practitioner Panayiotis Zavos created human cloned embryos by fusing human cells with empty cow oocytes.

[5] *See* Hwang, W.S., et al., "Evidence of a Pluripotent Human Embryonic Stem Cell Line Derived from a Cloned Human Blastocyst," *Science Express*, doi:10.1126/science.1094515 (2004).

[6] 45 C.F.R. § 46.204(d) (later repealed).

[7] Pub. L. No. 104-99, § 128, 110 Stat. 26.

[8] National Commission for the Protection of Human Subjects of Biomedical and Behavioral Research, *The Belmont Report: Ethical Principles and Guidelines for the Protection of Human Subjects of Research,* Bethesda, Maryland: Government Printing Office, 1978.

[9] *See* 45 C.F.R. § 46.101(b).

[10] *See* 45 C.F.R. § 46.101(b)(4).

[11] *See* 45 C.F.R. § 46.109(e).

[12] *See* OHRP Guidance on Continuing Review, July 11, 2002 (http://ohrp.osophs.dhhs.gov/humansubjects/guidance/contrev2002.htm).

[13] 18 Pa. Cons. Stat. Ann. §§ 3203, 3216.

[14] Mich. Comp. Laws Ann. § 333.2685.

[15] N.J. Stat. Ann. 26:2Z-2.

[16] N.J. Stat. Ann. 2C:11A-1.

[17] S. 303, 108th Congress.

[18] Ethics Committee of the American Society for Reproductive Medicine, "Donating Spare Embryos for Embryonic Stem Cell Research," *Fertility and Sterility* 78: 957-960 (2002).

[19] Ethics Committee of the American Society for Reproductive Medicine, "Informed Consent and the Use of Gametes and Embryos," *Fertility and Sterility* 68: 780-781 (1997).

[20] National Institutes of Health, Ad Hoc Group of Consultants to the Advisory Committee to the Director, *Report of the Human Embryo Research Panel*, September 1994, p. x.

[21] *Ibid.*, p. 80.

[22] *Ibid.*, p. 83.

6

Commerce

With advances and innovations in assisted reproduction, embryo research, and genetic screening and selection, there have arisen new markets for elements of these technologies and practices, including markets for gametes and embryos. Developments in patent law, meanwhile, have raised issues concerning the ownership of human genes, tissues, gametes, and embryos. These developments have significant implications for society's approach to reproductive biotechnologies, and for the formation of public and private attitudes about the ethical and social significance of these technologies and practices. They also have significant implications for the way we understand property in the human body more broadly.

This chapter discusses commerce involving (1) gametes and embryos (2) assisted reproductive technologies (ART) services and (3) the patenting of human organisms.

I. GAMETES AND EMBRYOS

A. Current Practices

There has long been a market for donated sperm in the United States.[1] According to one commentator, there are at present "thousands of sperm banks . . . in this country offering modest, yet significant remuneration."[2] In 2000, the average payment to sperm donors was between $60 and $70 per donation.[3] At the margins, there are individuals who aggressively market their sperm for thousands of dollars per vial, and Internet sperm brokers[4] such as ManNotIncluded.com, which offers baby-making kits to its customers.[5] In the early 1980s, multimillionaire Robert Graham established the "Repository for Germinal Choice," which offered infertile couples the opportunity to buy sperm donated by Nobel laureates.[*6]

Donated ova are generally procured by one of the following means: informally, from a close relative; indirectly, through a brokerage; or directly, from an individual or an ART clinic.[7]

In vitro fertilization (IVF) clinics, brokers, and infertile couples advertise for gamete donors.[8] The structures of the ensuing transactions vary. Typically donors are compensated for their time, efforts, and reasonable expenses, rather than for the gametes themselves. While there do not seem to be any definitive studies on the subject, it appears that the vast majority of donors provide gametes anonymously and without regard to specifically desired traits. There is, however, evidence of some noteworthy exceptions to this approach.

For example, some brokerages ("pooled brokerages") solicit a pool of potential donors, create individual profiles (including photographs, biographical data, information on physical characteristics, medical histories, etc.), and establish a database. One such brokerage, Egg Donation, Inc., seeks in a donor someone who is "bright and attractive, between the ages of 21 years to 30 years, of any ethnic background, preferably who has completed a college degree or is presently pursuing a college degree and is in excellent health."[9] Another brokerage, Tiny Treasures, specializes in Ivy League ovum donors. Its database includes photographs, SAT scores, grade-point averages, and compensation requests. Compensation for ovum donors from pooled brokerages varies. Egg Donation, Inc., advises potential donors that the donor fee "will range from $3,500 to $12,000." As to which variables drive cost, the website explains: "Asian and Jewish ovum donors are always in demand. A tall, attractive donor with a masters [sic] or doctor-

---

[*] The Repository closed its doors in 1998.

ate degree will always receive higher compensation than most other donors." Ivy League donors from Tiny Treasures seek anywhere from $8,000 to $20,000 compensation for a cycle of ova retrieval.

Pooled brokerages charge potential recipients a fee to browse their database of donors. Once a donor is selected, the brokerage begins the "matching process," which includes psychological screening, medical screening, and legal consultation. Thereafter, a contract is executed between the parties, and the process of stimulation and retrieval is initiated.

Some couples advertise directly for ovum donors. Many advertise in campus newspapers at prestigious colleges and universities. One such advertisement at Vassar College offered $25,000 in exchange for the ova of a "healthy, intelligent college student or college graduate, age 21-33 with blue eyes and blonde or light brown hair."[10] Another advertisement in the *Stanford Daily* offered $50,000.[11]

An alternative means of acquiring ova is through so-called "oocyte sharing," an arrangement by which women undergoing infertility treatment are given a price discount in exchange for agreeing to share their ova with other patients. According to the American Society for Reproductive Medicine (ASRM), few details are published on how these transactions are structured, but "[i]t seems that IVF patients in these sharing programs generally donate up to half the oocytes retrieved in a single cycle to another patient, in return for a 50%-60% reduction in the total costs of the IVF cycle."[12]

There does not seem to be a market in human embryos. There is no evidence that early extracorporeal embryos are bought or sold in the United States. As discussed in Chapter 2, individuals and couples may donate to researchers and to other infertile couples any "excess" embryos that remain after the completion of infertility treatment.

B. Ethical Considerations

Payments for human gametes raise several ethical concerns. Some argue that the commercialization of reproductive tissues might diminish respect for the human body and human procreation. By putting human reproductive tissue—the seeds of the next generation—up for sale in the marketplace, it is argued that we stand to introduce a commercial character into human reproduction, and to introduce commercial concerns into the coming-to-be of the next generation. If the essential materials of human procreation are regularly bought, sold, and esteemed in accordance with market valuations (and indeed valued differently based on the desirability of certain traits, as in ads in college newspapers that offer premium prices for donors with particular characteristics), the human meaning of bringing forward the next generation may be obscured or undermined.

Others see such concerns as misleading and unjustified. They argue that commerce in human gametes is no different from commerce in other meaningful activities of life (like paying one's doctor) or commerce in other articles of special significance (like a religious text or a wedding ring). They point out that the clinics and laboratories are making money from assisting reproduction, and they suggest that it is unfair that only the donor is excluded from financial benefit. They further argue that the ability to buy and sell gametes helps otherwise infertile couples to participate in the activities of human procreation and child-rearing.

Ovum sales raise additional ethical concerns. The process of retrieving ova is onerous and risky for donors. The high fees paid to ovum donors—who are often from financially vulnerable populations, such as full-time students—might create pressure to undergo these invasive procedures. For those undergoing infertility treatment themselves, incentive programs like oocyte sharing may reduce the probability of successful pregnancy, because such a program reduces the number of ova a donor has available for transfer during a given ART cycle. An additional concern is that a free market in ova could lead to discrimination and greater inequality. The 1994 National Institutes of Health (NIH) Human Embryo Research Panel speculated that an open market for ova would lead to a two-tiered system in which wealthy white ovum donors would receive high payments primarily from IVF patients, whereas poor minority women would receive substantially lower payments primarily from researchers.[13]

Finally, financial incentives for donation encourage individuals to become the biological parents—sometimes many times over—of children they will never know.* Alternatively, with the advent of laws providing children with the right to know their biological parentage, such donors may become involved in the lives of these children despite their wish to remain anonymous.

However, *not* compensating individuals for donating gametes raises still other ethical concerns. Financial incentives increase supply in other markets and are likely to do the same in the market for gametes for IVF. If there are no payments for gametes, some couples might remain childless because of an inadequate supply of eggs and sperm. Furthermore, given the sacrifice that is made by many gamete donors—especially ova donors—many argue that it would be unjust not to compensate them. Finally, some argue that a free market in gametes ultimately benefits all parties: those willing to provide their gametes get the compensation they desire, and those willing to pay for such gametes get the reproductive tissues they need to undergo assisted reproduction.

C. Regulation

There are now no federal laws directly regulating the sale of gametes. The National Organ Transplantation Act "makes it unlawful for any person to knowingly acquire, receive, or otherwise transfer any human organ for valuable consideration for use in human transplantation if the transfer affects interstate commerce."[14] While the term "organ" in this statute has been construed to include fetal organs, it has never been extended to include sperm, ova, or embryos. A number of states ban or otherwise restrict the sale of embryos.† Only Louisiana explicitly bans the sale of ova. Virginia, on the other hand, explicitly exempts ova from its prohibition on the sale of body parts. California bans the sale of ova for use in attempts at cloning-to-produce-children. Some states broadly prohibit or limit the

---

* This concern has been voiced for decades, prompted by the fact that, at least until recently, medical students were the primary source of sperm donation, sometimes with many children produced from a single sperm donor.

† See, for example, Florida, Illinois, Louisiana, Michigan, South Dakota, and Utah.

sale of organs or nonrenewable tissues, but it is an open question whether ova fall within the ambit of such prohibitions.*

ASRM has issued ethical guidelines for its members on financial incentives for oocyte donation. Following a discussion of the ethical considerations implicated in payment or oocyte-sharing programs, it concludes that these transactions are acceptable, subject to certain limitations. First, ASRM calculates a "reasonable" payment for oocyte donation by taking the average fee for sperm donation ($60 to $75 for one hour) and multiplying it by the number of hours spent in a medical setting during oocyte donation (fifty-six hours). Thus, ASRM concludes that the reasonable fee for an oocyte donor is $3,360 to $4,200. But because this calculus might not account for the more onerous nature of oocyte donation, ASRM concludes that "at this time sums of $5,000 or more require justification and sums above $10,000 go beyond what is appropriate."[15]

ASRM concludes that oocyte sharing is permissible provided that programs "formulate and disclose clear policies on how oocytes are allocated, especially if a low number of oocytes or oocytes of varying quality are produced." The Society advises that the reduction in fees resulting from oocyte donation should not be contingent on the number or quality of ova retrieved. Additionally, ASRM advises its members to adhere to certain guidelines: to ensure that there is a physician assigned to the oocyte donor (preferably not the fertility specialist for the ova recipient), to disclose policies regarding medical coverage for any complications experienced by the oocyte donor, to ensure that advertising is accurate and responsible, to avoid donors from recruiting agencies who have been paid exorbitant fees, and to limit the number of times a woman undergoes retrieval procedures "purely to provide oocytes to others."[16]

In a separate Practice Committee Report, ASRM advises its members to limit the number of stimulated cycles per oocyte donor to six, in light of health risks associated with the procedure. In the same document, ASRM advises its members to "strive to limit successful donations from a single donor to no

---

* Eggs, while they may be technically "nonrenewable" (since women are thought to be born with a finite number of them), could be said to be so numerous as to constitute renewable tissue.

more than 25 families per population of 800,000, given concerns regarding inadvertent consanguinity in offspring."[17]

II. SALE OF ART SERVICES

A. Current Practices

Assisted reproduction is a growing economic enterprise, with gross revenues of $4 billion per year, serving one in six infertile couples in the United States.[18] The costs of assisted reproduction services are variable, depending largely on the particular procedures undertaken. For example, at one prominent clinic, the cost of an initial consultation is $370, one IVF cycle using never-frozen embryos is $9,345 (while transfer of cryopreserved embryos is only $4,000 per transfer), preimplantation genetic diagnosis (PGD) (for sex selection or disease screening) is $4,000, and intracytoplasmic sperm injection (ICSI) (generally a prerequisite for PGD) is $2,000. Preconception sex selection (by sperm sorting) adds another $2,000. Most couples must undergo more than one cycle to achieve a successful result—the most recently reported percentage of live births per cycle (using never-frozen, nondonor embryos) was 27 percent.[19]

ART clinics advertise for business, emphasizing the range of procedures they offer to infertile couples.

Most infertility patients pay for ART services out-of-pocket, for reasons discussed below. To reduce their financial burdens, some clinics offer alternatives. One alternative, discussed above, is oocyte sharing. Another offered by some clinics is a "shared-risk" or "refund" program, in which infertile patients pay a higher fee, with the understanding that if they achieve an "ongoing pregnancy or delivery, the provider keeps the entire fee."[20] However, if the treatment fails, "90%-100% of the fee is returned."[21]

B. Ethical Considerations

The commercialization of ART services raises ethical concerns. Some of these are similar to those already raised in other contexts. Irresponsible clinicians may exploit the vulnerability and despair of the infertile with misleading advertisements and solicitations. As discussed in Chapter 2, commercial competition may induce IVF clinics to try to boost their success rates by adopting risky procedures (such as the transfer of an excessive number of embryos per cycle) or by selectively excluding certain types of patients (such as older patients or those whose chances of becoming pregnant are for other reasons low). Finally, given that infertility treatment is expensive and that in the United States insurance coverage for such services is rare, inequality becomes a real concern, with ART available only to those who can afford it. Many advocates for the infertile argue that the absence of insurance coverage for assisted reproduction is the single greatest problem facing such patients. They argue, for example, that the high costs to patients create incentives to transfer many embryos per cycle, leading to a greater incidence of multiple gestations.

Ethical questions may also be raised regarding ova sharing and shared-risk programs. Ova sharing might induce women who are providing the sharable supply of eggs to undergo risks in greater superovulation, in order to harvest as many ova as possible, or it may reduce a woman's ultimate chances for success, given that fewer ova are available for her own use. Ova sharing also causes individuals to become biological parents to children they will never meet. Shared-risk programs may promote unrealistic expectations for success. Such programs may induce clinicians to undertake unnecessary risks, or they may create a conflict of interest between doctor and patient.

Many see this range of concerns as unjustified or excessive. They argue that competition among clinics improves the quality of ART services, by making each clinic accountable in the marketplace. Some argue that the variety of treatment options—such as ova sharing and shared-risk programs—allow patients to choose which form of treatment and payment plan is best for them, and that normal informed consent procedures ensure against coercion and exploitation. To criticize irresponsible clinicians, they argue, is not to criticize the commercialization of assisted reproduction as such, but simply those who behave as irresponsible practitioners of medicine, who should be held accountable not through restrictions of commerce but enforceable standards for all ART practitioners. Some argue that the high cost of assisted reproduction is not a case against commerce as such, but rather a case for states to require insurance coverage of ART or for public subsidies for ART treatment. Finally, some argue that competition among ART clinics is the only way to control or reduce the cost of fertility treatment.

C. Current Regulation

Fourteen states now regulate insurance coverage of infertility treatment.* Some of these states mandate coverage of IVF, subject to certain conditions: for example, by requiring that the treatment be provided in conformity with guidelines of the American College of Obstetricians and Gynecologists and ASRM.[22] Certain states require coverage only of fertilization of a donor's own ova with her spouse's sperm.†

Although most states do not specifically mandate coverage of assisted reproduction services, an insurance company's failure to cover such services may in some cases be challenged by patients as a violation of the terms of their particular contract. For example, if the contract provides coverage for "illness" or "medically necessary procedures"—as most do—and does not specifically exclude infertility services, patients may argue that infertility falls into these categories and must be covered. Courts are divided on such questions. For example, in *Kinzie v. Physician's Liability Insurance Co.*, an Oklahoma appellate court held (as a matter of law) that IVF is not medically necessary but rather elective. In *Egert v. Connecticut General Life Insurance Co.*, the court rejected the defendant insurance company's claim that infertility is not an illness but rather the result of an illness, holding such a claim to be an improper construction of the insurance contract's provisions and the insurance company's internal guidelines. Some insurance companies have refused to cover IVF on the grounds that it is experimental, citing its less than 50 percent rate of success.[23]

---

* Arkansas, California, Connecticut, Hawaii, Illinois, Maryland, Massachusetts, Montana, New Jersey, New York, Ohio, Rhode Island, Texas, and West Virginia. (Source: ASRM website.)

† See, for example, Arkansas.

The Federal Trade Commission (FTC) has the authority to investigate deceptive claims in advertising by health care providers, including ART clinics, engaged in interstate commerce. It has jurisdiction, for example, to investigate claims of pregnancy success rates. FTC has the specific authority to investigate claims made in promotional materials, advertisements, contracts, consent forms, and other point-of-sale materials. To prove deception, FTC must show that there has been a "representation, omission, or practice that is likely to mislead the consumer" and that such deception is likely to affect the consumer's choice regarding the purchase of a service or product. For those clinics or individuals found to be engaged in deceptive advertising or unfair competition, FTC can impose civil penalties and cease-and-desist orders.[24*]

ASRM has issued guidelines on the subjects of advertising and shared-risk or refund programs. ASRM enumerates eight principles for advertising that should be followed by members: (1) advertising must comply with FTC guidelines; (2) claims must be supported by reliable data; (3) clinics should not rank or compare success rates; (4) advertisements should not unreasonably inflate expectations about success; (5) advertisements including references to outcomes may not selectively omit unfavorable data; (6) the method used to calculate success must be clear; (7) the Practice Director is ultimately responsible for all advertising content; and (8) when quoting statistics, the following statement must be included: "A comparison of clinic success rates may not be meaningful because pa-

* FTC has initiated disciplinary actions against fertility clinics for misrepresentation of reproductive service successes. For example, in October 1991 FTC charged Reproductive Genetics In Vitro, P.C., of Denver, Colorado, with making false and unsubstantiated claims about the success of its IVF program. The company claimed in its promotional brochure that women who make a single attempt at conception have a 25 percent chance of becoming pregnant and that the clinic's success rate was two-and-a-half times higher than the national average of 10 percent. FTC alleged that these claims were unsubstantiated and that the company was failing to disclose that it excluded from its success rate statistics those women who began the IVF program but did not become pregnant because they never reached the stage where a fertilized ovum was transferred into their uterus. The allegations were settled by consent agreement on January 15, 1992. In February 1992 FTC testified before Congress in favor of a success-rate formula that "takes into account all significant negative results."

tient medical characteristics and treatment approaches may vary from clinic to clinic."[25]

In a separate ethics opinion, ASRM sets forth the ethical concerns raised by "shared-risk" or "refund" programs, whereby patients pay a higher initial fee that is refunded if the treatment fails. Such concerns include the risks of exploitation, unreasonable expectations, overly aggressive and unsafe efforts to maximize chances for success, and conflict of interest. Following this discussion, ASRM concludes that shared-risk transactions may be ethically offered to patients lacking health insurance coverage for treatment, provided certain conditions are satisfied, namely, "that the criterion for success is clearly specified, that patients are fully informed of the financial costs and advantages and disadvantages of such programs, that informed consent materials clearly inform patients of their chances of success if found eligible for the shared risk program, and that the program is not guaranteeing pregnancy and delivery." Additionally, ASRM advises its members to clearly inform patients that "they will be paying a higher cost for IVF if they in fact succeed on the first or second cycle than if they had not chosen the shared risk program, and that, in any event, the costs of screening and drugs are not included." To prevent the danger that shared-risk programs may create incentives for clinicians to take actions that might harm patients in pursuit of success (and to avoid a refund), ASRM advises that patients be informed of the potential conflicts of interest. Moreover, such patients should not be given unusually high doses of hormones, and should be advised of the risks of multifetal gestation.[26] As with all other ASRM guidelines, these are suggestions rather than directives.

III. PATENTING HUMAN ORGANISMS

A. Current Practices

The Constitution confers upon Congress the authority to regulate patent rights: Article I, Section 8, provides in part that Congress shall have the power "To promote the Progress of Science and useful Arts, by securing for limited Times to Authors and Inventors the exclusive Right to their respective

Writings and Discoveries." Although the concept of patents (and intellectual property more generally) predates the Constitution, the patent is a form of property right expressly permitted by the Constitution.

A patent is an exclusive property right granted to an inventor for a limited time (currently, in most cases, twenty years from the filing date of the application). A patent grants an inventor the right to exclude all others from making, using, offering to sell or selling within, or importing into the United States the process or article that is the subject of the patent.[27] The holder of a patent has a right to bring an enforcement action in court against others who infringe the patent.[28] A patent is a right to exclude others, not necessarily a right to practice, make, or own the invention. A patent does not necessarily grant the inventor a right to the tangible product that results from the patented process. As a general matter, Congress may define and restrict what is patentable, and otherwise restrict patent rights by statute (for example, to promote national security[29]).

The Patent Act, which has changed little since it was authored by Thomas Jefferson and enacted in 1793, provides patent rights for three types of patents: plant patents, design patents, and utility patents. About 95 percent of all patents issued are utility patents.[30] A utility patent may be claimed by whoever "invents or discovers any new and useful process, machine, manufacture or composition of matter, or any new and useful improvement thereof."[31]

To receive a patent, an invention must be novel, nonobvious, and useful. A rich body of law, precedent, and agency practice defines these terms; but in general the bar for meeting them is not terribly high. Although traditionally, the inquiry into a proposed invention's "usefulness" might have considered the moral value of the invention, current U.S. patent practices do not take "morals" into account.

B. Ethical Considerations

To date, there have been patents issued on modified human tissues and cell lines, and DNA molecules of human origin. The future prospect of patenting human gametes and embryos is a source of much ethical disquiet. First, a patent creates a quasi property right, and the idea of one person or entity owning another—or part of another—raises deep worries. Second, patents imply a seal of state sanction, making it a matter of public concern which processes and products are made patentable; some question whether human organisms or human parts, modified or otherwise, ought to be among them. Finally, there is the practical concern that patents on genes and the like create a property right in a limited resource with wide utility, a resource that is arguably part of our common human heritage. Patents, in this way, erect a potential obstacle to the use of such resources for the benefits of many.

A powerful counterpoint to these claims, however, is that patents are a crucial mechanism to encourage the research and development of useful advances in biomedical science and biotechnology. By permitting researchers to protect the fruits of their labors for a limited time, patents give investors the incentive to commit resources to research and researchers the incentive to make discoveries that ultimately benefit the public by improving medicine and increasing the store of scientific knowledge. As Lincoln famously said, patents "add the fuel of interest to the fire of genius."

Yet a strong case can be made for drawing boundaries that limit patentability to parts of the human organism and that would exclude the developing human organism (embryos and fetuses) from the domain of patentable matter. It is one thing to have a property right in human cells or tissues; it is quite another to have a property right in a whole human organism, even at its earliest developmental stages.

C. Current Regulation

1. Patenting Living Things.

The foregoing analysis presupposes that the claimed invention consists of patentable subject matter. The test for determining this question is quite broad, with some limitations. The Supreme Court has relied on the assertion that the statutory subject matter for a patent includes "anything under the sun that is made by man."[32] The Court recognized that "laws of nature, physical phenomena, and abstract ideas" are not proper subject matter for patents.[33] For example, minerals found in the earth, plants found naturally occurring, and physical laws such as $E=mc^2$ are not patentable subject matter.[34] With respect, however, to those compositions of matter and manufactures that are not naturally occurring (but are made by man), the Court, interpreting the relevant existing patent laws, held that the nature of the subject—including whether or not the subject consists of a living organism—is irrelevant to the issue of patentability. These were statutory, not constitutional, interpretations. Congress, of course, retains its unquestioned authority to enact legislation that could exclude certain subject matter from patentability.

For about the first one hundred ninety years of its existence, the Patent and Trademark Office (PTO) declined to grant patents for inventions that were "products of nature," including living organisms.[*35] With a few possible exceptions, such as Pasteur's 1873 patent for a form of yeast, the "product of nature" doctrine prevailed. In 1980, the Supreme Court departed from the "rule of nature" doctrine in the landmark case, *Diamond v. Chakrabarty*. The applicant sought protection for a form of bacteria that had been genetically engineered to break down multiple components of crude oil, useful, for example, to clean up oil spills.[36] The patent examiner rejected the patent on two grounds: first, the bacterium was a "product of nature," and, second, as a living thing, the bacterium was not patentable. The PTO's Board of Appeals upheld the rejection on the basis that the bacterium was a living thing.[37]

The Supreme Court had to consider whether living organisms could constitute a "new and useful process, machine, manufacture, or composition of matter" within the meaning of the Patent Act. Reviewing the history of the Act and relevant case law, the Court embraced the notion that "anything under the sun that is made by man"—whether a chemical compound, a machine, a process, or a living organism—is proper subject matter for a patent.[38] The Court held that the nature of the subject matter for the patent—even if a living thing—was not a proper basis on which to deny an application. It concluded by noting that Congress was free to amend the law either to expressly exclude living organisms from coverage under the Act,

* The PTO did grant patents in 1967 and 1968 that covered microorganisms (*Chakrabarty*, 444 U.S. at 314, n.9).

or to add special provisions similar to those that exist for plants.

In 1988, the Court of Appeals for the Federal Circuit extended *Chakrabarty's* holding beyond microbial organisms to multicellular organisms (in this case, oysters), confirming that higher life forms may constitute "anything under the sun that is made by man" for purposes of patentability.[39] The PTO has adopted the position that "nonnaturally occurring, nonhuman multicellular living organisms, including animals, [are] patentable subject matter within the scope of 35 U.S.C. 101."[40] In 1988, the PTO issued the first patent granted on a higher animal, a transgenic mouse modified to be susceptible to cancer (the "Harvard Mouse").[41]

2. Patenting of Human Organisms.

Can a human organism at the embryonic, fetal, or any other stage be the subject of a patent? Until recently, the only express limitation on patents that cover human organisms was an interpretative ruling of PTO, which states that the agency will not grant a patent if "the broadest reasonable interpretation of the claimed invention encompasses a human being."[42]

It is not clear, however, what precisely the PTO meant by "human being." The PTO has issued at least one patent, US 6,211,429, which includes a "method for producing a cloned mammal" that also covers "the living, cloned products produced by each of the methods described." This patent lacks the "nonhuman" disclaimer that has previously been required for approval under the relevant provisions of the *Manual of Patent Examination Procedure*. While it is not clear how this broad patent squares with the PTO's policy of refusing to issue patents that "encompass a human being," a spokesman for the PTO has reiterated that this policy remains in force, and there will be no "patent claims drawn to humans."[43] A spokesman for the University of Missouri (the patent holder) has asserted that the University would not grant permission to use the patented process to clone a child.[44]

In 1997, a team of inventors sought to obtain a patent for an invention that covers the production of human-animal chimeras that could be up to (but not more than) 50 percent human.* Two years later, the PTO rejected the application, at one point during the process issuing a "media advisory" suggesting that a "morals" requirement still exists with respect to measurement of utility.[45] The PTO ultimately rejected the application on the grounds that a claimed invention that "encompasses a human being" is not patentable.[46] The then-Commissioner of the PTO, Bruce Lehman, declared: "There will be no patents on monsters, at least not while I'm commissioner." But the PTO did not explain why, given that the application sought to cover only those organisms that would be less than 50 percent human, the application "encompassed" a human being. The agency has given no guidance about whether there is a minimum threshold at which such a patent could be obtained (for example, organisms that are up to 10 percent human, or 5 percent human, or 1 percent human).

The only constitutional provision suggested to have any bearing on this question is the Thirteenth Amendment, which prohibits slavery and involuntary servitude; but it is possible this provision could be found by the courts to apply only to live-born humans, not human organisms at the embryonic or fetal stage.

Recently, Congress enacted a measure effectively prohibiting the issuance of patents on human organisms. The Consolidated Appropriations Act of 2004 provides, "None of the funds appropriated or otherwise made available under this Act may be used to issue patents on claims directed to or encompassing a human organism." [47] As further indication of the intended scope of this provision, the manager's statement for this amendment points to a June 22, 2003, colloquy wherein Rep. David Weldon (the amendment's sponsor) assured Rep. David Obey (the ranking minority member of the House Committee on Appropriations) that the amendment "would not interfere" with any existing patents on human genes or human stem cells. Weldon further noted that the purpose of the amendment

---

* See Magnani, T., *The Patentability of Human-Animal Chimeras,* 14 Berkley Tech. L. J. 443, 443 (1999). The inventors—Stuart Newman and Jeremy Rifkin—claim to have sought the patent for use in the purest form of a patent; that is, they stated that their intention was to prevent anyone from producing human-animal chimeras during the life of the patent, for the purpose of allowing greater policy discussions to occur before such creatures would be created.

was to affirm that "human life in any form should not be patentable." The Weldon Amendment thus proscribes the patenting of human organisms at any stage of development. It will remain effective for the duration of the relevant appropriations period, namely, for the fiscal year ending September 30, 2004. To continue in affect, it would have to be included in subsequent appropriations bills or be enacted as a freestanding, permanent law.

IV. CONCLUSION

Innovations in the reproductive biotechnologies and practices have given rise to new markets and opportunities for commercialization. There are currently no federal regulatory mechanisms that explicitly govern the sale of gametes. Very few states have laws that speak to this issue. There are voluntary professional standards that provide guidance relating to gamete-donor protections and financial incentives for gamete donation. The practice of assisted reproduction is subject to governmental regulations that relate to insurance coverage and truth in advertising. Professional societies have issued voluntary statements providing guidance on advertising and on various approaches to the payment for services. Finally, while patents have been issued for living organisms (and even for certain processes for creating human organisms), it is not now possible to patent a human organism itself at any stage, in light of the Weldon Amendment and the policy of the PTO.

ENDNOTES

[1] Alpers, A., et al., "Commodification and Commercialization in Human Embryo Research," *Stanford Law and Policy Review* 6: 39-45, 1995.

[2] Baum, K., "Golden Eggs: Towards the Rational Regulation of Oocyte Donation," *Brigham Young University Law Review* 107-166 (2001).

[3] Ethics Committee, American Society for Reproductive Medicine, "Financial Incentives in Recruitment of Oocyte Donors," *Fertility and Sterility* 74: 216-220 (2000).

[4] Andrews, L., "Changing Conceptions: Governance Challenges in the Engineering of Human Life," an unpublished draft paper, June 2003, cited with the author's permission.

[5] *See* www.mannotincluded.com (October 23, 2003).

[6] Plotz, D., "The 'Genius Babies,' and How They Grow," *Slate*, February 2, 2001, http://slate.msn.com/id/100331/ (accessed June 3, 2003).

[7] Baum, K., *op. cit.*

[8] Ethics Committee, ASRM, "Financial Incentives," *op. cit.*

[9] *See* http://www.eggdonor.com (February 26, 2004).

[10] Shanley, M., "Collaboration and Commodification in Assisted Procreation: Reflections on an Open Market and Anonymous Donation in Human Sperm and Eggs," *Law and Society Review* 36: 257-280 (2002).

[11] Healy, B., "Donors at Risk: The High Cost of Eggs," *U.S. News & World Report,* January 13, 2003, p. 44.

[12] Ethics Committee, ASRM, "Financial Incentives," *op. cit.*

[13] *Ibid.*

[14] 42 U.S.C. § 274e.

[15] Ethics Committee, ASRM, "Financial Incentives," *op. cit.*

[16] *Ibid.*

[17] American Society for Reproductive Medicine, Practice Committee Report, "Repetitive Oocyte Donation," November 2000, http://www.asrm.org/Media/Practice/oocyte_donation.pdf (accessed June 4, 2003).

[18] Andrews, L., "Changing Conceptions," *op. cit.*

[19] Centers for Disease Control and Prevention (CDC), *2001 Assisted Reproductive Technology Success Rates, National Summary and Fertility Clinic Reports*, Atlanta, Georgia: Government Printing Office, 2003, p. 17.

[20] Ethics Committee, American Society for Reproductive Medicine, "Shared-Risk or Refund Programs in Assisted Reproduction," http://www.asrm.org/Media/Ethics/shared.html (accessed May 16, 2003).

[21] *Ibid.*

[22] *See*, for example, Ark. Code Ann. §§ 23-85-137, 23-86-118.

[23] "In Vitro Fertilization: Insurance and Consumer Protection," *Harvard Law Review* 109: 2092-2109 (1996).

[24] *See* generally 15 U.S.C. § 45.

[25] American Society for Reproductive Medicine, Practice Committee Report, "Guidelines for Advertising by ART Programs," October 1999, http://www.asrm.org/Media/Practice/ArtAdvertising.pdf (accessed June 4, 2003).

[26] Ethics Committee, ASRM, "Shared-Risk," *op. cit.*

[27] 35 U.S.C. § 271(a).

[28] 35 U.S.C. § 281 et seq.

[29] *See*, for example, 42 U.S.C. § 2181(a).

[30] *R.R. Donnelly & Sons, Co. v. U.S.*, 40 Fed. Cl. 277, 279 n.6 (Ct. Fed. Cl. 1998).

[31] 35 U.S.C. § 101.

[32] *Diamond v. Chakrabarty*, 447 U.S. 303, 309 (1980) (quoting legislative history).

[33] *Ibid.*

[34] *Ibid.*

[35] *See*, for example, *Funk Bros. Co. v. Kalo Innoculant Co.*, 333 U.S. 127, 130-131 (1948).

[36] *See Chakrabarty*, *op. cit.*, at 305.

[37] *Ibid.*, at 305-306.

[38] *Ibid.*, at 309-311.

[39] *In re* Allen, 846 F. 2d 77 (Fed. Cir. 1988).

[40] U.S. Patent and Trademark Organization, *Manual of Patent Examination Procedure,* section 2105.

[41] 55 BNA Patent, Trademark & Copyright J. 1371 (April 9, 1998).

[42] *Manual of Patent Examination Procedure*, § 2105 (eighth ed., 2001).

[43] Gillis, J., "A New Call for Cloning Policy; Group Says Patent Would Apply to Human Embryos," *Washington Post*, May 17, 2002, p. A12.

[44] *Ibid.*

[45] 55 BNA Patent, Trademark and Copyright J. 1371 (April 9, 1998).

[46] 58 BNA Patent, Trademark and Copyright J. 1430 (June 17, 1999).

[47] Pub. L. No. 108-199, 118 Stat. 3.

7

Diagnostic Survey: Summary and Conclusion

I. SUMMARY

Chapters 2 through 6 describe in some detail the current regulatory activities governing the uses of biotechnologies that touch on human reproduction; this diagnostic survey reveals that the present constellation of regulatory mechanisms is broad but not uniform or systematic in its objectives, scope, or enforcement.

The practice of assisted reproduction is subject to oversight by a host of sources, governmental and nongovernmental. Governmental regulation is motivated by concerns for consumer protection, quality assurance in laboratory procedures, safety and efficacy of products according to their intended use, and the delivery of medical care according to accepted standards of practice. Nongovernmental oversight is aimed primarily at ensuring the satisfaction and privacy of those who seek assisted reproductive technology (ART) services. These standards, while extensive, are hortatory rather than compulsory. What seem to be missing from both governmental and nongovernmental regulations, individually or in the aggregate, are meaningful, enforceable rules directly aimed at safeguarding the health and well-being of the children who come to be born via ART.* Moreover, there do not seem to be significant oversight activities or effective guidelines that address larger ethical concerns relating to the enhanced control over human procreation. Finally, the system of regulation currently in place does not reflect the concerns many people have about the use and destruction of human embryos attendant on the practice of assisted reproduction.

New capacities to screen and select for specific genetic traits and characteristics are not regulated *as such* through governmental institutions. Insofar as they are regulated, they are governed by state, local, or institution-based standards for the practice of medicine or the conduct of embryo research. There do not seem to be any governmental authorities or regulatory efforts to comprehensively monitor the uses, applications, or long-term health effects of preimplantation genetic diagnosis (PGD) on children born after its use. And there is no public oversight or public guidelines with respect to the broader social and ethical implications of enhancing control of the genetic characteristics of children. At the nongovernmental level, there are guidelines that "strongly discourage" the use of PGD for elective sex selection, but these guidelines are not binding and, in fact, are not (at least as of this writing) followed by all of the prominent practitioners of assisted reproduction. There are also no guidelines regarding the permissibility of crossing the boundary between using PGD for producing a disease-free child and using it for so-called enhancement purposes or to produce siblings for children needing transplant donors.

The ability to genetically modify gametes or human embryos, today a merely speculative reproductive possibility, would likely be regulated under the existing federal guidelines for gene-transfer research. Current regulations in this regard include stringent protections for human subjects and rigorous standards requiring practitioners to demonstrate and document the safety and efficacy of such gene-transfer procedures. Moreover, most (if not all) such research is subject to federal

* It bears noting that extant safeguards relating to quality assurance, safety, and efficacy of products, etc., do bear indirectly on the health and safety of children born with the aid of ART.

guidelines that require submission of prospective research protocols to a body that publicly discusses the ethical implications of projects raising novel or important issues. Officially, it is the safety of the participants in such research that drives the federal regulation of genetic modification, but these regulations seem also to be informed by a regard for as-yet-unconceived future generations who may be affected (unintentionally) by such germ-line genetic modification. That being said, there is no positive authority that empowers the federal government to consider the safety of such future individuals. The absence of such authority might prove to be an obstacle to meaningful regulation of germ-line gene-transfer, should it ever be undertaken. At present, however, deliberate germ-line modification is not now being pursued in humans, due to concerns for safety and efficacy.

The use of in vitro human embryos for purposes of scientific research is not regulated by the federal government. The federal government neither promotes nor prohibits such research.* Regulation in the individual states varies widely, ranging from active endorsement to silent permission to strict prohibition. There is thus no uniformity in governmental regulation of embryo research. The nongovernmental regulation of this practice takes the form of ethical opinions and practice guidelines issued by professional societies. Subject to certain limitations discussed in Chapter 5, these authorities, in the main, endorse and promote such research based on their view that the embryo's moral status permits its use and destruction for certain scientific ends.

Commerce in gametes, embryos, and assisted reproductive services is subject to only a small degree of regulation. There is very little controlling law respecting the sale of gametes or embryos. Professional societies provide detailed yet merely hortatory guidelines regarding financial incentives and donor protections. The practice of assisted reproduction itself is subject to external regulation for purposes of consumer protection,

* One exception to this neutrality is the federal funding for research involving a limited number of embryonic stem cell lines derived before August 9, 2001. See the Council's report, *Monitoring Stem Cell Research*, especially Chapter 2. (The President's Council on Bioethics, *Monitoring Stem Cell Research*, Washington, D.C.: Government Printing Office, 2004, available at www.bioethics.gov.)

particularly with regard to truth in advertising and reporting the rates of success. Some states have laws concerning the provision of insurance coverage for assisted reproductive services, but the scope and substance of these laws vary widely. Professional societies offer some guidance as to how to structure compensation and some standards for truth in advertising. Regarding intellectual property protections, the recently enacted Weldon Amendment (along with the U.S. Patent and Trademark Office's policy) precludes the issuance of a patent directed to human organisms at any stage of development. The Weldon Amendment expires at the end of fiscal year 2004 and would have to be reauthorized if it is to have continuing effect.

II. CONCLUSION

Taken as a whole, the present system of regulation advances a number of goods and values. It allows for the robust and innovative practice of medicine, permitting physicians wide latitude to employ novel approaches in their efforts to help patients overcome infertility and experience the joys of parenthood. It promotes the safety and efficacy of products for their intended uses and provides an extensive system of protections for human subjects participating in clinical trials. Scientists are generally permitted (though not generally federally funded) to pursue most research relating to assisted reproduction or involving harm to human embryos. In many cases, scientists can secure patents to protect the fruits of their labors. The present system accords prospective parents a great deal of freedom to choose among a variety of approaches to assisted reproduction; it similarly confers upon them maximum freedom to make choices on behalf of their future children. Finally, present governance of commerce growing out of reproductive biotechnologies is largely left to the market, with all the attendant benefits of free enterprise and the freedom to contract.

The weaknesses of the present system in some ways grow out of its strengths. Practitioners and parents have such wide latitude to pursue the benefits of the new reproductive biotechnologies precisely because there are no governmental authorities or professional bodies formally charged with ensuring the well-being of children conceived and born with the aid of assisted reproduction. Tort liability for harm to children in this context is a crude (and, for the harmed children, necessarily after-the-fact) substitute for formal and effective guidelines. As with their treatment in other branches of medicine, protecting the interests of children is primarily the responsibility of parents. As we have seen, however, there are compelling reasons to believe that assisted reproduction—especially in light of new and emerging genetic technologies—raises unique ethical concerns and perhaps deserves more careful social oversight. No governmental bodies are today responsible for monitoring or assessing the broader ethical implications of the new reproductive biotechnologies, nor are there clear and accepted boundaries that would protect human procreation from possibly unwelcome innovations and degrading practices. Scientists in many states enjoy largely unlimited freedom regarding what they can and cannot do with human embryos in research because the current system of federal regulation is silent, neither promoting such research nor prohibiting it. Finally, as to commerce, the present regulatory system lacks a uniform approach to questions of access to reproductive services, and it sets no uniform, enforceable limits on the buying and selling of human gametes and embryos.

8

Findings

In this chapter, we enumerate the key findings growing out of our survey and analysis of the current regulation of biotechnologies that touch on human reproduction. Clearly, many human goods are well served by the current regulatory arrangements. Yet other goods are unmonitored or unprotected and may require further attention. Each of the findings listed below has been identified by a significant number of Council members as a matter of concern or at any rate worthy of note. The listing of findings here is not intended to imply that anything in particular, or indeed anything at all, is required by way of public policy response.

I. DOMAIN OF INQUIRY

The fields of assisted reproduction, human genetics, and embryo research are increasingly converging with one another. The integration of genomic knowledge with the practices of assisted reproduction is no longer speculative. Techniques and practices such as preimplantation genetic diagnosis (PGD) are already enhancing our control over human procreation, making it possible to screen and select specific genetic characteristics of our offspring.

II. GENERAL CONCLUSIONS

There is no uniform, comprehensive, and enforceable system of data collection, monitoring, or oversight for the biotechnologies affecting human reproduction. The present system is a patchwork of federal, state, and professional self-regulation.

A. Assisted Reproduction

1. Institutional Governance.

a. Governmental oversight. **There is minimal direct governmental regulation of the practice of assisted reproduction.** The primary animating values of current federal regulation are (1) consumer protection and (2) safety and efficacy of products when employed for their intended use. In the main, assisted reproductive technologies (ARTs) are regulated as the practice of medicine—with licensure, certification, professional oversight, and malpractice litigation as the chief means of regulation. Under this system, the children who will be born with the aid of these technologies are not technically considered patients, and parents are left solely responsible for safeguarding the interests of their children (though of course ART practitioners aim to help parents conceive healthy children). On the federal level, the Centers for Disease Control (CDC), acting pursuant to the Fertility Clinic Success Rate and Certification Act, collects and publishes some data on the practice of assisted reproduction at clinics in the United States; most of this information relates to the clinics' per-cycle success rates of initiating pregnancies and achieving live births. The CDC also provides a model certification program for embryo laboratories, although to date no states have adopted it. The federal Food and Drug Administration (FDA) regulates some of the products used in the practice of assisted reproduction, although this oversight is limited to insuring the safety and efficacy of a product in its intended use. Several experimental ARTs (for example, ICSI [intracytoplasmic sperm injection] and PGD) have entered clinical practice with limited prior testing and limited monitoring of their effects on the children produced with their aid. At the same time, there is at least one instance of the FDA asserting its authority to stop an experimental new technique (ooplasm transfer), the safety of which, for the resulting child, had been called into question. But the legal justification for doing so was not the protection of the child, as such, since the FDA has no explicit legal authority to regulate on such grounds.

b. Professional oversight. **There is extensive professional self-regulation of the practice of assisted reproduction, but compliance with the standards invoked is purely voluntary.** The animating ethical values of current professional self-regulation are safety, efficacy, and privacy for the individuals seeking infertility services. The standards are merely advisory, with no meaningful enforcement mechanisms. The professional societies do address some broader ethical issues—such as the permissibility of elective sex selection and cloning-to- produce-children—and recommend limiting or not engaging in certain practices. But these recommendations are also merely advisory.

2. Substantive Areas of Concern.

a. The well-being of children, egg donors, and gestational mothers. **There is no comprehensive, uniform, and enforceable mechanism for data collection, monitoring, or oversight of how the new reproductive biotechnologies affect the well-being of the children conceived with their aid, the egg donors, or the gestational mothers.** There is no definitive understanding of how ART or its adjuncts affect the well-being of children born with their aid. Some studies suggest that most children are normal and healthy; others raise serious concerns. No longitudinal controlled study has yet been undertaken to follow the long-term health and development of children born with the aid of ART. Multifetal gestations are significantly more common in pregnancies initiated with the help of ARTs as currently practiced; such pregnancies are associated with a higher incidence of serious health problems for both mothers and children. Yet there are at present no requirements to publish adverse health effects from the use of ARTs or their adjuncts.

b. Access to services and consumer protection. **There are no nationally uniform laws or policies relating to access to assisted reproduction.** State law relating to insurance coverage of ART services varies greatly; fourteen states have laws speaking to the question, the rest do not.* The federal Fertility Clinic Success Rate and Certification Act does not require the reporting of the average price (to the patient) of a successful assisted pregnancy.

c. Movement of techniques and practices from experimental to clinical use. **Given the present framework of regulation, novel technologies and practices that are successful move from the experimental context to clinical practice with relatively little oversight or deliberation. Once in practice, these techniques are used at clinicians' discretion, with little or no external oversight. Use of effective technologies becomes widespread rapidly.** Two examples: (1) ICSI was discovered by accident in 1992. Two years later it was in clinical practice. In 2001, ICSI was used in 49 percent of in vitro fertilization (IVF) treatment cycles. (2) PGD was developed in 1989. Since then, an unknown number of children have been born after undergoing PGD (estimates range between less than 1,000 and 10,000). Yet there have been no longitudinal studies of the effects of PGD on these children. Current professional guidelines dictate only that there be two peer-reviewed papers showing an acceptable risk-benefit ratio before the status of a new practice is elevated from "experimental" to "clinically acceptable." There is no system for reporting the reasons for using ICSI, PGD, and similar technologies. Nor is there any system for publishing and disseminating information regarding possible adverse effects.

---

* One published study concluded that in states where IVF is covered by insurance, there are associated "decreases in the number of embryos transferred per cycle, the percentages of cycles resulting in pregnancy, and the percentage of pregnancies with three or more fetuses." Jain, T., et al., "Insurance Coverage and Outcomes of In Vitro Fertilization," *New England Journal of Medicine* 347(9): 661 (August 29, 2002).

d. Public discussion and deliberation regarding the ethical significance of new technologies and practices. **In ART, as in other areas of medicine, there is no uniform system for public review and deliberation regarding the larger human or social significance of new reproductive technologies.** Practices combining assisted reproduction with genomic knowledge have come into clinical usage with little or no deliberation about their human, social, or ethical implications. Such practices include using PGD to screen and select genetic traits unrelated to the health of the child who is to be born—such as elective sex selection or compatibility with an older sibling in need of tissue donation. As genomic knowledge increases, the range of non-disease-related genetic traits for which PGD is feasible will potentially expand. There is today no system for data collection on the uses and applications of these or similar technologies.

B. Preimplantation Genetic Diagnosis

PGD is an unregulated practice. There is no system of data collection, monitoring, or oversight for preimplantation genetic diagnosis per se, and no system for reporting of possible adverse effects on children conceived following the use of PGD. Nor is there a mechanism for the collection of data regarding the frequency of specific applications of PGD (for example, screening for disease, for non-disease-related traits, or for the creation of compatible tissue donors).

C. Gene Transfer Research

Gene transfer research is regulated robustly. The federal government regulates gene-transfer research in regard to safety, efficacy, and protection of human subjects. Moreover, there exists a long-standing system for public discussion regarding novel protocols (through the Recombinant DNA Advisory Committee of the National Institutes of Health (NIH), commonly known as the RAC). But it is unclear whether this supervisory system would suffice to encompass safeguards for the health and well-being of children who might be conceived or born using gene-transfer techniques. This is, at present, a remote question, because the relevant techniques are for now entirely speculative.

D. Use and Disposition of Human Embryos in Research

There is no comprehensive, uniform, and enforceable mechanism for data collection, monitoring, or oversight regarding the use and disposition of in vitro human embryos in the context of clinical practice or research. A credible, recent estimate suggests that there are 400,000 embryos in cryopreservation in the United States. There are no federal limits or regulations governing what one can do to or with an ex vivo human embryo, so long as one is privately funded and so long as the embryos are acquired in a legal manner. There is no uniform guidance regarding the disposition of such frozen embryos, once their progenitors no longer want them. There are no federal limits on the creation of embryos solely for research, the creation of cloned or hybrid embryos, the implantation of human embryos into the bodies of animals, or the creation of embryos using fetal gametes or gametes derived from embryonic stem cells. Meanwhile, no federal funds may be used for research that involves the destruction of human embryos, but the law has been construed to permit federal funding of research on a limited number of human embryonic stem cell lines. Many in the research community believe that the current restrictions on funding of embryo–derived stem cell research create a chilling effect on embryo research generally.

E. Commerce

There is no comprehensive mechanism for regulation of commerce in gametes, embryos, and ART services. Professional guidelines exist that attempt to place limits on commerce in human reproductive tissue and human embryos, primarily in order to safeguard the health of women and the dignity of gamete donors, but these guidelines are unenforced. Regarding the sale of ART services generally, there are overall federal guidelines relating to truth in advertising, and professional societies have propounded guidelines on this matter as well.

Patenting of embryonic or fetal human organisms is prohibited for the fiscal year 2004. The Weldon Amendment to the Consolidated Appropriations Act of 2004 provides that no funds shall be made available "to issue patents on claims directed to or encompassing a human organism." Until October 1, 2004, no patents may be issued on human organisms at any stage of development. Congress may continue this policy, or not, as it sees fit. Additionally, it has for many years been the policy of the Patent and Trademark Office not to issue patents directed to or encompassing "human beings."

PART II

9

Policy Options

The findings drawn from our survey of the status quo, as presented in Chapter 8, suggest that a number of serious concerns may accompany the present and future uses of reproductive and genetic biotechnologies, and that there are potential deficiencies in our national system of monitoring, oversight, and regulation. But shortcomings in the present arrangement do not, in and of themselves, mean that new policies are called for. Any new form of regulation would surely come with costs, and in assessing prospective policies it is important to weigh their potential costs as well as their benefits; we must be sure that changes to the present system are not worse than doing nothing.

The appeal of doing nothing in this arena is, frankly, rather great, not only because the costs of regulation may be high (and, in their full proportions, incalculable in advance) but also because the areas of assisted reproduction, new genomic knowledge, and embryo research are socially and politically quite sensitive. Some prospective policies might touch on highly private matters of procreation, family life, and infertility, and we Americans are loath to intrude in these areas, even if our aim is to help and to protect those involved. Some potential policies may also involve questions of the character and status of human embryos—a crucial but highly charged subject in our politics. Parties on all sides have strong convictions to defend that reach well beyond the uses of reproductive biotechnologies; the ongoing national debate and struggle over abortion are never far from the surface in any discussion of reproduction and responsibility. Anyone contemplating new regulation in this field must acknowledge that there is no easy avenue to clear-cut policies or comfortable compromises, and perhaps that is as it should be.

But if action, any action, in this field has its financial, social, and political costs, inaction could surely prove costly as well. The most obvious costs of leaving the status quo untouched are reflected in the findings that have emerged from our survey of the field. These problems are real, and they demand serious public deliberation if not also improved public monitoring, oversight, or regulation.

Moreover, recognizing these problems, and detailing them as we have, places a burden upon us. While much remains unknown about the present state of technologies affecting human reproduction, we can no longer claim to lack a sense of the circumstances surrounding their use. We have a good grasp of the various concerns that might arise in these areas, and we have a sense of what sorts of benefits and difficulties will emerge as assisted reproductive technology (ART) becomes more integrated with the new genomic knowledge and technologies. We also have a reasonably well-developed understanding of what sorts of information we now lack. Having put together this picture of the status quo, we cannot now recommend that nothing further needs to be done without, in effect, declaring that the status quo is in all respects better than any realistic alternative.

The issues raised and the concerns described in our survey of the field make it difficult for us to make such a declaration; and it would be premature to allow the difficulties that might accompany new policies to foreclose any further discussion of regulatory or institutional change. At the same time, *we are in no position at this stage of our inquiry to offer any comprehensive suggestions regarding what, if anything, should be done regarding this field as a whole*. Before any such suggestions could be made, extensive further investigation and consultation would be needed. Further testimony and advice would need to be sought from the various identifiable stakeholders—

including research scientists and biotechnologists, ART practitioners and their professional societies, disease and disability organizations and advocates, religious organizations, bioethics and "watchdog" organizations, and the various governmental institutions already charged with some regulatory responsibility in this field—as well as from ordinary citizens. We would also need to carry out a thorough exploration of what could be done *within* the existing regulatory framework, limited though it may at present be. To offer suggestions that would be of genuine practical value, due attention would also have to be paid to the constraints imposed on any new policy by the special features of American political and economic life, medical and research practices, personal privacy protections, and the realities of public attitudes and domestic political struggles. To do this properly would take at least several years.

In the absence of such a thoroughgoing inquiry, we can however present in outline certain *institutional options* that might be considered for the field as a whole, indicating in general terms some of their strengths and weaknesses. And, more modestly, we can revisit some of the findings of our diagnostic assessment in order to consider certain *specific policy options* that might command some attention, even as people try to think through the desirability and feasibility of more thorough institutional changes. The remainder of this chapter takes up these matters in turn. *In each case, we are merely laying out the alternatives. We are not here endorsing any one of them.*

I. INSTITUTIONAL OPTIONS

What, then, might be done institutionally regarding this field as a whole? We begin by briefly offering a sense of what *sorts* of policy may be available to us. There is certainly something counter-intuitive about discussing institutional arrangements in the abstract without first articulating the substantive principles that should guide their design and operation. But it is nonetheless useful to approach the subject with a rough sense of the contents of our toolbox, so as to better organize our thinking about which particular substantive options are feasible. The actual design of oversight and regulatory mechanisms must of course begin from the substantive aims motivating the policy; but because such design is not our purpose at this stage, review of possibilities may usefully begin at the more general level of institutional forms.

It is worth emphasizing that we take a broad view of the meaning of the term "regulation." In employing that term, we do not refer merely to restrictions or enforced prohibitions, but to a broad range of potential actions that might be undertaken to encourage, facilitate, protect, oversee, restrain, or restrict a given activity. A government's regulatory stance may range from promoting (through funding), to permitting without restriction, to tolerating or permitting within enforceable limits, to discouraging (by withholding funding), to prohibiting. And particular regulatory policies may range from information-gathering and reporting, to monitoring, to oversight, to setting hortatory guidelines, to providing rules and regulations with penalties for violation, among others. An analogous range of regulatory stances and policy options (with some differences) is open also to professional societies and institutional ethics committees.

The array of national-level policy options that present themselves, and that have been examined by observers and critics in the past, may be divided roughly into five categories of potential institutional change: (1) a new regulatory agency; (2) new authority granted to existing regulatory agencies; (3) specific legislative action; (4) the use of government funding as a regulatory lever; and (5) increased oversight and self-regulation by the relevant professional societies. Let us briefly describe each of these in institutional terms, highlighting also what might be said for or against each alternative.

A. A New Regulatory Agency

One possibility, suggested by a number of observers and evident in the policies of several foreign countries, is the creation of a new administrative agency of the executive branch that would be authorized to monitor and administer the uses of biotechnologies discussed in this report. Such an agency would be charged by Congress with a number of specific tasks but would be also given some leeway in applying its mandate to particular circumstances that might arise. Its creation would therefore involve some delegation of regulatory authority. This, for instance, is the idea behind the Human Fertilization and Embryology Authority (HFEA) in Britain and the Assisted Human Reproduction Agency (AHRA) in Canada.

The logic of this approach is fairly straightforward: by creating a body whose business it is to oversee this arena of research and practice, we might ensure that the problems that worry us are at least noticed and at best addressed with appropriate policies. Many issues involved in assisted reproduction, genetic testing and screening, embryo research, and related fields are new and unprecedented, and they do not fall naturally into the purview of any existing government body or agency. Existing agencies, like the federal Food and Drug Administration (FDA), the National Institutes of Health (NIH), the Centers for Disease Control (CDC), to name just the most prominent ones, were designed and have evolved to serve different purposes, and authorizing them to oversee this field might not adequately address the important concerns that have emerged from our review of the present state of affairs.

Such a new agency would be granted some degree of latitude in making judgments in particular cases, so that each controversy in this emerging field would not turn into a legislative question requiring prolonged congressional debate.*

A new agency dedicated exclusively to monitoring or regulating this arena might ensure that all the relevant concerns are addressed. But the costs of such an agency, financial and otherwise, could be quite high. It would be very difficult for an institution along the lines of the British HFEA to function in the American system, since our approaches to embryology and human genetics, the practice of medicine, the financing of health care, private enterprise, reproductive freedoms, government regulation, and scientific progress are different from those of the British.

The potential wisdom or utility of such an agency would have to be judged in light of the tasks it would need to carry

* Erik Parens and Lori P. Knowles advocate the creation of a standing federal entity to "facilitate reasoned and systematic public and policy deliberation about the purposes of reprogenetic research and practice." This board would "resemble Britain's Human Fertilization and Embryology Authority." (Parens, E., et al., "Reprogenetics and Public Policy: Reflections and Recommendations," *Hastings Center Report*, July-August: S1-S24 [2003].)

out. In purely institutional terms, designing and establishing it would be a complex undertaking. It therefore marks the most ambitious of the potential institutional options before us.

B. Augmentation of Existing Agencies

Rather than establish a new agency, Congress might expand the scope and jurisdiction of one or more existing federal agencies to authorize them to exercise oversight over this field.

A number of potential candidates present themselves. The FDA, as discussed in our overview of the status quo, already exercises some limited oversight over certain elements of reproductive biotechnology, and its reach in this arena might reasonably be extended somewhat. In addition, the NIH, along with several of its subsidiary institutions (for example, the Recombinant DNA Advisory Committee, or RAC), might also be given some authority to monitor or even to regulate specific areas of research and, to a limited extent, of clinical applications. The CDC is already charged by statute with the task of gathering and publishing data on assisted reproductive technologies, and its authority in this regard, as well as other related ones, could be increased.

It may in principle be possible to delegate all or nearly all of the regulatory and oversight authority deemed appropriate in this field to one of these (or other) federal agencies. Alternatively, such authority might be divided among several existing agencies.

There would be several advantages to delegating any new authority to existing institutions. For one thing, it would circumvent the need to create a new federal regulatory body—a difficult and costly undertaking, with uncertain prospects of success and potential unintended consequences if it were to be established. A delegation of authority to an existing agency could probably be put into effect more quickly, as the basic mechanisms for oversight and enforcement would likely already exist, and the institutional resources for action would not need to be created from scratch. In addition, the authority could be delegated by integrating the new areas of oversight and regulation into existing patterns of regulatory activity, rather than, again, by beginning with a blank slate.

On the other hand, the delegation of oversight authority over reproductive biotechnologies to an existing federal agency would mean that no institution would have this arena as its prime or exclusive portfolio, and hence that the questions and concerns we have raised would not be anyone's principal business. In addition, the structure, authority, experience, and expertise of existing federal agencies might not be quite suitable for regulating in this area. Each existing federal agency was created, and has evolved, to oversee a particular sort of activity, and the issues that concern us may not be a good match with any of them. The questions before us do not, for the most part, involve food or drugs, the control of disease, or the funding of scientific research, for instance. While they touch on these subjects, these questions should not be understood primarily through lenses developed for viewing other problems. There is also the further difficulty, intrinsic to all attempts at regulation, that the regulators may be co-opted by the interests they seek to regulate.

If Congress deems it necessary to delegate some new regulatory authority over the technologies we have discussed, the choice between delegating such power to a new federal agency or to an existing agency or agencies should come down to the question of whether this arena of technology and activity raises (or is likely to raise) fundamentally new and different sorts of questions and challenges from those that have been dealt with by existing federal agencies in the past. This is a complex question that certainly cannot be answered in the abstract; rather, it must be considered with regard to each particular target of potential oversight and regulation.

C. Particular Legislative Action

The two previous options assume some degree of delegation of authority by Congress for the regulation of these technologies in particular instances. Congress, however, may also decide to address particular issues directly and specifically through legislation. Acts of Congress are necessarily broader and blunter instruments than the particular case-by-case decisions of a regulatory agency, but they can also speak with greater force and authority in the public eye.

Of course, the delegation of power to a regulatory agency would itself be an act of Congress, but what we have in mind in this category of potential institutional change is the passage of laws that lay down distinct and precise rules that do not require a great deal of complex regulation, or much case-by-case judgment to enforce them. The issues would be dealt with legislatively rather than administratively. Such policies could involve limitations or prohibitions, but they might also involve means of support for certain technologies and practices, or offers of funding that might be made available through existing funding agencies.*

Several advantages may be gained by proceeding through acts of Congress, rather than delegating judgment to an administrative agency. Such a process would be more democratic and more directly answerable to public wishes and concerns.

However, proceeding by acts of Congress would also limit the potential flexibility of oversight and legislation in this arena. It would make cast-iron prohibitions more likely and case-by-case judgment more difficult. It would also, of course, be slow and arduous, as past and present efforts to legislate policy regarding human cloning, genetic discrimination, and embryo research have already demonstrated. It may well be the appropriate means to achieve some potentially desirable reforms, but its limitations are apparent.

D. Federal Funding as a Regulatory Lever

A fourth institutional means for regulation involves the use of federal funding to encourage desirable practices and (by withholding funding) to discourage troubling ones. Federal funding can also be used as a more nuanced regulatory mechanism, since Congress can attach requirements to funding and compel all recipients to abide by certain rules. Indeed, this is an important way in which scientific research is currently regulated by the federal government. Researchers who receive federal funds, or whose institutions do, are required to abide by certain basic guidelines regarding clinical standards, human subject protections, the need to obtain informed consent, and other issues. Many people, including some members

---

* Regulatory possibilities tied to the awarding of federal funding are discussed in the next section of this chapter.

of this Council,* believe that the current paucity of oversight in this field is owed mainly to the absence of federal funding of in vitro fertilization (IVF) research, and that it is only through federal funding that the public can gain some control over this sensitive area of biotechnology.

The question of funding is, however, quite complex and controversial. By offering funding for a practice, the government at least implicitly expresses a public endorsement, in effect pronouncing the practice worthy of a share of taxpayer money. This becomes a problem when the work in question is controversial, or when it is deemed unethical or otherwise unacceptable by some significant portion of the public. Those who oppose the practice neither want their own tax money used to support it nor wish to have their government express approval of it. It is largely for this reason that much of the work in the fields taken up in this report has never been supported with federal funds.†

Of course, to refrain from offering funds is also a kind of policy decision, and certainly an act of Congress that expressly forbids federal funding of specific practices (as is the case with embryo research, for instance) is an explicit policy and a form of regulation.

Moreover, institutions that receive federal funds may sometimes be required to submit to government regulations even in their privately funded activities, so that the government can still reach and regulate those activities it does not fund directly. In such cases the costs of compliance to recipient institutions can be huge.

Federal funds, in one way or another, may therefore be used as a means of encouraging or opposing certain practices that are deemed to require government supervision. At the same time, there is no necessary relationship between regulation and direct funding: the government can and does regulate activities it does not fund.

---

* See, generally, the comments of Dr. Janet Rowley during session 2 of the January 15, 2004, meeting of the Council, available at www.bioethics.gov.

† This "failure to fund" was the issue that triggered public debate about embryonic stem cell research, a matter we have reviewed at length in our report on *Monitoring Stem Cell Research*.

E. Increased Oversight and Self-Regulation by Practitioners and Professional Societies

Finally, the status quo might be improved by augmenting and improving the mechanisms for self-regulation by practitioners and by the relevant professional societies. There is currently a fairly complex framework of self-regulation for the practice of assisted reproduction, administered by very well-organized and influential professional societies. These existing structures could be strengthened through increased oversight, enhanced penalties for noncompliance, and substantive changes to the content of the regulations themselves.

The potential benefits of this approach are manifold. First, because professional societies and practitioners have great institutional competence and expertise in the technical and practical aspects of their fields, they are uniquely situated to craft fitting and effective regulations and safeguards. Second, it would be symbolically very valuable to have the practitioners themselves draw boundaries and erect protective measures to defend against abuses and injuries to parents, to children, and to society at large. It would demonstrate that the mainstream community of practitioners is committed to preserving the human goods at stake and will not tolerate the transgression of ethical boundaries by irresponsible clinicians or scientists. Moreover, effective self-regulation could potentially insulate the mainstream community of clinicians and researchers from public criticism and from the possibly overbroad legislative response that might follow any disasters or tragedies flowing from the actions of renegade practitioners. Finally, it is likely (and reasonable) that practitioners would prefer to be regulated by their peers rather than by some external governmental body.

The possible drawbacks of self-regulation are fairly straightforward. There is the danger that some practitioners will not follow standards they regard as unduly burdensome, or that the professional societies will not enforce them.

II. SUBSTANTIVE OPTIONS

As we have already indicated, we are not now prepared to reach conclusions as to the best form of general regulation, not only because much remains unknown about the field, but also (and especially) because we must first decide what problems, if any, are sufficiently great to call for government action and, when they are, what sorts of action, if any, would be most beneficial. Nevertheless, the findings of our diagnostic inquiry identify several substantive areas of ethical and social concern that are of sufficient magnitude to warrant a consideration of the policy options currently available to address them. *Once again, we describe these options, and their perceived strengths and weaknesses, without endorsing any of them.*

The following, then, are some concerns that emerge from the diagnosis and findings laid out in Chapters 2 through 7, and some suggestions for possible ways of dealing with them. As will become apparent, in some instances we describe a variety of possible options, some of which may be mutually contradictory. In many cases, we do not yet have enough information to make a choice among the options (thus, the options include the gathering of such information). In other cases, there remain deep disagreements over matters of principle or between competing priorities. Our aim in presenting the following policy options is to map the landscape so that public discussion on these matters might proceed in a more informed manner, and to see whether some limited, specific, but perhaps much-needed action might be recommended by the Council.

A. Safety and Well-Being of Children Born Using ART

Among the ethical issues raised by the use of ARTs, the concern for the safety and well-being of children conceived through these technologies seems the one most in need of greater attention. Together with the safety of the women involved, it ought to be the first consideration (though surely not the only one) guiding the use of ART. But for various reasons described above, it appears to us that these concerns have not received sufficient attention.

It would of course be incorrect to say that no care at all is presently taken for the well-being of children later born, or to assume in any way that clinicians do not seek the well-being of the children who are to be conceived using ART. But institutional or public oversight in this area is limited, and those rules that have been set by professional societies tend to be vague and unenforced, although most clinicians are conscientious and try to follow them. And while most institutions, wary of malpractice suits, clearly try to avoid irresponsible or risky practices, we simply do not know how well they attend to the outcomes of interest here.

Several options for policy seem feasible in this arena:

1. Improved Annual Monitoring of ART Techniques and Outcomes.

The federal government could gather and compile more copious and specific data regarding the various techniques used and the outcomes related to such techniques in assisted reproduction procedures. The mechanism for collecting such information is already in place, through the CDC, and it could fairly easily be expanded or relocated as deemed necessary.* This information would provide more detailed data about what methods and materials are used in assisted reproduction procedures, with what effect on resulting outcomes.

2. Long-Term Longitudinal Studies.

The federal government might fund long-term longitudinal studies to track the health and well-being of children conceived using various ART techniques, as well as of mothers who undergo the procedures. Some information is currently available through relatively small-scale studies, mostly carried out abroad. More and better information is essential before further steps can be taken. Participation would of course be voluntary.

---

* Indeed, the CDC already collects some relevant data that it does not now publish; a simple requirement to publish the data in hand could be most helpful here.

3. Improved/Expanded Decision-Making.

State and federal government or ART practitioners themselves might put in place an improved and expanded informed consent process for prospective parents seeking ART procedures. Such a process might provide more complete information about the safety and well-being of children born through ART, including any and all available data about frequency of birth defects and other problems, in comparison to children in the general population. It might also seek to develop uniform consent procedures regarding the disposition and fate of any unused embryos generated in the process.

4. Requirements for Higher Standards and More Substantial Animal Research before Moving Experimental Procedures into Clinical Practice.

Since ART practices are largely unregulated at present, techniques can move from the experimental stage to clinical use quite quickly. One prominent technique, ICSI (intracytoplasmic sperm injection), was introduced into regular clinical use with minimal animal experimentation and with no studies to follow up on anecdotal reports of hazards for the children produced. More rigorous standards may well be called for, and these might be developed and enforced by a government body, by the professional societies (such as the American Society for Reproductive Medicine [ASRM]), or by some combination.

5. Enforcement Mechanism if Studies Show That Certain Procedures Are Insufficiently Safe.

Should the data collected by any of the above methods, or others, demonstrate that a particular ART procedure is sufficiently unsafe to be restricted only to patients with particular characteristics or needs, or halted altogether pending further review, some means should be available to formulate that judgment and to enforce it. The institutional layout presented above may provide some sense of the possible place and character of such an enforcement authority, though the question of who should be given that authority would of course be a controversial one. At present, we do not have sufficient information about whether such an agency might be required, and what might be required of it, to proffer more specific suggestions.

6. Expanded/Publicly Funded Research with a View to Improving ART Procedures.

The safety, reliability, and efficacy of ART procedures would be improved and better understood if more studies were conducted to test various methods and techniques of assisted reproduction. More and better-funded research could help to improve the reliability and effectiveness of existing techniques and to more thoroughly assess new ones before they are brought into practice. Such funding would also facilitate greater public oversight of the research in question. The extent, character, and funding of such research would likely be controversial issues, even if the benefits would be substantial.

B. Equal and Improved Access to IVF/ART

Among the concerns we have described are not only problems of practice, but also problems of access. Assisted reproduction procedures can be quite expensive, and at this point access seems to be fairly limited. The present situation varies by state (with some mandating that insurance companies cover it to various degrees, while most are silent) and by insurance company and policy. Such a situation may of course be deemed acceptable, but if policymakers were to see a need for action, at the state or federal level, several related avenues of recourse may be available.

The most commonly discussed policy option would be to require insurance companies to treat infertility as a medical condition like any other and to offer coverage for all assisted reproductive procedures. In most cases to date, proposed policies mandate funding only under certain circumstances (for instance, only for married couples, or for women of specified ages) or couple the funding with guidelines for practice (mandates regarding efficiency of the procedure, number of embryos created and implanted, etc.). As noted earlier, studies have shown a connection between availability of insurance coverage and decreases in the number of embryos transferred per cycle.*

C. Genetic Screening and Selection of Embryos for Non-Disease-Related Traits

The use of genetic screening and selection of embryos before implantation is, at the present time, unregulated and largely unmonitored. For the moment, to be sure, the options for such use are limited, since the technical capacity to select for particular traits is still relatively undeveloped. Today there are in general practice basically two uses for embryo selection outside the disease context: sex selection, and selection of embryos that could develop into genetically suitable organ or tissue donors. Both have already become quite controversial subjects, and as further techniques for selection are developed, new controversies are likely to emerge.

Should some oversight or regulation of this area prove necessary, it could take some or all of the following forms:

1. Increased Monitoring.

Regulation might begin with increased monitoring, to develop a clearer sense of the uses to which genetic screening and selection are being put and the degree and frequency of use. Such basic information is for the moment difficult to come by, and we may not have the kind of understanding of the status quo that would be required to make further judgments regarding regulation.

2. Review Mechanisms.

Beyond monitoring, Congress may establish new or improved mechanisms for reviewing non-disease-related uses of genetic screening and selection, setting a higher than usual bar for such techniques to pass before they are made generally available for clinical use or before they may be used in individual cases. Since very little information is available on the ef-

* For instance, see Jain, T., et al., "Insurance Coverage and Outcomes of In Vitro Fertilization," *New England Journal of Medicine* 347(9): 661 (August 29, 2002).

fects of screening and selection on the well-being of the child that results from the process, there may be a powerful case for such increased standards of scrutiny and care.

3. Limits on Non-Disease Uses.

Finally, Congress might consider placing limits or a moratorium on non-disease-related uses of screening and selection, whether in general or in relation to specific uses, such as non-disease-related sex selection. This would of course be quite challenging to implement, since it would require a fairly clear delineation of what are and what are not disease characteristics. It might also have certain unintended consequences, such as increasing the use of abortions (rather than preimplantation genetic diagnosis [PGD]) for elective sex selection. But policymakers may deem it sufficiently important nonetheless.

The various options along this continuum are not mutually exclusive; however, given our fundamental lack of data regarding the volume and popularity of such practices, and given the fact that most such practices are projected rather than current, it may be wise to begin with monitoring and data collection, so as to inform further decision-making in the future.

D. Intentional Germ-Line Modification of Embryos or Gametes to Produce Children

At present, germ-line modification of embryos and gametes with the intent to produce modified children is proscribed in practice by a decision of the RAC not to consider proposals for such work. But the moratorium could be overturned by a simple decision of the RAC, and it is also not clear whether it would apply to all potential modifications. Should it become technically feasible to safely correct single mutant genes in embryos or gametes, the RAC might relax its current proscription.

Given the fairly broad agreement in the country and Congress that germ-line modification should not now be attempted, Congress might institute, by statute, a national moratorium on germ-line modification to produce children, potentially including the following specific activities: (1) ooplasm transfer; (2) insertion of human genetic material into gametes or embryos with a view to fertilization and transfer to produce children; (3) insertion of animal genes or genetic material into gametes or embryos with a view to fertilization and transfer to produce children; and (4) insertion of artificial chromosomes, genes, or genetic material with a view to fertilization and transfer to produce children. Advances in technology and assurances of their safe and effective use could lead to a lifting of such a moratorium.

E. New Reproductive Possibilities That Alter the Biological Relationships between Children and Parents

A range of potential new reproductive technologies could mark a significant departure in human procreation, fundamentally altering the biological relationships between parents and offspring. In the future, for example, it might be possible to conceive a child using gametes obtained from an aborted human fetus or derived from embryonic stem cells. It might be possible to fuse blastomeres from two or more embryos to conceive a child with more than two genetic progenitors. It might be possible to conceive a child by transferring the nucleus from a person's somatic cell into an enucleated egg, producing a child who is virtually genetically identical to the somatic cell donor ("cloning-to-produce-children" or "reproductive cloning"). Or it might be possible to "activate" a human oocyte, producing a child whose genetic heritage is derived from a single progenitor ("parthenogenesis"). Under present law, these (and other) reproductive possibilities would be legal if they were technically feasible. All would mark a significant crossing of boundaries in human reproduction, either by denying children the natural connection to two human genetic parents or by giving children a fetal or embryonic progenitor. To secure for children born with the aid of assisted reproduction the same rights and attachments as children conceived in vivo, Congress could pass a ban or moratorium on attempts to conceive a child by any means other than the union of egg and sperm, attempts to conceive a child using gametes obtained from a human fetus or derived from embryonic stem cells, or attempts to conceive a child by fusing the blastomeres from two or more embryos.

F. Commercialization of Elements of Human Reproduction

The commercialization of various elements of human reproduction is, for some, a further cause for concern and an additional potential target for regulation. At present, the buying and selling of gametes is essentially unrestricted in most states, as is, in principle, the buying and selling of embryos, though there is no evidence to suggest the existence of any market in embryos. The potential patenting of human embryos is also a source of concern: the U.S. Patent and Trademark Office has traditionally refused to grant such patents as a matter of institutional policy, and an amendment to a recently passed appropriations bill prevents (through fiscal year 2004) the issuance of patents on human organisms at any stage of development.

Possible policies in this arena include:

1. Limits or Restrictions on the Buying and Selling of Gametes.

If the buying and selling of human gametes is deemed troubling, Congress, or state governments, could set certain limits, potentially including a ceiling on the price of eggs or sperm, limits on advertising for or by gamete donors, or perhaps even a restriction on the selling of gametes altogether.

2. Limits or Restrictions on the Buying and Selling of Human Embryos.

Similarly, Congress, or state governments, might set limits on the buying and selling of human embryos, whether for research or for implantation.

3. Prohibition on the Patenting of Human Embryos or Gametes.

In addition, Congress could *permanently* amend the patent laws to specifically forbid the patenting of human embryos, or of human organisms at any stage of development. It could also enact restrictions on the patenting of human gametes.

G. Biomedical Research Involving Early-Stage Human Embryos/Blastocysts

Embryo research is certainly among the most controversial and politically sensitive of the practices we have discussed, and therefore difficult to regulate. Those who believe it should be altogether prohibited often oppose regulating it, fearing that by doing so the government might implicitly sanction the practice and assure its continuation. Others see no need to regulate such research at all and fear that new regulations will only slow down or hinder new research. Still others worry that regulations founded in concerns about embryonic human life would set a precedent that might have implications for abortion law or scientific freedom in general.

The result has been essentially no regulation and almost no federal funding of embryo research, but rather an official policy of silently allowing such research in the private sector without public endorsement or support. All embryo research (including research on embryos left over from IVF procedures undertaken initially for reproductive purposes, embryos created by IVF solely for research, and cloned embryos produced solely for research) remains legal in the private sector. If it is regulated at all, it is regulated only by institutional review boards (IRBs), which generally do not have special rules for research involving human embryos used for research purposes, and whose oversight almost never takes into account the moral questions relating explicitly to the destruction of developing human life. We have only very limited knowledge of the numbers, uses, and commercial applications of embryo research in the private sector.

In the public sector, funding of research that involves the destruction of human embryos is prohibited by law, though current policy allows for the funding of research using certain embryonic stem cell lines that meet a series of qualifications: they must have been derived from human embryos originally created solely for reproductive purposes, with the informed consent of the donors, and without any financial inducements to the donors, and they must have been derived on or before

August 9, 2001.* These funding guidelines, combined with the broader restriction on all other federal funding of embryo research, are essentially the only federal regulations on the subject at present. Some individual states have crafted their own policies, ranging from sharp restrictions on embryo research to encouragement and even funding of such work. But most states have no explicit policy of any kind.

Should a national policy be deemed necessary, several options seem plausible, at least in theory:

1. Expanded Restrictions.

Congress might choose to impose new restrictions on embryo research, including restrictions on privately funded embryo research. For example: It might restrict embryo research exclusively to left-over IVF embryos. It might ban or pass a moratorium on the production of embryos solely for research purposes. It might ban or pass a moratorium on the creation of cloned embryos solely for research. It might ban or pass a moratorium on the creation of other "unnatural" embryos, such as man-animal hybrid embryos or embryos formed using fetal gametes or gametes derived from embryonic stem cells. It might allow research only on existing stem cell lines, and ban all future embryo destruction for biomedical research. Or it might set an upper limit on the age to which an embryo used in research may be grown or used for research purposes.

2. Expanded Funding.

Conversely, Congress might choose to relax existing restrictions and offer increased federal funding for embryo research. For example: The federal government might choose to fund all promising embryo research without restriction, including the creation of IVF or cloned embryos solely for research purposes. It might fund embryo research on left-over embryos that were originally created for reproductive purposes. Or it might fund research on all existing stem cell lines, including those lines produced since August 9, 2001.

---

* For a discussion of the federal policy regarding the funding of human embryonic stem cell research, see the Council's report, *Monitoring Stem Cell Research*, especially Chapter 2.

3. Expanded Regulation/Public Licensure under Certain Guidelines.

Congress might also explicitly permit or endorse embryo research within the framework of a regulatory system. This policy might involve requiring all embryo researchers to be licensed or registered; requiring embryo experiments to be approved case-by-case on the basis of whether they are deemed "scientifically compelling" by a panel of experts; or requiring each embryo used for research to be registered and the purpose of its use described and recorded. This regulatory option might be combined with new restrictions, new funding, or some combination of both. For example, the federal government might fund research on all existing embryonic stem cell lines while prohibiting future embryo destruction for research. Or it might fund research on both IVF and cloned embryos with extensive regulation, licensing, and approval requirements.*

H. Implantation of Human Embryos into Human or Non-Human Uteri for Biomedical Research

At present, there are no federal laws or rules restricting or prohibiting the transfer of a human embryo into a human or non-human uterus for the purpose of developing it solely for research.

If this is deemed sufficiently troubling to require action, two general options present themselves:

1. Restrictions on Embryo Transfer for Research.

Congress might put into effect a ban or moratorium on the transfer of human embryos to a woman's uterus purely for research purposes. The law could also be more narrowly tailored, if desired, to restrict specifically the transfer of embryos

* To repeat, there is no necessary connection between public regulation and public funding. The government often regulates activities that it does not fund—as is the case with workplace safety regulations, and rules governing air travel, telecommunication, broadcasting, banking, and numerous other industries.

into animals, human uterine material outside the body, (prospective) artificial wombs, or any combination of these, with the intent to keep such embryos alive purely for purposes of research.

2. Time Limit on Embryo Use.

Concerns on this score might also be addressed by prohibiting research on embryos beyond a certain age or stage of development.

III. CONCLUSION

At present, given the limited availability of data, we are not in a position either to recommend or to reject most of the options described in these pages, be they general institutional reforms or specific substantive policies. Some options may be deemed unacceptable on the basis of moral, ethical, or practical considerations independent of any information that might be gathered; others may turn out to be unwarranted or unwise as the nation learns more about the field; while yet others may prove to be desirable and sensible in light of new data still to be collected. No overarching policy direction in this arena can or should be set before substantially more and better information is gathered and before all interested parties are thoroughly consulted as potential policy options emerge.

There may, however, be some interim steps that would be advisable while the process of contemplating potential policies progresses. These involve both essential information gathering and some modest interim legislative action or policy reforms that may be deemed appropriate on the basis of the information we already possess and the findings of our preliminary inquiry. We offer some recommendations along these lines in the next (and final) chapter.

10

Recommendations

Over the past two years, the Council has devoted much time and energy to examining the current oversight and regulation of the uses of biotechnologies that touch the beginnings of human life—practices arising at the intersection of assisted reproduction, genetic screening, and human embryo research. The Council has heard from various experts and stakeholders, engaged in its own diagnostic review of current regulatory mechanisms and institutions, outlined the key findings emerging from that review, and surveyed various general and specific policy options. As the previous chapters indicate, the Council now understands a great deal about today's regulatory landscape and has identified concerns that suggest the need for improved monitoring and oversight and, perhaps, new forms of governmental regulation. Yet we are very far from being able to offer clear and well-considered recommendations regarding major institutional reforms. We do not know the precise costs and benefits of overhauling existing regulatory institutions and practices or of creating new regulatory authorities. We do not even know enough about the incidence and severity of some of the possible risks and harms that we have identified as causes of concern to decide whether they are serious enough to justify changing the present arrangements. We do not accurately know, for example, how the technologies and practices at the heart of our inquiry affect the health of those whose lives are touched by them—most notably, the children conceived with their aid. Similarly, we do not know how widely preimplantation genetic diagnosis or preconception (and preimplantation) sex selection will be practiced, and for which purposes. Without the answers to such questions, it would be premature at best to recommend dramatic legal or institutional changes. Further research and inquiry, and additional consultations with all those affected, are clearly needed.

Yet even as such inquiry and consultation proceed, the Council believes that some modifications can and should now be implemented to address some of the concerns identified by the present inquiry. The recommendations we offer fall into three general categories: studies and data collection, oversight and self-regulation by professional societies, and targeted legislative measures.

In Sections I and II of this chapter, the Council proposes several measures it believes the federal government and the various relevant professional societies should adopt immediately. Most of these suggestions are aimed precisely at addressing the remaining empirical questions described above. These include a call for comprehensive information gathering, data collection, monitoring, and reporting of the uses and effects of these technologies. They also address the needs for increased consumer protection, improved informed decision-making, and more conscientious enforcement of existing guidelines for practitioners of assisted reproductive technologies (ARTs).

In Section III of this chapter, we identify several matters that may warrant prudent interim legislative action, especially in light of rapidly emerging innovations that signal new departures in human reproduction. Familiar disquiet regarding human cloning or commerce in human embryos and gametes is augmented by recent reports of, for example, fusion of male and female embryos into one chimeric organism and of the derivation of gametes (in animals) from embryonic stem cells (in principle enabling embryos to become biological parents). Accordingly, while policymakers monitor and gather information and while deliberation continues about the need for better and more permanent monitoring and oversight arrangements, it may be necessary and desirable to enact a legislative moratorium on a few boundary-crossing practices, thereby providing interim prophylactic limitations. Such limitations would prevent the introduction of certain significant innovations into human procreation in the absence of full public discussion and deliberation about their ethical and social implications and consequences.

In offering these interim recommendations for improvements in data collection, monitoring, and professional self-regulation and in proposing limits and restraints on some potential applications of ARTs, the Council does not intend to challenge the current practices or impugn the ethical standards of most practitioners of assisted reproduction. The Council recognizes the efforts of professionals and patient groups working in this field to devise and implement appropriate ethical guidelines and standards of care. Yet we have identified areas of concern that have not been sufficiently studied or addressed. And there are at present no effective mechanisms for monitoring or regulating some of the more problematic practices or for preventing unwelcome innovations introduced by irresponsible practitioners. Indeed, it is our belief that responsible professional participants, patients, policymakers, and interested citizens should be able to recognize the merit of our proposals and work to see them implemented.

The recommendations we offer here are recommendations of the Council as a whole. Though we differ about certain fundamental ethical questions in this field, and especially about the moral standing of human embryos, we have nevertheless been able to agree on several policy suggestions that we believe should command not only the respect but also the assent of most people of common sense, good will, and a public-spirited concern for human freedom and dignity. These recommendations emerge quite naturally from the diagnostic survey and analysis presented in the previous chapters, and they are best understood only when read in that context. We have sought to frame the recommendations with sufficient specificity that they might be adopted by the relevant target audiences.

I. FEDERAL STUDIES, DATA COLLECTION, REPORTING, AND MONITORING REGARDING THE USES AND EFFECTS OF THESE TECHNOLOGIES

A. Undertake a Federally Funded Longitudinal Study of the Impact of ARTs on the Health and Development of Children Born with Their Aid

A most important unanswered question before the Council concerns the precise effects of ART and adjunct technologies on the health and normal development of children who are now being born or who will in the future be born with their aid. There have been a few studies, mostly undertaken abroad, reaching different and sometimes contradictory results. An effort has been undertaken, by the Genetics and Public Policy Center at the Johns Hopkins University, in collaboration with the American Academy of Pediatrics (AAP) and the American Society for Reproductive Medicine (ASRM), to review all of the existing literature on this question. This retrospective study is a laudable start, capable of identifying harmful health and development outcomes that should be monitored in the future. The Council strongly believes, however, that what is needed now is a *prospective* longitudinal study—national, comprehensive, and federally funded—that looks at both the short-term and the long-term effects of these technologies and practices on the health of children produced with their assistance, including any cognitive, developmental, or physical impairments. Such a study would require an adequate control sample, and a sufficiently large population of subjects to yield meaningful statistical results. Participation in such a study would, of course, be voluntary.

A seemingly ideal vehicle for this study is the National Children's Study (NCS) now being planned by a consortium of federal agencies led by the National Institute of Child Health and Human Development (NICHD). This study, which (if funded) is scheduled to begin in 2005, would track the health and development of 100,000 children across the United States from before birth until age 21. Given its great demographic, temporal, and substantive scope, the NCS would be uniquely suited to studying the health of children conceived with the aid of ART. It would be national in scope, it would not require the special recruitment of a population of children conceived with the aid of ART, and all participation would be voluntary. Correcting a major defect in other studies of the impact of ART, the NCS would have a built-in control sample, namely, children conceived without the aid of ART. It would allow researchers to observe and consider health impacts that reveal themselves only years after birth. It would analyze an exceptionally wide range of biological, physical, social, cultural, and other factors that may significantly influence a child's health and development. The NCS would have enormous resources at its disposal, as it would be undertaken by a partnership of federal, state, and local agencies; universities; academic and professional societies; medical centers; communities; industries; companies; and other private groups. Finally, the NCS would release its results as the study progresses; thus, it would not be necessary to wait until 2025 to review the information gathered. The study would publicize results as the children reached certain developmental milestones. In short, the NCS would offer an unprecedented and perhaps unrepeatable opportunity to answer questions relating to the well-being of children conceived with the aid of ART.

Should the planned NCS not go forward for any reason (or should it not include a suitable or statistically significant study of children conceived using ARTs), the Council recommends that an independent federally funded longitudinal study be undertaken on the health and development of children who are born with the aid of ARTs.

B. Undertake Federally Funded Studies on the Impact of ARTs on the Health and Well-Being of Women

Another area where better information is needed regards the health and well-being of women who use ARTs and of women who donate their eggs for the use of others. One or more studies, either in conjunction with or separate from the above-mentioned longitudinal study, should be conducted to discover the effects, if any, of the use of ARTs on women's health, including any short-term or long-term hormonal, physical, or psychological impairments. Participation in such a study would, of course, be voluntary.

C. Undertake Federally Funded Comprehensive Studies on the Uses of Reproductive Genetic Technologies, and on Their Effects on Children Born with Their Aid

As noted above, assisted reproduction and genomic knowledge are increasingly converging with one another. Practices such as preimplantation genetic diagnosis (PGD) and gamete sorting represent the first fusion of these disciplines. Before these practices become routine, it is desirable that policymakers and the public understand their present and projected uses and effects. To this end, there should be federally funded comprehensive studies, undertaken ideally with the full participation of ART practitioners and their professional associations, on how and to what extent such practices are currently and may soon be employed, and their effects on the health of children born with their aid. Mechanisms need to be developed for ongoing monitoring of the outcomes of these practices and other practices to which they may lead. Participation in any such studies would, of course, be voluntary.

D. Strengthen and Augment the Fertility Clinic Success Rate and Certification Act

As currently written, the Fertility Clinic Success Rate and Certification Act (FCSRCA) is aimed at providing consumers with key information about the pregnancy and live-birth success rates of assisted reproduction clinics in the United States. We believe that the Act should be augmented and strengthened, both to improve this original function of consumer protection and to allow for better public oversight (through the already existing ART surveillance program at the Centers for Disease Control [CDC]) of the development, uses, and effects of reproductive technologies and practices. Toward these ends, the Act, or the regulations propounded pursuant to it, or both, should be improved and strengthened in the following ways.

1. Enhance Reporting Requirements.

a. Efficacy. Provide more user-friendly reporting of data, including adding "patients" as an additional unit of measure.

Currently, data are reported only in terms of "cycles" of treatment (beginning when a woman starts ovarian stimulation or monitoring), rather than in terms of individual patients treated. Thus, it is impossible to know how many individuals undergo assisted reproduction procedures in a given year, how many patients achieve success in the first (or second or third) cycle, how many women fail to conceive, and the like. Presenting results in terms of "numbers of individuals" (in addition to "numbers of cycles") would be very helpful to prospective patients and would yield more precise information for policymakers.* Also, this information should be presented with any qualifying language or additional information that would help to avoid confusion for prospective patients or the public.†

b. Risks and side effects. Require the publication of all reported adverse health effects. Adequate consumer protection requires informing prospective users of the known hazards connected with the services or products they are using. Yet there is today no mechanism for the publication of information regarding adverse effects of ARTs, either on the health of adult patients or on that of their children. At the present time, the CDC does collect data on complications and adverse outcomes of pregnancy, including low birthweight and birth defects for each live born and stillborn infant, but this information is not made public. Knowledge of such adverse effects is of paramount concern for prospective patients, policymakers, and the public at large. The CDC should publish its data on the incidence of adverse effects on women undergoing treatment, as well as on the health and development of children born with the aid of ART. In order not to confuse or unduly alarm prospective patients or the public, the CDC should include in its publication comparative data on the incidence of such effects in

* The Council is not calling for the abandonment of "cycles" as a unit of measure. Rather, we urge the inclusion of "patients" as an additional unit of measure.

† The CDC collects but does not publish information regarding ART patients' prior attempts to conceive using assisted reproduction. This information might prove useful in helping the CDC to analyze and present information on a per-patient basis in a way that does not distort success rates and the like.

unassisted births, as well as any other relevant information that could help prevent misimpressions regarding the nature and magnitude of the hazards associated with ART.

c. Costs to the patients. Require the reporting and publication of the average prices of the procedures and the average cost (to patients) of a successful assisted pregnancy. There is currently no comprehensive source of information regarding the costs borne by the patients seeking treatment involving assisted reproductive technologies. Not surprisingly, prospective patients are keenly interested in this information. Moreover, policymakers interested in questions regarding equality of access, insurance coverage, and related matters would greatly benefit from such information. It would also shed light on whether incentives currently exist that may induce patients and clinicians to engage in potentially risky behavior, such as the transfer of multiple embryos in each cycle, in an effort to reduce costs (especially in those places where in vitro fertilization (IVF) is not covered by insurance). While the publication of such information may cause some confusion or, worse, may create a perverse incentive to cut costs at the expense of health and safety, the Council believes that the consumer benefits of providing such information outweigh such speculative harms. This is especially true if this information about costs to the patient is published alongside the information, recommended above, regarding patient health and safety.

d. Innovative techniques. Include information on novel and experimental procedures. A key area of concern for the Council is the ease and speed with which experimental technologies and procedures (such as intracytoplasmic sperm injection [ICSI] or PGD) move into clinical practice, even in the absence of careful clinical trials regarding their efficacy and their long-term effects on children born with their use. It would be useful for consumers and policymakers to understand more fully how each clinic manages the process of introducing new technologies and practices and what safeguards are employed. Such information would include the human subjects protections in place; the extent to which technologies are first tested in animals; the standards that must be satisfied before a given procedure is deemed fit for clinical use; and the measures taken to evaluate safety and efficacy.

e. Adjunct technologies. Require more specific reporting and publication of the frequency of, and reasons for, uses of specialized techniques such as ICSI, PGD, and sperm sorting for sex selection. Little is understood about the frequency and uses of the various adjunct technologies and practices complementing standard IVF. Under the present system, the CDC already collects and reports information relating to the incidence and uses of some adjunct technologies.* The present approach could be greatly improved, however, by modestly changing the relevant law to require information on additional adjunct procedures (particularly those that combine assisted reproduction with human genetic technologies), as well as to require the reporting and publication of somewhat more detailed information relating to the reasons patients elect to use those procedures that are already subject to reporting requirements. For example, the present system of reporting sheds little light on precisely *why* patients chose ICSI as their preferred method of fertilization. Also, because results are reported in terms of cycles rather than patients (as discussed above), it is impossible to know how many *individuals* used ICSI.

Other techniques, particularly those fusing reproductive technology and genomic knowledge, are not reported at all under the present version of the Act. There is no requirement to report the number of cycles using PGD, much less the reasons for using PGD. For example, how many patients using PGD are infertile? How many have family histories of genetic disorders? What sort of genetic screening is being done? For aneuploidy and single-gene mutations? For donor siblings? For non-disease-related traits? There is also no reporting of any practices in which sex selection occurs or of the reasons for undertaking them. Consumer protection and public policy would be enhanced if this information

---

* For example, the CDC publishes information on the percentage of IVF cycles involving ICSI (49.4 percent in 2001); the CDC also reports the percentage of the cycles using ICSI that involve patients with male factor infertility (57.8 percent in 2001).

were available and published. Consumers would benefit from knowing how much experience a given clinic has in performing such procedures. The public would benefit from knowing how, why, and to what effect genomic knowledge is being used in human reproduction.

2. Enhance Patient Protections: Informed Decision-Making.

a. Provide model forms for decision-making. The present Act would be greatly improved by providing for the promulgation of easy-to-read model consent forms that include information on the possible health risks to mother and child, the novelty of the various procedures used, the number of procedures performed to date, the outcomes, and the various safeguards in place to ensure that such procedures are safe and effective.

3. Improve Implementation.

a. Enforcement. Provide stronger penalties to enhance compliance with the Act's reporting requirements. Under the Act as currently written the only penalty for noncompliance is the publication of the names of nonreporting clinics. This is insufficient, given the importance of clinic compliance to ART consumers and the greater public. The penalties should reflect the magnitude of harms to be avoided. We leave to legislators the question of what precisely these should be.

b. Funding. Increase funding for implementation of the Act. CDC's budget should be augmented sufficiently to enable it to undertake the additional measures suggested above. In this way, the increased oversight called for will be borne by the government rather than by the individual patient. We leave to legislators the question of how much additional funding would be required.

II. INCREASED OVERSIGHT BY PROFESSIONAL SOCIETIES AND PRACTITIONERS

Professional oversight has traditionally been the principal mechanism of regulation for the practice of medicine, and the practice of reproductive medicine is no exception. There is a well-developed body of professional guidelines and standards for the clinical practice of assisted reproduction, and as far as the Council can determine (in the absence of a more comprehensive investigation of physicians' actual conduct), the vast majority of practitioners abide by these guidelines and standards and are dedicated to the welfare of their patients. Yet the Council has identified the following substantive areas that it believes require attention and improvement:

A. Strengthen Informed Patient Decision-Making

Clinicians and their professional societies should make efforts to improve the current system of informed decision-making by patients to conform to the concerns and suggestions described above. ASRM and SART (the Society for Assisted Reproductive Technology) should pay attention not only to helping devise improved consent forms, but also to recommending procedures to their members for discussing the subject properly with patients and for securing their meaningful consent. For this purpose, they should consider making training sessions on this subject a requirement of membership.

B. Treat the Child Born with the Aid of Assisted Reproductive Procedures as a Patient

ART clinicians should take additional measures to ensure the health and safety of all participants in the ART process, *including the children who are born as a result*. Thus, in making decisions and undertaking clinical interventions, such practitioners should carefully consider how these actions will affect the health and well-being of these children. We recognize, of course, that health care services tend in general to be disaggregated among different specialties, and that collaboration is not always feasible. In the domain of assisted reproduction, once pregnancy has been achieved, the prenatal care of the pregnant woman is transferred to her obstetrician. But the Council urges clinicians and professional societies to seek out ways to improve the continuity of the services offered to their patients and their children. ART clinicians and their professional societies should consult with pediatricians (and their professional societies) to learn how their practices may be affecting the health and safety of the children born as a result. Clinicians and professional societies should also cooperate fully and vigorously with any efforts (such as the studies described in Section I of this chapter) to ascertain the effects of ART and related practices on the health and development of such children. In addition, the Council strongly endorses a specific substantive recommendation: clinicians and professional societies should take additional concrete steps to *reduce the incidence of multiple embryo transfers* and resulting multiple births, a known source of high risk and discernible harm to the resulting children.

C. Improve Enforcement of Existing Guidelines

There are today a host of reasonable guidelines in place for clinicians and practitioners engaged in ART, and, to repeat, they are apparently followed by most practitioners. However, the relevant professional societies need to take stronger steps to ensure that these guidelines are followed. For example, one such professional society "actively discourages" the use of PGD for sex selection for nonmedical purposes, yet several prominent members of that society openly advertise the practice. Professional societies must clarify the contours of appropriate conduct and adopt reasonable mechanisms of enforcement.

D. Improve Procedures for Movement of Experimental Procedures into Clinical Practice

Professional societies and clinicians should develop a more systematic mechanism for reviewing experimental procedures before they become part of standard clinical practice. Such a system might include requirements for animal studies, institutional review board (IRB) oversight, and formal discussion and ongoing (and prospective) monitoring of the significance and results of novel procedures.

E. Create and Enforce Minimum Uniform Standards for the Protection of Human Subjects Affected by Assisted Reproduction

At present there is no systematic, mandatory mechanism for protecting human subjects who are engaged in experimental ART protocols not affiliated with institutions receiving federal funds. This problem is compounded by the fact that in the practice of assisted reproduction (as in the practice of medicine more generally), there is not a clear distinction between research and innovative clinical practice. Investigational interventions that could affect the health and well-being of children born with the aid of ART should be subjected to at least as much ethical scrutiny and regulatory oversight as investigational interventions affecting other human subjects of research. Current research policies establish special protections for children and fetuses in research. For similar reasons, there is a need for special protections when research involves interventions in embryos that could later affect the health and welfare of the resulting live-born children. Clinicians and their professional societies should adopt measures (such as IRB-like oversight) to provide necessary safeguards.

F. Develop Additional Self-Imposed Ethical Boundaries

Clinicians and professional societies would be well-advised to establish for themselves additional clear boundaries defining what is and what is not ethically appropriate conduct, regarding both research and clinical practice. Without such guidance, irresponsible clinicians and scientists may engage in practices that will, fairly or unfairly, bring opprobrium on the discipline as a whole. Practices such as, among others, the fusion of male and female embryos, the use of gametes harvested from fetuses (or produced from stem cells) to create embryos, and the transfer of human embryos to nonhuman uteri for purposes of research fall squarely into this category. The relevant professional societies should preemptively take a firm stand against such practices and back that stand up with meaningful enforcement.

III. TARGETED LEGISLATIVE MEASURES

In the course of our review, discussion, and findings, we have encountered and highlighted several particular practices and techniques (some already in use, others likely to be tried in the foreseeable future) touching human procreation that raise new and distinctive challenges. Given the importance of the matter, we believe these practices and techniques require special attention, not only from professional societies but also from the people's representatives. Especially because technological innovations are coming quickly and because there are today no other public institutions charged with setting appropriate limits, we believe Congress should consider some limited targeted measures—bundled together perhaps as a "Reproduction and Responsibility Act"—that might erect boundaries against certain particularly questionable practices.* These measures, proposed as moratoria, would remain operative at least until policymakers and the public can discuss the possible impact and human significance of these new possibilities and deliberate about how they should be governed or regulated.

The benefits of such congressional legislation, as we see it, are multiple:

(a) It could help educate the public about the transformative character of some new reproductive biotechnologies; and it could enhance public awareness of the need for research and practice in this area to be guided by respect for the women using assisted reproduction and for the children born with its aid (on which see below).

---

* The listing (below) of these activities should not be taken to imply that we believe that the reputable practitioners of assisted reproduction are interested in engaging in them. Our goal is rather to establish boundaries and guidelines for future practice, and barriers against those irresponsible practitioners who, indifferent to the standards of the profession and the community, might not only endanger patients and the public, but also unfairly cast a pall over the entire field.

(b) It would institute a temporary moratorium on certain practices, imposing a few carefully defined boundaries on what may be done and preventing any individual from committing acts that could radically alter what the community regards as acceptable in human reproduction without prior public discussion and debate.

(c) If carefully drafted, it would not interfere with important scientific research. On the contrary, it could serve to protect the reputation of honorable scientists and practitioners of assisted reproduction against the mischief done by "rogues," whose misconduct might invite harsh and crippling legislative responses.

(d) Practically, it would place the burden of persuasion on those innovators who are inclined to transgress these important boundaries without adequate prior public discussion or due regard for social or moral norms.

(e) It would show that there is a way forward for continuing public oversight in these areas, and it would demonstrate that scientists and humanists, physicians and laymen, liberals and conservatives, "pro-lifers" and "pro-choicers," can find certain shared core values that they are willing to defend collectively and by deliberate agreement.

Legislative interest in responsible reproductive practices might give rise to a fairly wide range of specific provisions, and Congress should consider these in their full array. But the concerns we have taken up in this report, and which emerge from our findings, suggest to us a few that are especially crucial, and also especially likely to command fairly broad assent. They may be usefully grouped under four principles or desiderata, each pointing to one or two particular provisions that we believe to be in order and that we now recommend*:

* The particular provisions that follow below (in boldface type) have been carefully drafted, with a view to specifying accurately the Council's concerns. Yet they are to be read not as precise legislative provisions but as articulations of possible boundaries that we would like to see erected and defended.

A. Preserving a Reasonable Boundary between the Human and the Nonhuman (or, between the Human and the Animal) in Human Procreation

The question of the human-animal boundary in general can, in some respects, be quite complex and subtle, and the "mixing" of human and animal tissues and materials is not, in the Council's view, by itself objectionable. In the *context of therapy and preventive medicine*, we accept the transplantation of animal organs or their parts to replace defective human ones; and we welcome the use of vaccines and drugs produced from animals. Looking to the future, we do not see any overriding objection to the insertion of animal-derived genes or cells into a human body—or even into human fetuses—where the aim would be to treat or prevent a dread disease in the patient or the developing child (although issues would remain about indirect genetic modification of egg and sperm that could adversely affect future generations). Likewise in the *context of biomedical research*, we now see nothing objectionable in the practice of inserting human stem cells into animals—though we admit that this is a scientifically and morally complicated matter. But in the *context of procreation*—of actually mixing human and nonhuman gametes or blastomeres at the very earliest stages of biological development—we believe that the ethical concerns raised by violating that boundary are especially acute, and at the same time that the prospects for drawing clear lines limiting permissible research are especially favorable. One bright line should be drawn at the creation of animal-human hybrid embryos, produced ex vivo by fertilization of human egg by animal (for example, chimpanzee) sperm (or the reverse): we do not wish to have to judge the humanity or moral worth of such an ambiguous hybrid entity (for example, a "humanzee," the analog of the mule); we do not want a possibly human being to have other than human progenitors. A second bright line would be at the insertion of ex vivo human embryos into the bodies of animals: an ex vivo human embryo entering a uterus belongs *only* in a *human* uterus. If these lines should be crossed, it should only be after clear public deliberation and assent, not by the private decision of some adventurous or renegade researchers. We therefore recommend that Congress should:

- **Prohibit the transfer, for any purpose, of any human embryo into the body of any member of a nonhuman species; and**

- **Prohibit the production of a hybrid human-animal embryo by fertilization of human egg by animal sperm or of animal egg by human sperm.***

B. Respect for Women and Human Pregnancy, Preventing Certain Exploitative and Degrading Practices

Respect for women with regard to assisted reproduction encompasses many things, including respect for their health, autonomy, and privacy; these are by and large properly attended to in current assisted-reproduction practices. But in the face of some new technological possibilities, we recognize that respect for women also involves respecting their bodily integrity. A number of animal experiments using assisted reproductive technologies have shown the value of initiating pregnancies solely for the purpose of research on embryonic and fetal development or for the purpose of securing tissues or organs for transplantation. We generally do not object to such procedures being performed on other animals, but we do not believe they should, under any circumstances, be undertaken with humans, or that human pregnancy should be initiated using assisted reproductive technologies for any purpose other than to seek the birth of a child. A woman and her uterus should not be regarded or used as a piece of laboratory equipment, as an "incubator" for growing research materials, or as a "field" for growing and harvesting body parts. We therefore recommend that, in an effort to express our society's profound regard for human pregnancy and pregnant women, Congress should:

---

* It bears noting that, in testing for male-factor infertility, practitioners of assisted reproduction now use hamster eggs to test the capacity of human sperm to penetrate an egg; yet there is no intent to produce a human-animal hybrid embryo and there is a negligible likelihood that one might be formed, given the wide gap between the species. Thus, we do not believe that such procedures run afoul of the letter or spirit of the above recommendations.

- **Prohibit the transfer of a human embryo (produced ex vivo) to a woman's uterus for any purpose other than to attempt to produce a live-born child.**

C. Respect for Children Conceived with the Aid of Assisted Reproductive Technologies, Securing for Them the Same Rights and Human Attachments Naturally Available to Children Conceived In Vivo

We believe that children conceived with the aid of ARTs deserve to be treated like all other children and to be afforded the same opportunities, benefits, and human attachments available to children conceived without such assistance. If some care is taken, this can surely be accomplished, as it largely has been for twenty-five years with IVF as ordinarily practiced. But as we have seen, certain applications of embryo manipulation and assisted reproductive techniques could deny to children born with their aid a full and equal share in our common human origins, for instance by denying them the direct biological connection to *two* human genetic parents or by giving them a fetal or embryonic progenitor. We believe that such departures and inequities in human origins should not be inflicted on any child. We therefore recommend that, in an effort to secure for children who are born with the help of ARTs the same rights and human attachments naturally available to children conceived in vivo, Congress should:

- **Prohibit attempts to conceive a child by any means other than the union of egg and sperm.***

- **Prohibit attempts to conceive a child by using gametes obtained from a human fetus or derived from human embryonic stem cells.***

- **Prohibit attempts to conceive a child by fusing blastomeres from two or more embryos.***

---

* Operationally, in each of the three cases listed, the prohibited act comprises the creation ex vivo of any such human embryo *with the intent* to transfer it to a woman's body to initiate a pregnancy.

D. Setting Some Agreed-Upon Boundaries on How Embryos May Be Used and Treated

What degree of respect is owed to early human embryos will almost certainly continue to arouse great controversy, as it does among members of this Council. But we all agree that human embryos deserve, as we have said, "(at least) special respect." Accordingly, we believe some measures setting upper age limits on the use of embryos in research and limits on commerce in human embryos may be agreeable to all parties to the ongoing dispute over the moral status of human embryos. Along these lines, we believe that Congress should:

- **Prohibit the use of human embryos in research beyond a designated stage in their development (between 10 and 14 days after fertilization);[*] and**

- **Prohibit the buying and selling of human embryos.[†]**

Furthermore, these concerns about commerce in the domain of human reproduction suggest to us the need for legislation

---

[*] Some members of the Council are opposed to any experimentation that harms or destroys human embryos, but, recognizing that it is legal and active, they see the value in limiting the practice. Other members of the Council favor allowing such experimentation during the early stages of embryonic development, but nonetheless recognize the need to establish an upper age limit beyond which such research should not proceed. Some Council members believe that this upper limit should be 14 days after the first cell division; others favor 10 (or fewer). *This recommendation should not be construed as silently endorsing (or opposing) embryo research at earlier stages.*

[†] This provision is not intended to preclude those patients who receive donated embryos from reimbursing donors for reasonable expenses, storage costs, and the like. Also, because the compensated giving of sperm is a long-established practice, and because payment to egg donors is now also fairly common, efforts to ban payment to gamete providers would likely prove controversial and untenable for purposes of actual legislation. Thus, we decline to recommend such a ban here. That is not to say, however, that the Council approves of the buying and selling of gametes. Indeed, many Council members have raised serious concerns regarding this species of commercialization in the domain of human reproduction.

instructing the United States Patent and Trademark Office **not to issue patents on claims directed to or encompassing human embryos or fetuses at any stage of development**; and amending Title 35, United States Code, section 271(g) (which extends patent protections to products resulting from a patented process) **to exclude these items from patentability**. The language of any such statute would in our view need to take some care not to exclude from patentability the processes that result in these items, but only the products themselves. Similar language has been included in a component of the federal budget for fiscal year 2004 (the Consolidated Appropriations Act of 2004, H.R. 2673, 108th Congress [January 23, 2004], Division B, § 634), but we believe this provision should also be made a clear and permanent element of the patent law.

These recommendations indicate the kinds of specific measures that could give concrete expression to widely shared goals and that might serve as safe interim boundaries, as public deliberation tries to catch up with rapidly changing technologies. We do not presume here to make detailed suggestions regarding specific legislative language or the assignment of penalties, as Congress, should it choose to take up these recommendations, would most appropriately determine these in accordance with its usual procedures. Also, of course, these are by no means the only possible legislative measures Congress might take up to limit practices that put at risk important shared public values. But we offer these recommendations for what in our view are reasonable and moderate measures, which could do genuine good and which might command relatively broad assent across the usual spectrum of opinion on these subjects.

APPENDIX

Personal Statements

The preceding ten chapters constitute the official body of this report; it stands as the work of the entire Council. In the interest of contributing further to public discussion of these issues, and of enabling Members of the Council to speak in their own voice on one or another aspect of this report, we offer in this Appendix personal statements from those Members (and groups of Members) who have elected to submit them:

Personal Statement of Professor Dresser, Professor Glendon, Dr. Krauthammer, and Professor Wilson

This document represents a singular achievement. To achieve unanimity on any issue in bioethics is difficult enough. To achieve it on an issue as contentious as the treatment of a human embryo is more difficult still. Yet, this Council has found unanimous consensus on the recommendations in this report. Even more remarkable is that this unanimity has been achieved on a Council of such extraordinary philosophical and ideological diversity.

Regardless of our different positions on the moral status of the embryo and on the autonomy that ought to be granted to science, it turns out that we can agree on certain fundamental human goods that are at stake and that deserve not just moral but legal protection. As a result, we are in a position to recommend to Congress, which represents a similar diversity of philosophical and ideological inclinations, a concrete roadmap on how to proceed.

These recommendations establish basic guidelines—"fences"—defining activities that lie outside the bounds of decency, while at the same time providing the converse service of defining the boundaries within which we continue to contend and disagree.

We are proud to associate ourselves with this document.

REBECCA S. DRESSER
MARY ANN GLENDON
CHARLES KRAUTHAMMER
JAMES Q. WILSON

Personal Statement of Professor Dresser

Reproduction and Responsibility makes several major contributions. First, it is a detailed and comprehensive account of existing policy and professional standards relevant to assisted reproductive technologies (ARTs). Second, it highlights significant gaps in the current oversight system.

One such gap concerns safety. The federal regulatory system fails to ensure that newly developed ART interventions receive the same level of scientific and medical review as do other novel interventions with potential human applications. As a result, novel ART interventions may be attempted in human subjects without sufficient preclinical data showing that the approach is safe enough to try in humans. Such interventions may also enter the medical arena without the rigorous evidence of safety and efficacy normally required before drugs and other products are approved for clinical use.

Protection of human subjects can also be inadequate. Infertility specialists developing new approaches are not always affiliated with an academic or other medical center mandating institutional review board evaluation prior to human applications. Thus, there is no assurance that prospective parents will be informed of a technique's unproven status, its risks, and the alternative measures that might be available to them. Another problem is that federal agencies lack policies explicitly addressing situations in which investigational modifications affecting embryos could have health consequences to a later-born child. The children whose health could be affected by ART innovations, as well as the parents of such children, should benefit from the same regulatory protections governing human research and introduction of new medical interventions as do other human beings.

More extensive oversight by the Food and Drug Administration would be one way to address these regulatory gaps. Yet as *Reproduction and Responsibility* observes, more assessment and analysis are needed to determine which specific regulatory actions would be most effective and least burdensome. At the same time, this report supplies a solid foundation for moving forward with oversight to protect people affected by ART in the research and clinical settings.

Reproduction and Responsibility makes a third contribution in offering additional guidance for federal oversight. One activity the report discusses is stem cell and other research that requires the destruction of human embryos. I agree with my colleagues Daniel Foster, Michael Gazzaniga, Janet Rowley, Michael Sandel, and James Wilson that certain legislative recommendations in this report could be helpful in advancing the current national debates over cloning and human embryonic stem cell research. The longstanding congressional restrictions on federal funding for embryo research and similar longstanding disputes over the ethics of creating embryos for research suggest that meaningful policy changes will require those with diverse views to cooperate and to seek common ground. The report's recommendations emerged from this sort of process.

Members of this Council know all too well the impediments to achieving consensus among individuals with very different positions on the moral status of early human life. Barriers to consensus also exist when group members disagree on the moral and social value of technologies that enable more people to have biologically related children, expand opportunities to test embryos and fetuses for genetic traits, and offer researchers new avenues for studying preimplantation embryos. *Reproduction and Responsibility* represents a deliberative success, for it includes a collection of recommendations endorsed by people with extremely diverse values and beliefs about these matters. Thus, its greatest contribution may be to demonstrate that mutual respect, accommodation, and compromise on embryo research and acceptable ART practices are possible in this pluralistic and polarized country of ours.

REBECCA S. DRESSER

Personal Statement of Dr. Foster, Dr. Gazzaniga, Dr. Rowley, Professor Sandel, and Professor Wilson

We endorse the legislative recommendations contained in this report, on the following grounds: First, the limitations these regulations impose on the treatment of embryos in assisted reproduction and research give proper expression to the moral significance of human embryos. Although we do not regard embryos as the moral equivalent of fully developed human beings, we believe that they are more than mere things, and should not be used wantonly or treated with moral indifference. The proposed regulations offer a way to prevent such wanton or casual treatment, and so accord human embryos the respect they are due.

Our second reason for supporting these regulations is that they point to a possible solution to the vexed issues of cloning and stem cell research that could overcome the current impasse in the U.S. Senate. Despite widespread opposition to reproductive cloning, the Senate has been unable to ban it because of disagreement about cloning for biomedical research. The obvious solution is to detach the two questions, but until now, it has proven difficult to do so. One way of banning reproductive cloning alone would be simply to prohibit the transfer of a cloned embryo into a woman's uterus, as Britain has done. Some object, however, that such a law would effectively make it a crime not to destroy a cloned embryo.

The formulation proposed in this report offers a way of banning reproductive cloning that avoids that difficulty. It proposes that Congress "prohibit attempts to conceive a child by any means other than the union of egg and sperm." We believe that this language provides a way for Congress to ban reproductive cloning while agreeing to disagree on the question of cloning for biomedical research; such a solution would prevent attempts to created cloned children while allowing debate to continue about cloning for stem cell research and regenerative medicine.

The proposed regulations, taken together, also point toward a possible compromise on federal funding of stem cell research. Some object to embryonic stem cell research on the grounds that embryos are persons and therefore inviolable. But others object on different grounds. They worry that, in the absence of clear limits, embryo research could lead down a slippery slope of exploitation and abuse: if today we derive stem cells from blastocysts, tomorrow some might seek to transfer embryos into a women's uterus, or even a pig's uterus, to grow organs for transplant, creating the nightmare prospect of embryo farms, fetuses exploited for spare parts, and the commercialization of human life.

One great merit of the regulations contained in this report is that, if implemented, they would address the slippery slope argument against embryonic stem cell research by assuring that such research is done responsibly, within carefully prescribed limits. No embryos used for research could be used or preserved beyond a 10-14 day limit, or transferred into a woman's uterus or an animal's body to grow organs for harvest; nor could embryos be bought and sold. Regulations such as these will not fully satisfy the objections of those who oppose stem cell research on the grounds that blastocysts are morally equivalent to babies. But by assuring that stem cell research is conducted within carefully prescribed limits, these regulations effectively address the concern that stem cell research today will lead us down a path to exploitation and abuse tomorrow. The proposed regulations could, therefore, point the way toward a compromise on federal funding along the lines that Senator Bill Frist proposed in July 2001:

> After grappling with the issue scientifically, ethically and morally, I conclude that both embryonic and adult stem cell research should be federally funded within a carefully regulated, fully transparent framework. This framework must ensure the highest level of respect for the moral significance of the human embryo. Because of the unique interaction between this potentially powerful new research and the moral considerations of life, we must ensure a strong, comprehensive, publicly accountable oversight structure that is responsible on an ongoing basis to moral, ethical and scientific considerations.

Senator Frist proposed a number of regulations, similar in spirit to the ones proposed in this report, that would permit federal funding of embryonic stem cell research, at least on cell lines derived from blastocysts from in vitro fertilization (IVF) clinics that would otherwise be discarded. Although we would not restrict stem cell research to blastocysts left over from IVF clinics, we realize that this remains a controversial question. The compromise toward which the regulations in this report point might leave aside the question of funding for stem cell research on cloned embryos, and move forward on areas of potential agreement.

Recent scientific developments illustrate the need to adjust federal funding policy along the lines Senator Frist proposed in 2001. Only 17 cell lines are currently on the NIH Registry and available for federally funded research, and many of those are subject to stringent licensing requirements. In March, Harvard biologist Douglas Melton announced the creation of 17 new embryonic stem cell lines that he is making available free of charge to scientists for noncommercial research purposes. The Harvard stem cell lines meet all the criteria proposed by Senator Frist: They were derived, using private funds, from blastocysts left over from IVF clinics that would otherwise be discarded, with the consent of the donors. And yet, under current federal policy, research on these cell lines is ineligible for federal funding. The reason: Unlike the 17 stem cell lines currently available for federal funding, the new Harvard cell lines were derived after 9:00 P.M. on August 9, 2001, the deadline announced by President Bush in his address to the nation on stem cell research.

Whatever one's view of the moral status of the embryo, it is difficult to understand the moral distinction between research on stem cell lines created before 9:00 P.M. on August 9, 2001, and research on stem cell lines created since. We endorse the regulations proposed in this report in the hopes that these regulations can point the way to a national compromise on cloning and stem cell research that will enable this country to promote the promise of stem cell research while upholding the highest ethical standards.

DANIEL W. FOSTER
MICHAEL S. GAZZANIGA
JANET D. ROWLEY
MICHAEL J. SANDEL
JAMES Q. WILSON

Personal Statement of Professor Fukuyama and Professor Wilson

We believe that the *Reproduction and Responsibility* report is a very important document that articulates a broad moral consensus over the limits that our society should place on new reproductive procedures now made possible by technology. The proposed legislation, if passed, would ban certain clearly unacceptable techniques (including reproductive cloning) while at the same time neither prohibiting nor condoning research cloning or other forms of embryo research. As such, it shows a way to get past the current deadlock that leaves the United States as one of the few developed countries without guidelines on these issues.

Appropriate as these guidelines are, we believe that they represent only a first step toward a more complete regulatory approach needed to deal with new technological possibilities. Today we can foresee possibilities like reproductive cloning or human-animal hybrids that should be banned. But technology will move quickly and in the future pose ethical challenges, as well as scientific and medical opportunities, that we cannot today imagine. It will be difficult and inappropriate for Congress to intervene seriatim as these developments occur. What is called for instead is a modernization of our existing regulatory structure to allow it to respond with flexibility in such cases, taking account not simply of the safety and efficacy of new procedures but of ethical concerns that would be widely shared in our society.

Our hope is that the current report will represent not the final word on the subject of legislative limits but the beginning of a broader discussion of regulatory oversight of new reproductive technologies. As a general rule, we do not welcome government intrusion into scientific inquiry and into the reproductive choices made by parents. But regulation frequently facilitates scientific advance and individual choice by reassuring the public that it is being done responsibly. That is the light in which the current report should be seen, as well as hoped-for future efforts to update and modernize our regulatory system.

FRANCIS FUKUYAMA
JAMES Q. WILSON

Personal Statement of Dr. Gazzaniga

This is a complex report. The explicit objective of this report is to propose some sort of regulatory mechanism that monitors the possible uses and misuses of a variety of existing artificial reproductive techniques. The policy recommendations made at the end of the report are presented in that context. At the same time the importance of this report is the implicit implications of those recommendations. While unstated, the implication is to ban reproductive cloning, but is silent on biomedical cloning. It is hoped that this will allow stem cell research to go forward in some way that is advancing this biomedical pursuit and public good. I accept the foregoing rationale for concurring with this report as articulated by Foster, Rowley, Sandel, Wilson and myself, but I do so reluctantly. I much prefer a more broad and bold explicit statement.

What overhangs this discussion is the question of the moral status of the embryo. In what follows, I present my thoughts on that issues as concurrently published in a letter to *Science*. In the meantime I feel obliged to stake out a far more assertive position. The current compromise does not capture the goods that can be achieved by allowing biomedical cloning to go forward with the full support of the federal government for not only research on spare IVF embryos, but also biomedical cloning that allows somatic cell nuclear transfer procedures. The report does not make explicit that federal funding for research should go on for all of these endeavors.

The reason the explicit aspects of this report are now proposed is because federal funding has been withheld from embryo research of any kind in the past. It is now clear proper epidemiological studies would be good not only for ART but also for a wide variety of other current medical practices. By not explicitly allowing federal funding for biomedical cloning as well as new stem cell lines we are painting ourselves into yet another corner down the road.

I firmly believe that the problems underlying all of these social and medical dilemmas derive from a profound misunderstanding of what an embryo is and is not. If greater understanding could be brought to that issue, we all could move forward in a reasoned and rational way. The following forthcoming letter to *Science* ("Human Being Redux," April 16, 2004) was prompted by the recent advances in biomedical cloning in Korea and addresses this issue:

> Here we go again. It was two years ago that as one of the member's of the President's Council on Bioethics, I among others outlined a logic for letting biomedical cloning go forward.

No one is for reproductive cloning—or cloning for baby making as it is sometimes called. But cloning for biomedical research, a process that only involves cells in a Petri dish and might well relieve untold human suffering is another matter.

Now, two years later, the good scientists of South Korea have made a major advance in biomedical cloning. They have shown the world that careful and caring biomedical cloning, cloning that allows for the production of stem cells, which might lead to breathtaking remedies for horrible diseases, is possible. Two years ago the reason many people were against letting the American biomedical community into this intellectual and scientific hunt was that by allowing biomedical cloning, the human race would lose its dignity. Tell me, does any reader feel diminished in the past few days? Do the one million Americans who suffer from Parkinson's disease, whose human dignity has been brutally robbed from them, feel an even greater affront?

How did we get into this mess, the position that the greatest biomedical discovery machine in the history of the world, the American basic science enterprise, is sitting on the sidelines? It is in part due to religious zealotry and in part due to superficial reasoning by well meaning people. At the center of the discussion is the belief on the part of some that a blastocyst, the entity in the Petri dish, is morally equivalent to a living post-natal human being. For those who simply assert that equivalence, no matter what the scientific data might be, there is nothing more to be said. But for those who think the equivalence is due to 'scientific fact' there is hope they may come to a deeper understanding of the nature of the problem.

Many people recognize that the human embryo, the entity that is created by the union of an egg and sperm, carries all the genetic information of a member of the human species. Thus, they call the embryo a human being. Of course, to develop into a human being, the embryo has to become implanted into the uterus of a woman and be allowed to develop. This potential to become a human being is what sticks in the minds of the supporters of the moral equivalence argument and this is why manipulations of embryos for anything but normal reproduction is not acceptable to them.

Looking at a minuscule ball of cells in a Petri dish, so small that it could rest on the head of a pin finds one hard pressed to think of it as a human being. After all, it has no brain or capacity to think and feel. The ball of cells has the potential if it was to be implanted into a woman but so do the egg and sperm 'set' before they meet. Why don't we revere those entities? Well, it is argued, because they don't have the full compliment of genetic material that could make up a human being. Those that see a bright line here, the line between an entity with the combined genetic material versus the uncombined entities, are forgetting the central discoveries of neuroscience and developmental psychology.

Merely possessing the genetic material for a future human being does not make a human being. The developing embryo that becomes a fetus that becomes a baby is the product of a dynamic interaction with its in vivo environment, its post-natal experiences, and a host of other factors. A pure genetic description of the human species does not describe a human being. A human being represents a whole other level of organization as distinct from a simple embryo as an embryo is distinct from an egg and sperm. It is the dynamics between genes and environment that make a human being. Indeed, most of us are willing to grant this special status to a developing entity way before it actually exists, but surely not before the entity even has a brain.

The South Korean scientists seem to understand these distinctions. They are not in the baby making business and want no part of it. They have constructed a great fence around developing embryos through a cloning process unfolding in a Petri dish. Their embryos are allowed to develop for only a few days whereupon the all-important stem cells are harvested for possible therapeutic use and at the exact same time the rest of the cell mass dies. There is no slippery slope here, there is no beginning of the much-feared world of cloned humans and the like. The Koreans have found a way to let biomedical cloning go forward with all of its spectacular promise for restoring human dignity to the seriously diseased and infirmed patients of the world while at the same time not in any way creating a social atmosphere to use such advances for baby making. What could be better?

America can solve its dilemma quickly and easily. Congress could vote to outlaw reproductive cloning. At the same time, they could allow biomedical cloning to go forward. The definitional problem of what it means to be a human being is becoming clearer and the much feared slippery slope argument has been put to rest. Biomedical cloning, *Si*, reproductive cloning, *No*!

MICHAEL S. GAZZANIGA

Personal Statement of Professor George, Professor Glendon, Dr. Gómez-Lobo, Dr. Hurlbut, and Professor Meilaender

With the release of this report, the President's Council on Bioethics has continued and advanced the development of its position on difficult and controverted questions that arise at the beginning of human life. We append these comments in order to offer a brief analysis of what the Council has said and to place what it says here into the context of its earlier work. In particular, we think it important to highlight a few recommendations for interim legislation offered by the Council at the very end of the report. It is essential to see what the Council has said and equally essential to note where it has been silent.

Among the Council's recommendations is the following: Congress should "prohibit attempts to conceive a child by any means other than the union of egg and sperm." Were such legislation enacted, it would be unlawful to attempt to produce a child through cloning. Readers should note with care the definition given in a footnote of the act prohibited here. It is "the creation ex vivo of any such human embryo *with the intent* to transfer it to a woman's body to initiate a pregnancy." Two important implications follow:

> (a) One might, of course, produce a human embryo by somatic cell nuclear transplantation or some other cloning technique with no intent whatsoever to transfer it to a uterus (no doubt in order to conduct research on such an embryo, what the Council has elsewhere called "cloning-for-biomedical-research" and for which some use the incorrect language of "therapeutic cloning"). About this possibility the Council is entirely silent. It does not recommend or endorse such action. Nor does it take a position about whether it should be legally permitted or forbidden. In the absence of any new recommendation, readers may therefore rightly conclude that the Council's earlier majority recommendation (in its report, *Human Cloning and Human Dignity*) that a four-year moratorium on all cloning-for-biomedical-research should be instituted continues to be the Council's position.
>
> (b) Because the prohibited act would be the "creation ex vivo" of a human embryo by any means other than the union of egg and sperm "*with the intent* to transfer it to a woman's body to initiate a pregnancy," the Council's recommended legislation would never require the destruction of any embryo. The prohibited act is not—it is crucial to note—implantation in a woman's uterus of embryos,

but, rather, creation of such embryos *with the intent* to implant. Implantation, apart from creation with the intent to transfer, is not in any way prohibited. Hence, this actually provides additional clarity to the Council's recommendations in *Human Cloning and Human Dignity*.

There is one important issue on which the Council has not yet achieved sufficient agreement to offer a recommendation—and on which it, therefore, is entirely silent in the recommendations of this report. That is the issue of the use in research of human embryos at an early stage of development that have been conceived ex vivo by union of egg and sperm (i.e., embryos that are not created by SCNT or other asexual process of reproduction). The Council has been able to agree that research on human embryos should be prohibited beyond a designated stage of their development. (Some members of the Council would extend the period up to fourteen days after fertilization, but none favors permitting research on embryos that have developed beyond that point. Others would draw the line at ten days or earlier. We, and perhaps other members of the Council, have grave concerns about research that destroys human embryos at any stage of their development.) But the Council says no more than that. In particular, we should note two significant silences:

(a) The Council is entirely silent about whether research on human embryos before the 10/14 day limit should be conducted or legally permitted, and, hence, the Council has in no way endorsed such research.

(b) Because of its silence on this matter, the Council does not endorse the destruction of human embryos at any stage of their development.

Although the Council's earlier report, *Human Cloning and Human Dignity*, dealt only with embryos produced by cloning, these silences cohere well with the position endorsed by the Council majority in that report and with current policy of the federal government to prohibit federal financing of any research using stem cells derived from human embryos produced after August 9, 2001 (the date of the institution of that policy). Chapter 2 of the Council's earlier report, *Monitoring Stem Cell Research*, has explored the moral underpinnings and legal significance of that policy, and the recommendations the Council now makes in this new report represent a further advance in drawing out some of the implications of that moral commitment.

We are, therefore, happy to join all our colleagues on the Council in endorsing the recommendations in *Reproduction and Responsibility*, and we are pleased that we have been able, especially in areas of great controversy, to agree on the matters we have briefly outlined above.

ROBERT P. GEORGE
MARY ANN GLENDON
ALFONSO GÓMEZ-LOBO
WILLIAM B. HURLBUT
GILBERT C. MEILAENDER

Personal Statement of Professor George and Dr. Gómez-Lobo

In our statement attached to the Council's report *Human Cloning and Human Dignity* and in other writings, we have set forth our reasons for holding that human beings are entitled to full respect and legal protection, irrespective of age, size, location, stage of development, or condition of dependency. We reject the proposition that human beings may at certain stages of development, for example, the embryonic, fetal, and infant stages, legitimately be treated as disposable research material. So we support the ban on federal funding of experimentation and research involving the deliberate destruction of human beings in the embryonic stage, or any other, and we hope that the day will come when such experimentation and research is effectively prohibited. At the same time, we understand and fervently share the desire of those who favor embryo-destructive experimentation and research to develop cures for dreaded diseases and add to the sum of human knowledge. We believe that biomedical science should move forward aggressively by every ethically legitimate means. We do not, however, believe that deliberate embryo killing is morally defensible.

Our nation is divided on the question whether human beings in the embryonic stage deserve full respect and legal protection, and that division is reflected on our Council as it is in the Congress. However, the nation is not divided, nor is the Council or the Congress, on the question whether *some* limit must be placed on the destruction of nascent human life for purposes of experimentation and biomedical research. There is near unanimity in rejecting the idea of generating human embryos and gestating them for the purpose of harvesting their tissues and organs. Even those of our colleagues and fellow citizens who are prepared to countenance the destruction of human embryos in the blastocyst stage for what they regard as a greater good agree that the law should forbid damaging or deadly experimentation on embryos at later stages of development. Yet federal law currently establishes no limit. In the present report, we join in unanimously recommending that Congress establish a certain number of days beyond the first cleavage after which embryo-destructive experimentation is legally prohibited.

Our report does not designate a particular number of days, though no member of the Council has suggested that embryo-destructive research should be permitted beyond fourteen days after the first cleavage. Some would set the limit at ten days, others perhaps earlier. As noted, we ourselves are among the members of the Council who favor protecting human life from the very beginning by banning the use of living human embryos at any stage of development as disposable research material. Until this becomes politically feasible, we support efforts to accord as much protection as possible by limiting the number of days beyond which the law tolerates deliberate embryo killing. It is important to understand that the Council's recommendation here is *not* to authorize embryo-destructive research up to a certain limit. It is only to prohibit such research beyond a certain limit. Because in the absence of legislation this research remains unrestricted, a prohibition of embryo-destructive research beyond a certain limit does not amount to authorizing research up to that limit.

It is our hope that citizens who share our fundamental commitment to the principle of the full and equal dignity of every member of the human family will join us in endorsing the Council's unanimous recommendation to Congress to establish a limit on embryo-destructive research. We pledge to join with them in working to establish yet more complete protection for human life in all stages and conditions.

ROBERT P. GEORGE
ALFONSO GÓMEZ-LOBO

Personal Statement of Dr. Kass

The intersection of assisted reproduction and genomic knowledge confronts us with a daunting array of new opportunities and new questions. But the question of questions in this field is this: Can human beings find a way to govern the uses of biotechnology, so as to have it serve worthy human ends without eroding human freedom and dignity? And if we can, *how* shall we do it? This report on the regulation of biotechnology is offered as the first step in what I hope will be a serious and vigorous national attempt to answer these questions.

The report begins that attempt by properly defining the field, and asking questions not just about one or another technique, but about the ways in which biotechnologies of reproduction touch the lives of children, women, and men. This report is not about cloning, stem cell research, or the moral status of human embryos, though it certainly bears on them. Those topics the Council addressed in previous reports. This report is about the larger whole of which those controversies are parts, and by looking at the whole the Council has managed to find common ground in particular areas where before none seemed to exist.

Although its recommendations may be helpful in making progress on some familiar and contested policy questions, the report's major contribution is to show how a heterogeneous group of individuals, whose opinions range almost as widely as those of the American people, has agreed on the need to set limits on some uses of some biotechnologies, in order to protect common values.

Such agreement has been lacking in the past because people on very different sides of the issues have feared or opposed formal governmental oversight and regulation in this area. Some scientists and biotechnologists want no interference with scientific research and medical progress, and oppose especially those restraints that rest on moral grounds. On the other hand, some people with profound moral objections to certain types of research do not want to see governmental regulation of this field, fearing it would implicitly sanction the activity being regulated. I appreciate the reasons and principles behind these two stances. But I respectfully submit that both groups have principled reasons to seek and support public policies that defend shared values. Prudent scientists, technologists, and entrepreneurs should realize that it is in the interest of responsible science for them to join the regulatory discussion and propose some principles and boundaries that they themselves could welcome and would like to see upheld. And prudent defenders of the sanctity of human life should realize that it is a Pyrrhic victory to keep the federal government out of certain activities, if the price of such a stance means that worse practices are allowed to proceed without oversight or regulation in the private sector.

This report demonstrates that when people of such different views do pursue some common ground, practical ways forward can be found, even while serious disagreements remain. I hope that people on all sides of these issues, in the Congress and the public, will take up the challenge posed by this report, will take the first steps recommended in this report, and will take further steps along these lines as well.

Those further steps should try to expand the scope of common agreement, and also to seek more lasting ways to turn agreement into concrete policy. After all, bioethics commissions come and go. They take up important issues. They write reports. Sometimes, as in this case, the reports contain recommendations that may find a willing audience. But they have no oversight or regulatory authority. Their power consists only in their ability to persuade, and that is as it should be.

But in this rapidly developing world of biotechnology, where the human import of the changes we are undergoing is hard to discover and where social institutions lag far behind in their ability to cope with the new challenges that innovations may bring, a case can be made for the importance of trying to devise suitable regulatory institutions and activities that could help protect society's basic values, even as we continue to treasure the benefits that biotechnology will continue to bring us. Legislation and prohibitions are suitable only for a few rare violations (such as human cloning, or euthanasia, or some of the prospects taken up in this document). Laissez-faire, while reflecting the honored American principles of freedom and choice, offers no guidance other than the market. Regulation would seem to offer a superior alternative, even if it is far from clear what form it should take or how it might be effected.

Concrete steps like those proposed in this report might begin to pave the way toward greater clarity on such questions, and they may help us to see whether or not further regulation is called for, what forms it might take, and what common goods it should seek to uphold.

The path forward is difficult, but people on all sides have something vital to defend, not only for themselves but for all of us. I would hope that people might join together, as we have tried to do here, to seek out the common ground and to try to gain greater understanding of and control over where biotechnology is taking us.

LEON R. KASS

Personal Statement of Dr. McHugh

I am pleased to endorse the legislative recommendations that have emerged from our Council's discussions and are contained in this report. I believe the report will help move our governmental representatives toward important solutions in a most problematic arena. I also think this publication will encourage the American public to believe that thoughtful and coherent policies can and will emerge from these disputed matters, in part because of the enterprises of this Council.

I do, though, want to take this opportunity to repeat a point I made during our meetings about the President's regulatory decision on August 9, 2001, when he permitted some stem cells derived from embryos produced by in vitro fertilization to be used in federally funded research. In essence I see that effort as a prototypic example of an attempt to balance out "conflicts of goods" that can arise with biotechnology regulation.

I hold that President Bush (in trying to respond to concerns that the previous administration's and Congress's decisions banning destructive human embryonic research were holding back crucial work) presented American scientists not just with some identified stem cell lines but also with the opportunity to prove their points. Since many Americans (including me) along with governments of other Western nations believe that the use of in vitro fertilization as a source of experimental tissues is seriously problematic, our best scientists could treat the approach offered by President Bush as they might any priority decisions over federal support and funding. They could take the partial support offered at the moment and return to the source after employing that support to develop more compelling data demonstrating what has been accomplished and what is now more clearly in prospect and not to be denied. Anyone who has worked on an NIH grant review board knows and expects just such behavior from scientists who receive less financial support than they requested and a priority score that they find perverse.

I sense from our conversations that scientists resent the idea that in this arena "non-peers"—i.e., people lacking their scientific credentials—are voting on the "priority score" and so may influence the outcome. But not only are other matters in question here than the quality of the science, we are now accustomed to representatives from the public on institutional review boards and hospital ethics committees dealing with biotechnology, and we have occasionally celebrated the wisdom these people bring to the enterprises. I think the most helpful and productive stance is to presume that the President's regulatory proposal is a good-faith effort to define the problems and priorities on the basis of contemporary knowledge as he sees it. Disagreements with him should be supported with new results from the research his proposal permits.

In essence I support the regulations as proposed here and am honored to have had the opportunity with my colleagues on the Council to play a small role in their development.

PAUL MCHUGH

Personal Statement of Dr. Rowley

The latest report of the Council on Bioethics focuses on the ethical issues surrounding aspects of assisted reproductive technology (ART) and the potential misuses of the technology. The report is a review and restatement of previous reports with a relatively complete review of the agencies, government and others, who have an interest in and potential jurisdiction over various aspects of ART. In my view, the report should have done much more to applaud the medical advances that have occurred leading to the effective treatment of an important medical problem, namely infertility, rather than focus primarily on the potential hazards and misuses of the new technologies. *In addition, I think it is important to note plainly that some of the major concerns highlighted in the report could be resolved relatively painlessly by changes in current governmental regulation, at the state and at the federal level. I am also disappointed that the report does not call for federal funding of basic and clinical research seeking improved methods of assisted reproduction or for mandated health insurance for ART services. Both of these measures would help to reduce the risks of ART to women and children.*

One area of concern includes the lack of comparative data on the outcome of in vitro fertilization (IVF) both with regard to long-term health effects on the women involved and on the children born using the various techniques. Because this is a rapidly moving area of medical practice, meaningful comparisons between older techniques and current practices and the impact of the changes on the success rate (full-term pregnancies) and health of the child are not as complete as one would like. However we are not as ignorant as indicated in the report. There are solid data from other countries with more integrated health care systems that the risk of ovarian cancer is not increased in women using IVF; hyperovulation syndrome is rare (as this report notes, it may be as low as 0.5 percent), relatively easily treated and mostly occurs if the woman becomes pregnant. Nowhere in the report is it indicated that the risks to women of a natural pregnancy are far greater than the procedures associated with IVF. Adequate federal funding (as recommended) would allow accurate data collection on the effect of ART on the women who have participated and the health and performance status of children born using ART, correlated with the various techniques used in the early stages before implantation. Such data are important, and, as the Council insists in this report, participation in such a longitudinal study should be voluntary, rather than required by law.

In addition, these medical practices are generally not covered by insurance so the costs are born by couples desperate for a biologically related child of their own. This restricts ART to only those families that can afford it. The report criticizes professional societies for inadequate and conflicting guidelines in Chapter 2. In contrast, in Chapter 10, the report says that there are a host of reasonable guidelines in place. Many ART clinics follow the guidelines established by the societies but some (the number is uncertain) flaunt them, apparently with impunity. I believe that having ART covered by insurance would be the most effective means of oversight because if clinics did not conform to agreed upon guidelines, they would not get paid. As shown by a recent study in the *New England Journal of Medicine* (347: 661, 2002), fewer embryos are implanted in states with insurance coverage for ART and multiple births are one of the major causes of maternal and infant morbidity and mortality. Informed discussions to create guidelines with effective means of enforcement, as well as federal funding in certain areas, are a far more rational route than Congressional legislation.

The report also sounds alarms about privately funded research, raising the fear that because there are no federal laws regulating research, individuals are free to pursue avenues of research of their own choosing using human embryos. In fact, some of these privately funded researchers have already developed new embryonic stem cell lines that are likely to help advance our understanding of the potential of human embryonic stem cells for better treatment. Allowing these cell lines to be used for federally funded research is required if we are to make meaningful progress.

The report identifies other areas of research that appear to be irresponsible, namely attempts to fuse two species to try to form a human/animal chimera. Such experiments are rare and are unlikely to succeed beyond a preliminary mixing of cells because of the genetic incompatibility of the two species. Other bioethical issues relate to the possible use of preimplantation genetic diagnosis for non-medical indications, especially for sex selection. This is not done by reputable clinics and could be abolished by vigorous oversight. I believe that promoting data collection and availability of insurance coverage would be far more effective than opposing these highly uncommon practices. Some futuristic scenarios discussed in Chapter 3 that consider the prospect of increasing control over the genetic characteristics of children seem to me very far-fetched, and the ethical issues raised are, therefore, not in my view anything to be concerned about.

Providing data on the costs and results of individual clinics is, at first glance, a worthy proposal. Data gathering in this field involves complicated issues of privacy, as well as a need for strict controls in data analysis. For instance, data should be obtained and presented in a manner that reflects the patient population and should include most especially maternal age. Are some clinics willing to accept couples that have failed at other clinics and may be likely to fail again? In other words, are the populations seen at different clinics comparable?

Much of the final part of the report's description of the options and recommendation is related to concerns for human dignity and what is seen by some as the trumping of this concept by technology. At present there is unanimous agreement that (1) human embryos should never be transferred to the body of nonhuman species or to a human womb except to produce a live-born child and that (2) a child should only be the result of the union of egg and sperm. There is less agreement on how long human embryos should be cultured ex vivo, although current practice is no longer than 14 days.

Yet legislating in this area, even when well meaning, is a tricky and risky business, and there is a danger of overreaching and excessive zeal that could, if unchecked, interfere with sound research and beneficial treatment. There are many other areas of concern that are probably not suitable for being considered as an option for legislation; and although the Council's final recommendations avoid them, the presentation (in Chapter 9) of possible *substantive* policy options puts forth dubious suggestions that might seduce the careless or the zealous legislator. For example, the question of ooplasm transfer is not as clear-cut as it might seem. If infertility is due to defects in maternal mitochondrial DNA, the fusion of the nucleus from her oocyte with ooplasm from a normal donor cell might be a rational treatment. So why ban it? Should there be legislation related to non-disease-related genetic screening? How serious a problem is it in the U.S.? Should we restrict gene therapy in embryos with single gene disorders if it becomes safe? These are all questions that need thoughtful discussion before moving headlong into a legislative ban, and although this report does not call for such bans, some observers and commentators would surely like to enact them. Thus, I am concerned that, despite the limited character of the final recommendations in Chapter 10, Congress might make use of the report's outline of some *possible substantive* legislative options in Chapter 9 to do real damage to beneficial research and medical treatment.

In my personal view, what should the Council recommend? In addition to the two items listed above, the top priority is for increased federal funding for basic research to develop the best conditions that will result in healthy babies as well as collecting data on the health of mothers and children involved in IVF. Responsible professional societies and patient advocates should be more forceful in developing comprehensive practice guidelines and then enforcing them. As indicated, universal insurance coverage for infertility would provide a strong lever for such enforcement.

JANET D. ROWLEY